The Transatlantic Economy 2011

Annual Survey of Jobs, Trade and Investment between the United States and Europe

Daniel S. Hamilton and Joseph P. Quinlan
Center for Transatlantic Relations
Johns Hopkins University
Paul H. Nitze School of Advanced International Studies

Hamilton, Daniel S., and Quinlan, Joseph P., *The Transatlantic Economy 2011: Annual Survey of Jobs, Trade and Investment between the United States and Europe*
Washington, DC: Center for Transatlantic Relations, 2011.

Center for Transatlantic Relations
American Consortium on EU Studies
EU Center of Excellence Washington, DC
The Paul H. Nitze School of Advanced International Studies
The Johns Hopkins University
1717 Massachusetts Ave., NW, Suite 525
Washington, DC 20036
Tel: (202) 663-5880
Fax (202) 663-5879
Email: transatlantic@jhu.edu
http://transatlantic.sais-jhu.edu
ISBN 978-0-9841341-7-5

Table of Contents

Preface and Acknowledgements

This annual survey offers the most up-to-date picture of the deep and intricate economic relationship binding European countries to America's 50 states. This year we have added a number of "Special Focus" features that look at the global role of the dollar and the euro; transatlantic innovation; and the impact of rising powers on the transatlantic economy.

This annual survey supplements our earlier work and other recent publications of ours in which we use both geographic and sectoral lenses to examine the deep integration of the transatlantic economy, and the role of the U.S. and Europe in the global economy, with particular focus on how globalization affects American and European consumers, workers, companies, and governments. Daniel Hamilton's latest book, *Europe 2020: Competitive or Complacent?* (Washington, DC: Center for Transatlantic Relations, 2011) assesses the EU's global competitive position and maps its connections to 12 other world regions in terms of goods, services, money, energy, people and ideas. Joseph Quinlan's recent book, *The Last Economic Superpower: The Retreat of Globalization, the End of American Dominance, and What We Can Do About It* (New York: McGraw Hill, 2010), analyzes the global aftershocks of the "Made in America" financial crisis, the attendant rise of developing countries and the impact on the standard bearers of the global economy: the United States and Europe.

We would like to thank Jessica Martin, Andrew Vasylyuk, James Medaglio, Peter Lindeman, Gretchen Losee, and Peggy Irvine for their assistance in producing this study.

We are grateful for generous support of our annual survey from Daimler AG; the American Chamber of Commerce to the European Union and its member companies Caterpillar, Fleishman-Hillard, SAS and UPS; and the European-American Business Council and its member companies BT, CA Technologies, DHL, Grant Thornton, Hewlett-Packard, and Medco.

The views expressed here are our own, and do not necessarily represent those of any sponsor or institution. Other views and data sources have been cited, and are appreciated.

Daniel S. Hamilton
Joseph P. Quinlan

The Transatlantic Economy 2011
Executive Summary

- Despite the recession, the United States and Europe remain each other's most important foreign commercial markets. No other commercial artery in the world is as integrated and fused together as the transatlantic economy.
- We estimate that the transatlantic economy generates close to $5 trillion in total commercial sales a year and employs up to 15 million workers in mutually "onshored" jobs on both sides of the Atlantic.
- Ties are particular thick in foreign direct investment, portfolio investment, banking claims, trade and affiliate sales in goods and services, mutual R&D investment, patent cooperation, technology flows, and sales of knowledge-intensive services.
- The transatlantic economy is the largest and wealthiest market in the world, accounting for over 54% of world GDP in terms of value and 40% in terms of purchasing power.
- Even following the financial crisis, U.S. and EU financial markets continue to account for well over two-thirds of global banking assets; three-quarters of global financial services; 77% of equity-linked derivatives; more than 70% of all private and public debt securities; almost 80% of all interest-rate derivatives; almost 75% of all new international debt securities; and 70% of all foreign exchange derivatives transactions. 92.8% of global foreign exchange holdings were either in dollars (62.1%), euros (26.5%) or sterling (4.2%) in mid-2010.
- As globalization proceeds and emerging markets rise, however, transatlantic markets are shifting from a position of preeminence to one of predominance—still considerable, but less overwhelming than in the past. In the last decade the transatlantic share in global stock market capitalization declined from 78% to just over 50%. Its share in stock trading fell from 86% to just over 70%. Asia's share of investment banking revenues rose from 13% to more than 20%. BRIC stock markets grew more than 40% per year while EU and U.S. markets contracted. The BRIC share of listed companies worldwide jumped from just over 2% in 2000 to 22% today. More than half of the world's IPOs in 2009 were listed in China alone.

The Rocky Road to Recovery

- In 2010 the transatlantic economy rebounded sharply from the depressed levels of 2009. Trade, foreign investment, foreign affiliate income, and mergers and acquisition all enjoyed positive growth rates and in some cases, record growth.
- Green shoots of economic recovery are appearing on both sides of the Atlantic in 2011 and consumer and business confidence is improving. But most areas of the U.S. and Europe face stubborn unemployment, impaired financial systems and mounting fiscal debts.
- Global trade volumes rose 12% in 2010 after plunging by nearly 11% in 2009.
- 2011 is likely to be the year of a three-speed global economy, with Europe and Japan stuttering forward with less than 2% growth, emerging markets roaring ahead with growth of 7% or more, and the U.S. somewhere in between.

- The economic crisis destroyed 7.3 million American jobs and cut U.S. GDP by 4.1%. It cut more than 7 million European jobs and erased almost €150 billion from EU output. Between 2008 and 2010 the eurozone lost about 2.5% in per capita GDP relative to the U.S. and barely kept par with Japan, even though Japan's recession was more severe.
- Government debt is likely to exceed 100% of GDP in Greece, Italy, Ireland, Belgium and France by 2012. The EU's public debt is around 80% of GDP. Eurozone budget deficits average 6.2% of GDP.
- U.S. federal debt has tripled over the past decade, from $3.5 trillion in 2000 (35% of GDP) to $9 trillion in 2010 (62% of GDP) and could reach 100% of U.S. GDP by 2015, about the relative indebtedness of Greece and Italy today. The U.S. federal budget deficit for fiscal year 2011 is expected to total $1.5 trillion, a record high, and equating to roughly 10% of GDP.

The Dollar Reigns, the Euro Will Survive

- The Greek and Irish crises of 2010 have exposed fundamental weaknesses in the mechanisms governing the eurozone, testing European unity. The potential for a sovereign default or debt rescheduling in one of Europe's most indebted countries remains a real risk in 2011.
- A sovereign debt crisis in Europe would not spare U.S. banks. While U.S. banks do not have much direct exposure to Europe's debt-laden periphery, they are highly leveraged to UK banks, which in turn are highly leveraged to some of Europe's most indebted countries.
- Despite the global financial crisis and the Greek and Irish dramas of 2010, the euro has held its own, accounting for 26.5% of total allocated global foreign exchange holdings at mid-year 2010, significantly higher than its 18.3% share in 2000. Demand for the euro among developing countries is even higher—28.3% percent of allocated reserves (18.1% in 2000).
- The dollar's share of global reserves fell from 71.1% at the end of 2000 to 62.1% at mid-year 2010. The pound sterling boosted its share from 2.8% to 4.2%. The yen's share declined from 6.1% to 3.3%. Global claims in all other currencies amounted to only 3.9%.

Transatlantic Investment: Still Driving the Transatlantic Economy

- Trade alone is a misleading benchmark of international commerce; mutual investment dwarfs trade and is the real backbone of the transatlantic economy. Together the U.S. and Europe accounted for only 28.2% of global exports and 33.4% of global imports in 2009. But together they accounted for 62.9% of the inward stock of foreign direct investment (FDI), and a whopping 75.3% of outward FDI stock. Moreover, each partner has built up the great majority of that stock in the other economy.
- Foreign investment and affiliate sales are the engine powering transatlantic trade. 61% of U.S. imports from the EU in 2009 consisted of trade between the European and U.S. branches of the same company. The percentage was even higher in the case of Ireland (85%) and Germany (65%). Over half of total U.S. exports to the Netherlands and 31% of U.S. exports to the EU consisted of this intra-firm trade.
- The U.S. and Europe are each other's primary source and destination for foreign direct investment.

- U.S. FDI to the EU jumped nearly 30% during the first nine months of 2010, a solid rebound from the depressed levels of 2009.
- The 2010 spike in U.S. FDI to Europe was far greater than the increase in global FDI; overall FDI inflows rose just 1%, to $1.1 trillion.
- U.S. FDI worldwide totaled an estimated $350 billion in 2010, a significant improvement from the prior two years but still down from its peak of $394 billion in 2007.
- Direct U.S. FDI flows rose sharply to the UK (243%), Belgium (172%), Italy (48%), and Germany (22%) in the first nine months of 2010 versus the same period a year earlier. U.S. inflows to France rose just 1%. In dollar terms, U.S. outflows to the UK totaled $39.6 billion; to the Netherlands $38.2 billion; Germany $4.2 billion; Italy $2.4 billion; and France $1.5 billion.
- U.S. FDI to Ireland plunged 17.5% and U.S. FDI to Spain declined by 6% in 2010. U.S. firms *dis*invested $157 million in Greece in 2009 and $18 million in 2010.
- Between 2000 and 2010 U.S. firms sunk roughly $1.3 trillion into Europe—over 60% of total U.S. FDI for the decade. Europe's share of total U.S. FDI in 2010 was roughly 52%.
- Over the past decade 5 of the top 10 overseas markets for U.S. investment were in Europe. The Netherlands ranked #1, UK 2nd, Ireland 4th, Switzerland 5th, and Germany 8th. Belgium ranked 11th, France 13th, and Spain 15th. Also ranking in the top ten were Nafta members Canada (3rd) and Mexico (6th). Singapore ranked 8th, Australia 9th and Japan 10th.
- Since 2000 U.S. firms have sunk $4.3 billion in Poland, more than double U.S. flows to Portugal; and nearly $7 billion in Turkey, on par with U.S. investment levels in Russia.
- Ireland's share of U.S. investment to the EU more than doubled from 4.6% in the 1990s to roughly 10% since 2000 ($120 billion). Yet U.S. FDI to Ireland plunged 17.5% in the first nine months of 2010.
- France received just 2.9% and Italy only 2.2% of U.S. FDI to the EU over the past decade.
- U.S. FDI outflows to the BRICS between 2001 and 2009 accounted for only 3.7% of global U.S. FDI outflows.
- U.S. investment inflows into Brazil, India and China surged in 2010, but from relatively low levels and a comparatively small base. U.S. firms sank more capital into Brazil in the first nine months ($7.2 billion) than either China ($6.3 billion) or India ($4.7 billion).
- U.S. firms invested more capital in Belgium ($7.9 billion) than either Brazil, China, or India in the first nine months of last year. Total U.S. investment in the three BRIC countries ($18.2 billion) was just slightly higher than total U.S. investment in Ireland ($17.5 billion) and less than half of U.S. flows to either the Netherlands or the UK.
- U.S. firms invested $37 billion into China between 2000 and 2010, putting China 12th as a destination of U.S. FDI, behind Belgium, France, Germany, Switzerland, Ireland, the UK and the Netherlands.
- U.S. investment in the Netherlands 2000-2010 was 9 times more than in China. U.S. investment in the UK was over 7 times more and in Ireland nearly 3 times more than in China.

- Since 2000 U.S. firms have invested more in the Netherlands alone than in South and Central America, the Middle East and Africa combined.
- America's cumulative investment in Brazil since 2000 ($27 billion) is less than half of total U.S. investment in Germany. U.S. investment of $7 billion in Russia was roughly a quarter of the amount of U.S. investment in Italy, itself only 2.2% of U.S. FDI in the EU overall.
- The roughly $19 billion sunk in India by U.S. firms since 2000 was just 60% of total U.S. investment in Norway during that period.
- Roughly 60% of U.S. investment assets were located in Europe, with the largest share, by far, in the United Kingdom. U.S. assets in the UK totaled $1.6 trillion in 2008, 14% of the global total, and an amount greater than total combined U.S. assets in Asia, South America, Africa and the Middle East.
- U.S. assets in the Netherlands ($1.2 trillion) were the second largest in the world in 2008. More than half of U.S. affiliate sales in the Netherlands are for export within the EU.
- America's asset base in Germany ($547 billion) was nearly double its asset base in all of South America in 2008.
- America's collective asset base in Poland, Hungary, and the Czech Republic (roughly $85 billion) was twice the size of corporate America's assets in India.
- U.S. assets in Ireland totaled $650 billion in 2008, more than total U.S. assets in either Germany or Switzerland. Ireland accounted for 9.5% of total U.S. assets in Europe in 2008.
- On a historic cost basis, the U.S. investment position in Europe was nearly 14 times larger than in the BRICs in 2009.
- U.S. investment in Europe ($2 trillion) was nearly four times larger than Corporate America's investment position in all of Asia at the end of 2009.
- U.S. investment stakes in Belgium at the end of 2009 ($70 billion on a historic cost basis) were on par with the combined U.S. investment position in China and India ($68 billion).
- Corporate America's investment stakes in Ireland ($166 billion) are much greater than total U.S. investment in South America ($125 billion).
- U.S. investment in Spain ($51 billion) is greater than U.S. investment in all of Africa ($45 billion).
- America's FDI stock in China in 2009 ($49 billion) was more than 20 times larger than China's investment presence in the U.S. ($2.3 billion). The EU's investment position in China ($81 billion) was 10 times larger than China's in the EU ($8.1 billion).
- BRIC companies combined in 2010 spent 3 times more on cross-border mergers and acquisitions in developed Europe ($44 billion) than in the U.S. ($14.4 billion). That compares to just $1 billion in combined acquisitions in Europe and the U.S. in 2001.
- Nonetheless, FDI by the BRICs in the EU is miniscule, accounting only 3.5% of EU FDI inflows 2002-2007—about the same as Norwegian FDI in the EU, and only about 9% of U.S. FDI in the EU.
- Total output of U.S. foreign affiliates in Europe ($638 billion in 2008) and of European affiliates in the U.S. ($423 billion) is equivalent to the total output of South Korea or Mexico.

- Aggregate output of U.S. affiliates reached nearly $1.2 trillion in 2008; Europe accounted for 53% of the total. The UK accounted for 26% of total U.S. affiliate output in Europe, followed by Germany (15%) and France (9%). These 3 countries accounted for roughly half of total U.S. affiliate output in Europe in 2008. Output was split between services and manufacturing.
- U.S. affiliates accounted for 21% of Ireland's total output in 2008; 7.2% of Norway's output, 6.2% of the UK's output, 5.7% of Switzerland's output, and 4.5% of Belgium's total output.
- U.S. foreign affiliate output in Belgium in 2008 ($22.5 billion) was more than double U.S. foreign affiliate output in India ($9.2 billion) and higher than in Indonesia ($14.3 billion).
- U.S. affiliate output in Poland in 2008 totaled $8.3 billion, exceeding U.S. output in more developed markets like Austria, Portugal, and Denmark. U.S. affiliate output in Hungary ($5 billion) was larger than output in Portugal ($4.7 billion) or in Greece ($4 billion); U.S. output in Turkey ($8 billion) was similar to that in Russia ($8.3 billion).
- Europe remains the most profitable region of the world for U.S. multinationals. U.S. foreign affiliate income earned in Europe rose to an estimated $196 billion in 2010—a record high—after collapsing in 2009.
- Even in recession year 2009 Europe accounted for just over 53% of total global affiliate earnings for U.S. companies. Since 2000, Europe has accounted for nearly 57% of the total.
- U.S. affiliates in 2009 earned over 6 times more in the Netherlands alone ($53 billion) than they did in China and India combined ($8.7 billion).
- U.S. affiliates earned $2.6 billion in Poland, Hungary, and the Czech Republic in recession year 2009, four times the level of 2000. Earnings were robust in 2010, with affiliate earnings in the Czech Republic 7% greater in the January-September 2010 period versus a year earlier; over the same period, affiliate earnings in Hungary and Poland rose 52% and 34%, respectively.
- Sales of U.S. affiliates in Europe were roughly double comparable sales in the entire Asia/Pacific. Affiliate sales in the UK ($622 billion) exceeded sales in all of Latin America.
- While U.S. affiliate sales in China have soared over the past decade, they do so from a low base, and still remain well below comparable sales in Europe. For instance, U.S. affiliate sales of $131 billion in China in 2008 were slightly above those in Italy ($129 billion) but well below those in Germany ($347 billion) or France ($232 billion).
- U.S. foreign affiliate sales in Ireland ranked fourth in Europe at nearly $250 billion in 2008, more than sales in France or the Netherlands.
- U.S. FDI flows to China rebounded last year, to $6.3 billion in the first nine months of 2010, following actual disinvestment of $7 billion in 2009. Since 2000, China has attracted just 1.8% of total U.S. FDI flows versus the following shares in Europe's major markets: Belgium (2.3%), Germany (3%), Ireland (5.9%), the UK (13.2%) and the Netherlands (16.2%).
- The U.S. was the top recipient of EU FDI outflows in 2010. European inflows totaled $106 billion in the first nine months of 2010, a 70% rise from the same period a year earlier. That equates to an annualized figure of around $140 billion—a marked improvement from 2009, yet still well below 2008 ($202 billion).

- The upturn in U.S. inflows from Europe was led by the Netherlands (+391%), the United Kingdom (+93%), Switzerland (+87%), Ireland (+85%), Germany (+53%) and France (+17%). Combined, these six countries accounted for nearly two-thirds of total EU investment in the U.S. the first nine months of 2010.
- In dollar terms, Swiss, French, German, and British firms led the way, with Swiss firms investing $18.2 billion in the U.S. in the first nine months of 2010, followed by France ($18 billion), Germany ($17.4 billion), and the UK ($17 billion). Dutch investment totaled $13.6 billion, while inflows from Ireland totaled $3.4 billion.
- In recession year 2009 Europe's investment stakes in the U.S. totaled a record $1.7 trillion, a 13% rise from 2008 and more than triple the level of a decade earlier. Corporate Europe accounted for 74% of total foreign direct investment in the U.S. in 2009 ($2.3 trillion).
- In 2009 EU FDI in the U.S. (€1.1 trillion) was almost 13 times more than EU combined investment in China and India (€85.5 billion). EU FDI in China totaled €58.3 billion in 2009, up from €47.2 billion in 2008, while EU FDI in India tallied just €27.2 billion in 2009, up from only €19.3 billion in 2008.
- In 2008—the last year of comparable global data—the amount of EU FDI flowing to the U.S. was more than to the next 6 destinations combined. Switzerland ranked 2nd, registering about 43% of the amount going to the United States. Canada was 3rd and Mexico 12th, bolstering the importance of Nafta as the EU's preferred FDI destination.
- EU FDI in China in 2008 was 26 times less than in North America; over 15 times less than in Wider Europe; almost 6 times less than in Rising Asia; 5 times less than in the Caribbean and in Latin America; almost 3 times less than in Africa; and half of EU FDI in Russia.
- Between 2001 and 2009 EU FDI outflows to the BRICS represented only 8.4% of global EU FDI outflows, and most of that was to Brazil and Russia, not China and India.
- Although EU FDI in North America was considerably more than to other world regions (38%), the 2008 levels were 14% lower than in 2001, whereas FDI in all other regions except Central and South America increased. 22.5% went to other parts of Europe outside the EU—about 6% more than in 2001.
- EU FDI outflows to the BRICs are focused primarily on Russia, and then Brazil, rather than China or India. While EU FDI outflows to Russia dropped off to only €9 million in 2009, flows to Russia in 2007, 2008 and 2009 totaled €45 billion, nearly 1.5 times EU FDI to Brazil, 2.5 times EU FDI to China and 4 times EU FDI to India.
- Although the share of EU FDI going to the BRICs still remains small—and has increased only moderately since 2002—overall the EU is the largest single provider of FDI to each of the BRICs. Germany and the UK are the EU's main FDI investors in the BRICs, followed by France and the Netherlands.
- The EU is by far Russia's major commercial partner, accounting for over half of its overall trade turnover. It is also by far the most important investor in Russia, accounting for up to 75% of FDI stocks in Russia.
- Nonetheless, EU investment assets in the U.S. are 3 times the size of those in the BRICs.
- Of the BRICs, EU investment assets are greatest in Brazil, with 4% of EU investment, mainly from Spain and Germany. The value of that EU investment, however, was only one-

tenth of that in the U.S. in 2009. EU investment assets in Russia were about 8% of those in the U.S. In China, the comparable figure was 5% of EU investment stock in the U.S.

- EU FDI links to India are particularly thin. India accounted for less than 1% of EU investment stock in 2009. In 2008, the last year of comparable global data, the EU total of €19 billion in FDI in India was 40% of its FDI in China; 28% of its FDI in the Middle East; 25% of its FDI in Japan; about 20% of its FDI in Russia; 14% of its FDI in Africa; 8% of its FDI in Latin America and 8% of its FDI in the Caribbean; 7% of its FDI in Rising Asia; less than 3% of its FDI in Wider Europe; and less than 2% of its FDI in North America.

- Services account for about 60% of EU projects and accumulated FDI stocks in the BRICS, compared to about 33% for manufacturing.

- Europe's direct investment stock in the U.S. in 2009 was nearly a record $2 trillion, up 7.9% from the prior year and more than triple the level a decade earlier. British and Dutch firms are the largest foreign investors in the U.S., with U.S. investment stock of both nations totaling $471 billion in 2009. In 1999 British stock in the U.S. totaled $216 billion and Dutch stock tallied $121 billion.

- Since 2000, European firms have invested roughly $1.4 trillion into the U.S., more than double that of the 1990s. Europe accounted for roughly 76% of total U.S. investment inflows 1990-1999 and 72% from 2000-2010.

- Europe's stakes in the U.S. are sizable yet declined to $8.6 trillion in 2008 from $9.3 trillion in 2007, a 7.5% decline. The United Kingdom ranked first as the largest holder of U.S. assets in 2008 ($2.1 trillion), followed by Swiss firms ($1.6 trillion). France and Germany ranked third and fourth, respectively, in 2008.

- The U.S. remains the most important market in the world in terms of earnings for many European multinationals. European foreign affiliate income earned in the U.S. rebounded impressively to total $105 billion in 2010, following recession year 2009.

- French affiliate income in the U.S. in 2010 soared 344% from the dismal levels of 2009, totaling nearly $15 billion. Affiliate income among German ($12 billion), British ($18.6 billion), and Dutch affiliates ($12.8 billion) rose 83%, 23%, and 33%, respectively.

- The output of British firms in the U.S. in 2008 reached nearly $108 billion—roughly a quarter of the European total. German affiliate output totaled $83 billion, or one-fifth of the total. French affiliate output accounted for 14% of the total.

- U.S. output of British, French and Germany affiliates declined 10%, 9.1%, and 5.8%, respectively in recession year 2008.

- Beyond European affiliates, only Corporate Japan has any real economic presence in the United States—Japanese affiliate output totaled $87 billion in 2008, well below output from British affiliates but slightly above output from German affiliates.

- Overall, foreign affiliates contributed nearly $670 billion to U.S. aggregate production in 2008, with European affiliates accounting for nearly two-thirds of the total.

- The Southeast and Mid-Atlantic states account for one-third of all EU FDI in the U.S. The Southeast's share was roughly 17% and the Mid-Atlantic's share 16.2% in 2007.

- The UK was the top foreign investor in terms of employment in 23 U.S. states. Germany and the Netherlands each ranked #1 in 3 states, while France was the #1 foreign employer in 2 states.
- Texas, California and New York are the top three destinations of European FDI. They account for nearly one-third of total European FDI in the U.S., even though they represent only about one-fourth of the U.S. population. European affiliates directly employed the most U.S. workers in California (287,000), New York (255,300) and Texas (212,200).
- Affiliate sales are also the primary means by which European firms deliver goods and services to consumers in the United States. In 2008 European affiliates sales in the U.S. ($2 trillion) were more than 4 times larger than U.S. imports from Europe (roughly $500 billion).
- Sales of British affiliates in the U.S. rose 6.5% and sales by French affiliates in the U.S. rose by 5% in 2008. Sales among German affiliates dropped sharply by 12.3%. Swiss affiliates posted a decline of 6%.

Transatlantic Trade

- The U.S. remains the #1 country market for EU exports of goods, accounting for 20% of EU goods exports in 2009. The U.S. also imports most services from the EU—43% of all U.S. services imports in 2009.
- North America was the largest destination for EU goods exports (23%) in 2009: 7% more than to Wider Europe; 2½ times more than to Africa; 2.2 times more than to Rising Asia; about 3 times more than to China (U.S. share 2.4 times more); almost 4 times more than to Russia; almost 7 times more than to Japan; almost 9 times more than to India.
- North America accounts for 23% of EU exports—the same as the Asia-Pacific region.
- Total U.S. exports to the EU rose 7.1% in the first eight months of 2010 vs. the same period a year earlier. U.S. exports to the world rose by over 22% over the same time frame, making Europe a relative laggard in terms of U.S. export growth in 2010.
- China has become the most important source of goods imported by the EU. Between 2000 and 2009, China's share of EU goods imports grew to 18.2% from 7.7%, while North America's share shrank to 15.9% from 23.9%.
- China's imports from the EU totaled $80 billion in the first eight months of 2010, a rise of 17.5% from the same period in 2009, while imports from the U.S. tallied $56 billion, a jump of 35%. Imports from Japan rose at an even faster rate—43% in the first eight months of 2010.
- Chinese imports from the EU15 in 2009 totaled $110 billion, vs. $109 billion from Japan and just $70 billion from the U.S.
- China has always imported more goods from the EU than the U.S., but the gap has widened over the past decade. Chinese imports of EU goods were 43% larger than U.S. imports in 2000 and 57% larger in 2009.
- Even though EU goods exports to China have been growing at a 30% annual average growth rate over the past decade—faster than any other goods export destination—China is only the

6th largest regional destination for EU goods exports. The EU exports more to Switzerland than to China.

- U.S. goods exports plunged 43% to crisis-stricken Greece, fell 3.3% to Ireland, and declined 2% to France in the first eight months of 2010. U.S. exports rose 15.7% to Italy, 11.2% to Germany and to Switzerland, and 7.6% to Spain. The UK and Germany were far and away the largest markets in the EU for U.S. goods.
- The Pacific coast state of California is Europe's largest trading partner among U.S. states, and exported roughly $25 billion in goods to Europe in 2009.
- Texas exports to Europe totaled $24.2 billion in 2009, almost double those in 2000.
- New York exports to Europe totaled nearly $20 billion in 2009, a significant decline from the more than the $30 billion the state exported to Europe in 2008.
- The UK was the top European export market for 15 U.S. states in 2009. Germany was second, the top European export market for 13 states, including Michigan and California.
- North America was the #3 regional source of EU goods imports (15.9%) in 2009, 87% of EU goods imports from China (U.S. share 70%) and 88% of EU goods imports from Wider Europe; 40% more than from Russia; 74% more than from Rising Asia; almost 2 times more than from Africa, over 3 times more than from Japan; and over 7 times more than from India.
- The U.S., EU and Japan all run massive trade deficits with China. The EU's trade deficit with China topped $160 billion in 2009, compared to $37 billion in 2000. The U.S.: $240 billion in 2009, up from $90 billion in 2000. Japan: $12 billion in 2009, down from $25 billion in 2000.
- Over the past 15 years the EU has essentially maintained its 19% market share of world exports, despite the rise of China, which tripled its performance and on the eve of the recession accounted for 16.1% of world market shares. In contrast, Japan and the U.S. each lost around 6% in market shares, so that the U.S. accounted for 12.5% and Japan 8.6% of world market shares in 2007.
- The EU is the most important trading partner for the BRICs—especially for Russia, Brazil and India. Of the major developed economies, the EU is the top supplier of goods to the developing world—by a significant margin—and has enjoyed far greater growth rates than either the U.S. or Japan.

Services: The Sleeping Giant of the Transatlantic Economy

- The United States and Europe are the two leading services economies in the world. The U.S. is the largest single country trader in services, while the EU is the largest trader in services among all world regions.
- The U.S. is the world's top exporter of commercial services, with a global export share of 14.1% in 2009, the U.K. ranks second (7%), followed by Germany (6.8%) and France (4.3%).
- Europe registered 10% annual average growth in commercial services exports between 2000 and 2009, 1% more than the global average, 1% less than Asia, but 4% more than North America. The EU15 almost quadrupled their services trade balance over the past decade; the

EU in 2009 had a trade surplus in services with every world region except North America and the Caribbean. 18 EU member states ranked among the top 40 exporters of services in 2009, accounting for 43.4% of world market share.

- The EU has sustained or expanded its share of world trade in most broad service categories except transport services, in contrast to developments in the United States. Regarding services exports, the EU ranked #1 in the world in 8 of 11 categories of services exports, and in fact boosted its position between 2005 and 2008 in communications, telecommunications, construction, computer and information services. The U.S. leads in 3 categories: royalties and license fees; personal, cultural and recreational services; and audiovisual services.
- The U.S. and Europe are also each other's most important commercial partners when it comes to services trade and investment. The services economies of the United States and Europe have never been as intertwined as they are today in financial services, telecommunications, utilities, insurance, advertising, computer services, and other related activities.
- North America was the largest destination for EU services exports (29.6%) and the largest source of EU services imports (36.9%) in recession year 2009 (down from 32% of exports and 39% of exports in 2008).
- EU services exports to North America in 2009 were 31% higher than to Wider Europe; over 3.5 times more than to Rising Asia and Latin America; 4 times more than to the Middle East and to Africa; almost 5 times more than to Oceania; over 7 times more to Russia, China and Japan; almost 15 times more than to India; and 29 times more than to the Caribbean.
- EU services imports from North America in 2009 were 43% more than from Wider Europe; over 4.5 times from Rising Asia; over 5 times from Africa; over 6 times from the Middle East; over 9 times more than from Oceania, China and Latin America; over 12 times more than from Japan and Russia; over 18 times more than from India; and 37 times more than from the Caribbean.
- 5 of the top 10 export markets for U.S. services in 2009 were in Europe. The UK ranked #1, Ireland 4th, Germany 5th, Switzerland 7th and France 8th. The same 5 countries ranked among the top 10 service providers to the U.S.
- The EU accounted for just over 41% of total U.S. services exports and for 43% of total U.S. services imports in recession year 2009.
- U.S. services exports to the EU more than doubled from around $100 billion in 1997 to nearly $200 billion in 2009. Yet in 2009 U.S. services exports to Europe plunged by 11.5%. Still, the U.S. enjoyed a $54 billion trade surplus in services with Europe in 2009, compared with its $73 billion trade deficit in goods with Europe.
- U.S. services imports from Europe peaked at $162 billion in 2008, more than double the levels of 1999. Yet in 2009 U.S. services imports from Europe declined by nearly 10%.
- Sales of services by U.S. foreign affiliates in the EU in 2008 rose to a record $638 billion, more than double the level of 2000. U.S. affiliate sales of services in the EU were nearly triple U.S. services exports to the EU.

- Europe accounted for nearly 57% of total U.S. services sales.
- The UK accounted for 36% of all U.S. affiliate sales in the EU; U.S. services sales in the UK ($229 billion) alone were not that far behind total U.S. affiliate sales of services in all of Asia ($268 billion).
- U.S. affiliate sales of services in the EU ($638 billion) in 2008 exceeded European affiliate sales of services in the U.S. ($447 billion). However, on a country-by-country basis, French, German, and Dutch affiliates sold more services in the U.S. in 2008 than U.S. affiliates sold in France, Germany, and Switzerland.
- European affiliate sales of services in the U.S. were more than 2.5 times larger than U.S. services imports from Europe.
- The U.S. and EU each owe a good part of their competitive position in services globally to deep transatlantic connections in services industries provided by mutual investment flows. A good share of U.S. services exports to the world are generated by European companies based in the U.S., just as a good share of EU services exports to the world are generated by U.S. companies based in Europe.

Transatlantic Jobs

- Despite stories about U.S. and European companies decamping for cheap labor markets in Mexico or Asia, most foreigners working for U.S. companies outside the U.S. are Europeans, and most foreigners working for European companies outside the EU are American.
- The combined number of workers employed by U.S. affiliates in Germany, France and the United Kingdom is more than double those employed in China.
- European companies in the United States employ millions of American workers and are the largest source of onshored jobs in America. Similarly, U.S. companies in Europe employ millions of European workers and are the largest source of onshored jobs in Europe.
- Roughly 42% of the 10.1 million people employed by U.S. majority-owned affiliates in 2008 lived in Europe—most in the UK, Germany and France, and almost evenly split between manufacturing and services.
- U.S. affiliates employed just as many manufacturing workers in Europe (1.9 million) in 2008 as they did in 1990. Yet the geographic distribution has shifted within Europe towards lower cost locations like Ireland, Spain and Poland. Between 1990 and 2008 U.S. affiliate manufacturing employment fell in the UK by roughly 34% and in Germany by 14%. Meanwhile, manufacturing employment in Ireland soared over 27% over the same period, while rising by over 18% in Spain.
- Even with the decline of manufacturing employment in Germany, the manufacturing workforce of U.S. affiliates in Germany alone totaled 387,000 workers in 2008—15,000 more than the year before and not far from the number of manufactured workers employed in China by U.S. affiliates (410,000).
- European majority-owned foreign affiliates directly employed roughly 3.6 million U.S. workers in 2008—over 100,000 more workers than U.S. affiliates employed in Europe. The top five employers were firms from the UK (957,000), Germany (614,000), France (550,000),

Switzerland (394,000) and the Netherlands (371,000). European firms employed two-thirds of all U.S. workers on the payrolls of majority-owned foreign affiliates in 2008.

- French firms employed 34,000 more people in the U.S. in 2008 than in 2007, while German firms employed 39,000 less and Dutch firms 20,000 less.

The Transatlantic Innovation Economy

- U.S.-based companies account for 34.3% and EU-based companies for 30.6% of the top R&D companies in the world, with Japan accounting for an additional 22%.
- Of the global top 20 companies spending on innovation, 9 are in the U.S. and 7 in Europe.
- 18 of the top 20 knowledge regions in the world are in the U.S. and Europe.
- The EU, the U.S. and Japan also lead in internationalization of patents. The U.S. and the EU are by far each other's most important host for overseas patents. The U.S. accounts for 60% of all overseas patents applied for by EU entities at the European Patent Office. This share is virtually unchanging over time.
- Private R&D spending in 2009 declined by 11% in Japan, 3.8% in the U.S. and 0.2% in Europe, while combined private R&D spending soared 41% in India and China. Nonetheless, Asia's twin emerging giants account for only 1% of global private R&D spending, versus 38% for the United States and 31% for Europe. China's R&D spending is largely from the public sector.
- The transatlantic share of global patents has fallen from 70% in 1999 to 62% today. Six Asian firms now rank among the top ten private sector recipients of U.S. patents.
- In 2008, U.S. affiliates sunk $24 billion on research and development in Europe, or nearly 65% of total R&D expenditures by U.S. foreign affiliates of $37 billion. R&D expenditures by U.S. affiliates were greatest in the UK, Germany, France, Sweden and Ireland. These five countries accounted for nearly three-fourths of U.S. global spending on R&D in 2008—a 30% increase over 2007.
- In the U.S., R&D expenditures by majority-owned foreign affiliates totaled nearly $40.5 billion in 2008—around 15% of total R&D spending in the U.S. A significant share emanated from world-class leaders from Europe.
- British-owned affiliates were the largest foreign source of R&D in the U.S. in 2008 ($7.4 billion), yet nearly one-quarter less than in 2007. UK firms accounted for 18% of total affiliate R&D in the United States.
- Swiss-owned affiliates were second with a 17% share in 2008, followed by France with a 15% share. French and Swiss R&D investment rose 7% and 7.8%, respectively.
- The R&D of German affiliates totaled $5.5 billion, and was mainly concentrated in transportation equipment, pharmaceuticals and machinery. Given recessionary conditions in the U.S., German investment fell 5.1% in 2008.

The Potential of an Open Transatlantic Marketplace

- A U.S.-EU zero-tariff agreement on trade in goods alone could boost annual EU GDP by up to .48% and 1.48% for the U.S.; generate welfare gains of up to $89 billion for the EU and $87 billion for the U.S.; and push EU exports to the U.S. up by 18% and U.S. exports to the EU up by 17%.
- A 75% reduction of services tariffs would yield almost $13.9 billion annually for the EU and $5.6 billion for the U.S.
- Aligning half of relevant non-tariff barriers and regulatory differences between the EU and U.S. would push EU GDP .7% higher in 2018, an annual potential gain of €122 billion; and boost U.S. GDP .3% a year in 2018, an annual potential gain of €41 billion. An average EU household would receive an additional €12,500 over a working lifetime, and an average U.S. household would receive an additional $8,300 over a working lifetime. U.S. exports would increase by 6.1% and EU exports by 2.1%.

Chapter 1

The Transatlantic Economy in 2011: On the Mend—But Still Hurting

Green shoots of economic recovery are appearing on both sides of the Atlantic in 2011, but both the United States and Europe face another difficult year as job losses, impaired financial systems and mounting fiscal debts continue to plague even the most robust areas of the transatlantic economy. The financial storm that slammed the global economy in 2009 has passed, but the U.S. and many European economies are still cleaning up the debris and dealing with the devastation left in its wake. 2011 is likely to be the year of a three-speed global economy, with Europe and Japan stuttering forward with less than 2% growth, emerging markets roaring ahead with growth of 7% or more, and the United States somewhere in between.

In 2010 the United States and Europe recovered gingerly from the depths of 2008/09 recession. Despite fears about a double dip recession in the United States, the U.S. economy posted growth of roughly 3% in 2010—good, but not great. Ditto for the European Union (EU)—the economy expanded by roughly 1.8% in 2010 but growth was quite variable, with 3.6% real growth in Germany, for instance, juxtaposed against declining output in Greece and Ireland.

Greece was the first to buckle under the weight of government overspending, mismanagement and corruption, and the EU and IMF were forced to provide a multibillion euro rescue package. Some months later, a second rescue package had to be cobbled together to save the Irish economy from imploding.

Greece's woes are different from Ireland's crisis, which stemmed largely from deeply troubled banks riddled with bad loans from a massive real estate bust. In response the Irish government nationalized three banks, backing them with a €50 billion euro bailout. This unaffordable expenditure of taxpayer funds, combined with a severe 7.6% contraction of the economy in 2009, pushed the Irish government's fiscal deficit to 32% of GDP and its public debt to 100% of GDP. Massive cuts in budgets, wages and prices failed to staunch the bleeding. Loans outstanding at Irish banks were more than 11 times the size of the economy. European banks had half a trillion dollars in outstanding loans in Ireland, nearly more than 3 times European exposure in Greece.[1]

Despite the different nature of the two crises, their combined effect has been to impose severe pain on each economy and to expose fundamental weaknesses in the mechanisms governing the eurozone, testing European unity as angry German taxpayers rebel against

[1] See Anders Aslund, Peter Boone, and Simon Johnson, "The Debt Problems of the European Periphery," Peterson Institute for International Economics, November 17, 2010; Address by Governor Patrick Honohan to the Chartered Accountants Ireland Financial Services Seminar, 23 November 2010; Anthony Faiola, "Humbled Ireland asks for bailout," *The Washington Post*, November 22, 2010; Landon Thomas Jr. and James Kanter, "Europe Fears That Debt Crisis Is Ready to Spread," *The New York Times*, November 16, 2010.

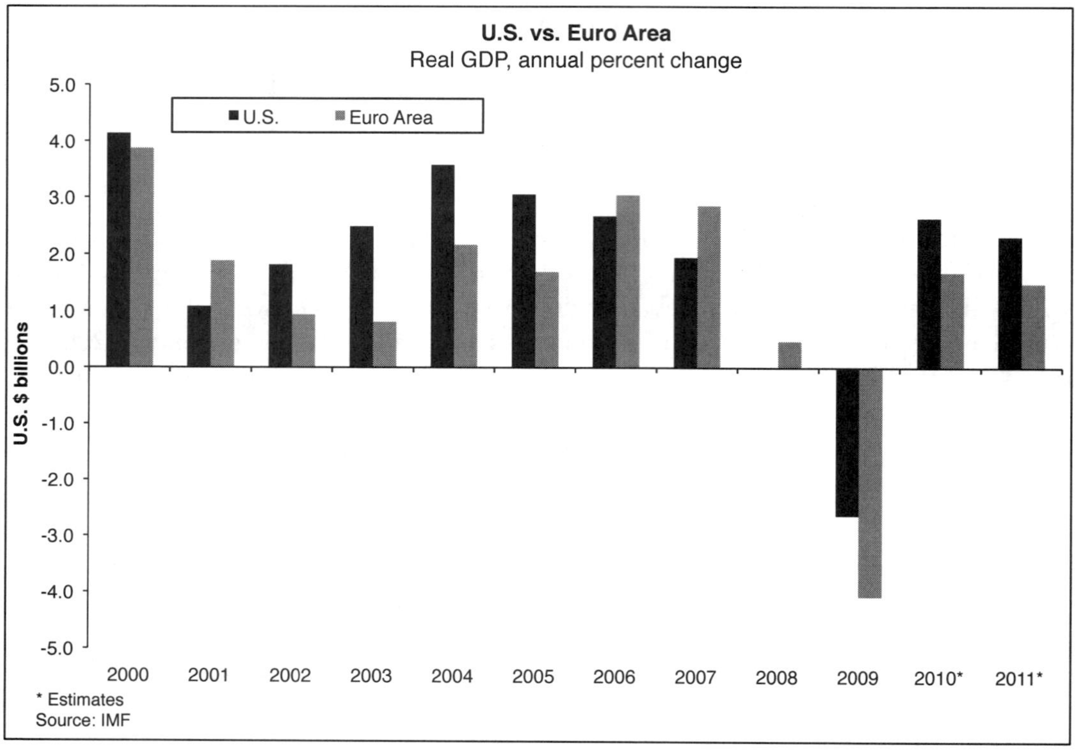

paying for what they believe to be Greek corruption and Irish greed. Images of protestors setting Athens ablaze remain fresh in the minds of many investors and business leaders.

Overall, however, economic conditions in the transatlantic economy have improved, with the United States and most of Europe emerging from recession in late 2009. The rebound was courtesy of aggressive monetary and fiscal policies on both sides of the Atlantic. Super-low interest rates helped to recapitalize the transatlantic banking sector, generating greater stability and confidence in global capital markets and a sharp rebound in transatlantic equity markets. Consumer and business confidence gradually improved over 2010 and is less frail in 2011. Global trade volumes have picked up sharply, rising 12% in 2010 after plunging by nearly 11% in 2009. Meanwhile, robust corporate earnings have sparked more transatlantic merger and acquisition (M&A) deals, a sure sign that corporate confidence is rebounding.

It will not be easy, however, to escape the Great Recession's wreckage. The economic crisis destroyed 7.3 million American jobs and cut U.S. GDP by 4.1%. It also cut more than 7 million European jobs and erased almost €150 billion from EU output. Between 2008 and 2010 the eurozone lost about 2.5% in per capita GDP relative to the United States and barely kept par with Japan, even though Japan's recession was more severe.[2]

[2] See Celine Allard and Luc Everaert, et al., "Lifting Euro Area Growth: Priorities for Structural Reforms and Governance, " IMF Staff Position Note, November 22, 2010 (Washington, DC: International Monetary Fund, 2010); David Cameron and Fredrik Reinfeldt, "Reining in Europe's deficits is just the first step," *Financial Times*, June 17, 2010.

The housing market remains the Achilles Heel of the U.S. economy, with millions of American homeowners struggling to come to grips either with mountains of debt, negative home equity, or no jobs. Some are coping with all three simultaneously. Despite record corporate profits in 2010, U.S. companies have been slow to rehire and remain relatively cautious about putting capital to work. Unemployment remains stuck at over 9%. Many U.S. states confront massive budget deficits that are forcing them to cut public sector jobs and services. On the plus side, U.S. consumer spending, which accounts for 70% of the U.S. economy, increased by 3.5% in 2010. With U.S. interest rates at historically low levels, corporate profits at all-time highs, and with the tone of the Obama administration less hostile to big business, the pieces are falling into place for accelerated U.S. growth in excess of 3% in 2011.

In Europe, the picture is less clear and more fragmented. Europe's periphery—notably Ireland and Greece—remains problematic, which in turn has made investors and policy makers nervous about Portugal and Spain. The potential for a sovereign default or debt rescheduling in one of Europe's most indebted nations remains a real risk in 2011. Bank profits on both sides of the Atlantic have improved, although the transatlantic capital markets remain fragile and are becoming increasingly fragmented. Despite super-low interest rates and government financial assistance, the financial health of both the United States and Europe remain key concerns in 2011.

Financial Sector Write-downs & Credit Losses vs. Capital Raised*
(Regional aggregates, Billions of $)

Period	Worldwide		Americas		Europe		Asia	
	Loss	Raised	Loss	Raised	Loss	Raised	Loss	Raised
Prior	(5.0)	0.0	(4.3)	0.0	(0.3)	0.0	(0.4)	0.0
3Q07	(60.3)	16.0	(43.1)	3.1	(15.8)	12.9	(1.4)	0.0
4Q07	(224.2)	76.0	(128.7)	47.1	(83.4)	28.9	(12.1)	0.0
1Q08	(229.8)	90.2	(135.6)	64.7	(81.7)	21.4	(12.6)	4.2
2Q08	(182.1)	203.2	(114.3)	103.8	(63.9)	84.9	(3.9)	14.5
3Q08	(273.6)	109.8	(206.8)	44.1	(60.5)	56.0	(6.3)	9.8
4Q08	(406.6)	445.8	(245.3)	266.9	(156.7)	147.0	(4.6)	31.8
1Q09	(153.9)	231.1	(103.9)	117.1	(46.1)	92.9	(4.0)	21.2
2Q09	(162.5)	123.9	(102.2)	90.2	(60.2)	11.4	(0.1)	22.2
3Q09	(48.1)	72.2	(31.3)	16.1	(17.2)	34.1	(0.4)	22.0
4Q09	(96.7)	129.2	(50.3)	21.2	(46.9)	102.0	(0.6)	6.0
1Q10	(59.6)	40.2	(44.1)	23.8	(15.4)	0.5	0.0	15.9
2Q10	(38.6)	14.9	(21.8)	11.1	(16.8)	3.8	0.0	0.0
3Q10	(29.9)	3.2	(17.0)	3.2	(13.0)	0.0	0.0	0.0
4Q10	(12.5)	34.5	(12.5)	0.0	0.0	34.5	0.0	0.0
1Q11	0.0	20.0	0.0	20.0	0.0	0.0	0.0	0.0
Total	**(1,983.4)**	**1,610.2**	**(1,261.2)**	**832.4**	**(677.9)**	**630.3**	**(46.4)**	**147.6**

Sources: Bloomberg
Data through January 26, 2011
* Includes all banks, brokers, insurers and GSEs; Reflects amounts reported or announced for the respective calendar quarter.

Since the financial crisis began in 2008, Europe banks have written off over $680 billion in bad loans. That is a large figure, yet by some estimates European banks have written off only half of their bad loans. U.S. banks are thought to have written off a larger percentage after suffering losses in excess of $1.2 trillion.

Spain, in particular, remains a huge "known unknown" factor in 2011, since a sovereign debt crisis in one of the EU's largest member states would rattle European capital markets and the transatlantic economy to its core. Spain's economy is larger than those of Ireland, Greece and Portugal combined, which means that the ripple effects from a debt crisis in Spain would reach much farther and wider than the others. Spain's gross debt in relation to GDP is expected to approach 75% in 2012, up from 40% in 2008. The country's weak regional savings banks (Cajas) remain a key concern, and a variable the financial markets are watching very carefully. Notably worrisome is the fact that European banks are massively exposed in Spain. According to the Bank for International Settlements, European banks have $657 billion of exposure to Spanish banks (28% held by German banks, 25% by French and 17% by British banks). U.S. banks have claims of $47 billion in Spain.

Countries' banks: cross-border exposure

As at end June 2010 **Exposure to...**	**French banks**	**German banks**	**Greek banks**	**Irish banks**	**Italian banks**	**Portuguese banks**	**Spanish banks**	**UK banks**	**Belgian banks**	**U.S. banks**
France		$196.8 bn	$1.9 bn	$18.1 bn	$31.6 bn	$8.2 bn	$26.3 bn	$257.1 bn	$29.7 bn	$161.5 bn
Germany	$255 bn		$5.7 bn	$32.1 bn	$254.4 bn	$3.9 bn	$39.1 bn	$172.2 bn	$20.9 bn	$152.1 bn
Greece	$53.5 bn	$36.8 bn		$7.8 bn	$5.3 bn	$10.0 bn	$925 m	$12.0 bn	$2.0 bn	$7.5 bn
Ireland	$50.1 bn	$138.6 bn	$461 m		$15.3 bn	$19.4 bn	$14.0 bn	$148.5 bn	$54 bn	$68.7 bn
Italy	$418.9 bn	$153.7 bn	$485 m	$40.9 bn		$3.4 bn	$32.6 bn	$66.8 bn	$24.6	$32.5 bn
Portugal	$41.9 bn	$37.2 bn	$101 m	$5.1 bn	$4.7 bn		$78.3 bn	$22.4 bn	$2.6 bn	$3.2 bn
Spain	162.4 bn	$181.6 bn	$673 m	$25.3 bn	$25.6 bn	$23.1 bn		$110.8 bn	$18.8 bn	$47.1 bn
UK	$327.7 bn	$462.1 bn	$19.7 bn	$209 bn	$44.0 bn	$7.7 bn	$386.4 bn		$43.1 bn	$572.7 bn
Belgium	$253.1 bn	$35.1 bn	$5.7 bn	$90.5 bn	$3.7 bn	$400 m	$5.7 bn	$172.2 bn		$40.0 bn

Source: Bank for International Settlements, Financial Times
Data for Foreign claims by nationality of reporting banks, immediate borrower basis

In Ireland, U.S. bank claims as of early February 2011 totalled $69 billion. European banks are even more exposed, with claims on Irish banks totaling $509 billion, 29% of which is held by UK banks, 27% by German banks, and 10% by French banks. As the accompanying figure highlights, cross-border banking exposure in Europe is widespread and cuts across all countries. While U.S. banks do not have much direct exposure to Europe's debt-laden periphery, American banks are nevertheless highly leveraged to British banks, which in turn are highly leveraged to some of Europe's most indebted nations. Hence, a sovereign debt crisis in Europe would not spare U.S. banks. Moreover, German banks have enormous exposure to the rest of Europe, making it highly likely that in the end the German government, despite its own great reluctance, will be compelled to ante up the necessary capital to keep the eurozone intact.

Reflecting the poor shape of public finances, the OECD projects government debt to exceed 100% of GDP in Greece, Italy, Ireland, Belgium and France by 2012. The EU's public debt is presently around 80% of GDP, and will only stabilize at these levels if Europe's most indebted countries can stomach severe budget cuts and maintain austerity measures with populations that are increasingly angry over how governments have managed state finances over the past decade. Budget deficits as a percent of GDP are quite high across Europe, averaging 6.2% for the eurozone as a whole. This average, however, masks wide variation: while the budget deficit is 3% of GDP in Germany, one of Europe's most fiscally conservative states, deficits are relatively larger in the United Kingdom (10.1%), Greece (9.7%), Spain (9.1%), and France (7.8%).

Not to be outdone, U.S. federal debt has tripled over the past decade, from $3.5 trillion in 2000 (35% of GDP) to $9 trillion in 2010 (62% of GDP) and could reach total U.S. GDP by 2015, about the relative indebtedness of Greece and Italy today. If the government does not act to alter this trend, global capital markets are likely to do it instead. The U.S. federal budget deficit for fiscal year 2011 is expected to total $1.5 trillion, a record high, and equating to roughly 10% of GDP.[3]

[3] See Ben S. Bernanke, "Rebalancing the Global Recovery," November 19, 2010, available at http://www.federalreserve.gov/newsevents/speech/bernanke20101119a.htm; Terrence Checki, "Challenges Facing the U.S. Economy and Financial System," November 17, 2010, available at http://www.newyorkfed.org/newsevents/speeches/2010/che101119.html; Roger C. Altman and Richard N. Haass, "American Profligacy and American Power: The Consequences of Fiscal Irresponsibility," *Foreign Affairs*, November/December 2010.

Given all of these figures, it is little wonder that the specter of sovereign debt defaults looms large over the transatlantic economy. At worse, one or two countries of the transatlantic economy may opt—or be forced—to reschedule some of their debt this year, an event that would dramatically increase financial volatility and economic uncertainty on both sides of the Atlantic. At best, the heavily debt-laden countries of Europe will muddle through, condemned to years of slow or very little growth—the penalty for living well beyond their means for years.

Unemployment remains another key concern for the transatlantic economy. The unemployment rate in the United States peaked at around 10% but still hovers at an uncomfortable rate of 9.4%. Nearly two years into recovery, the U.S. economy is struggling to create new jobs. The same holds true for most of Europe—despite a rebound in growth last year, the unemployment rate in the eurozone was 10.1% at year-end 2010. Germany is the outlier, with the jobless rate dropping to 7.5% in December. But in France, 9.8% of the workforce was without a job in November; in Belgium 11.5%, Greece 13.5%, Spain 20.6%, Poland 12.3%, and Hungary 10.7%.

The End Game in Europe

If there is a silver lining to Europe's financial crisis, it is this: policymakers—many of whom denied any problems a year ago—are becoming more aggressive with each policy response. The European Central Bank is expected to step up its bond purchases and the EU's rescue fund is expected to be increased in size. Some top European leaders are even expressing interest in issuing "eurobonds." The latter, thus far, have been rejected by Germany. There is even talk of a eurozone fiscal union, although we believe that the prospects of this happening at this juncture are slim. The EU's December 2010 announcement that a permanent crisis resolution mechanism (bail-out fund) would be created helped to reduce some of the pressure on Europe, but the size and nature of the fund remains in contention. Other options being explored include the creation of a pan-eurozone sovereign debt market; tapping the sovereign wealth funds of the Middle East; borrowing more capital from China and Japan, two huge surplus countries; and expanding European Central Bank purchases of various debt, following in the footsteps of the U.S. Federal Reserve.

The key point to be drawn from the above is that there are plenty of tools left in the eurozone tool box. The eurozone will be sustained and with any luck, could be even more integrated and intertwined when the financial crisis finally does pass. There is little probability that Germany, Greece, or any member for that matter, would leave the eurozone, as the costs would simply be too high. The eurozone will survive. The question is whether the right mechanisms can be put in place to stave off future financial crises among eurozone members.

Rebounding from the Great Recession

By most measures, 2010 was a vast improvement over 2009, the year the bottom fell out of the transatlantic economy. Whether in terms of trade, foreign investment, foreign affiliate

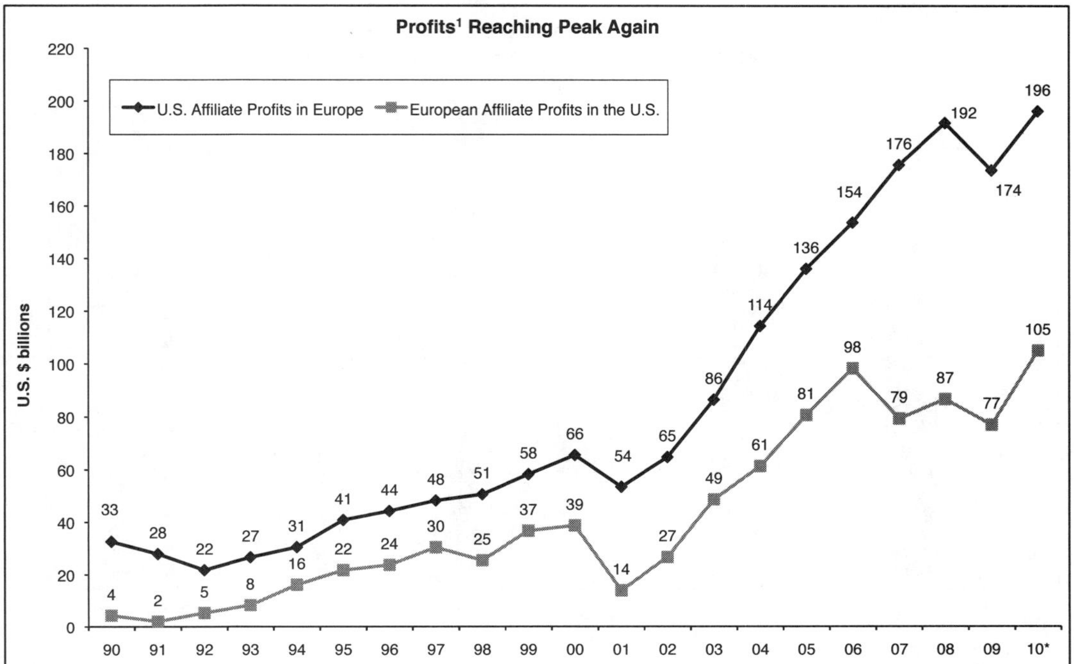

[1]Income of affiliates
Source: Bureau of Economic Analysis
Data through 3Q2010, Data annualized for full year estimate

income, or mergers and acquisition, the transatlantic economy rebounded sharply from the depressed levels of 2009.

For instance, U.S. foreign affiliate income earned in Europe rose to an estimated $196 billion in 2010—a record high—after collapsing in 2009, Similarly, European affiliates in the U.S. also saw their fortunes improve last year. As the U.S. economy rebounded in 2010, so did the income of European companies in the U.S., to the tune of $105 billion.

Because affiliate income (earnings) is a significant component of foreign direct investment, as affiliate income rose on both sides of the Atlantic last year, so did transatlantic foreign direct investment flows. To this point, in the first nine months of 2010 versus the same period a year earlier, U.S. FDI flows rose sharply to Germany (22%), the United Kingdom (243%), Italy (48%), and Belgium (172%). In contrast, U.S. inflows to France rose just 1% during the period. Meanwhile, the damage was far more extensive in Ireland, with U.S. foreign investment plunging by 17.5%. Ireland's banking crisis and tough austerity measures have dramatically reduced economic activity in a number of sectors, resulting in less investment capital from U.S. companies.

Not surprisingly, U.S. firms *dis*invested $18 million in Greece in 2010, following their even larger disinvestment of $157 million in 2009. U.S. firms decreased their investment in Spain by nearly 6% in 2010—not bad given all the market worries and concerns about Spain's slumping construction, troubled banks and less than ideal economic prospects.

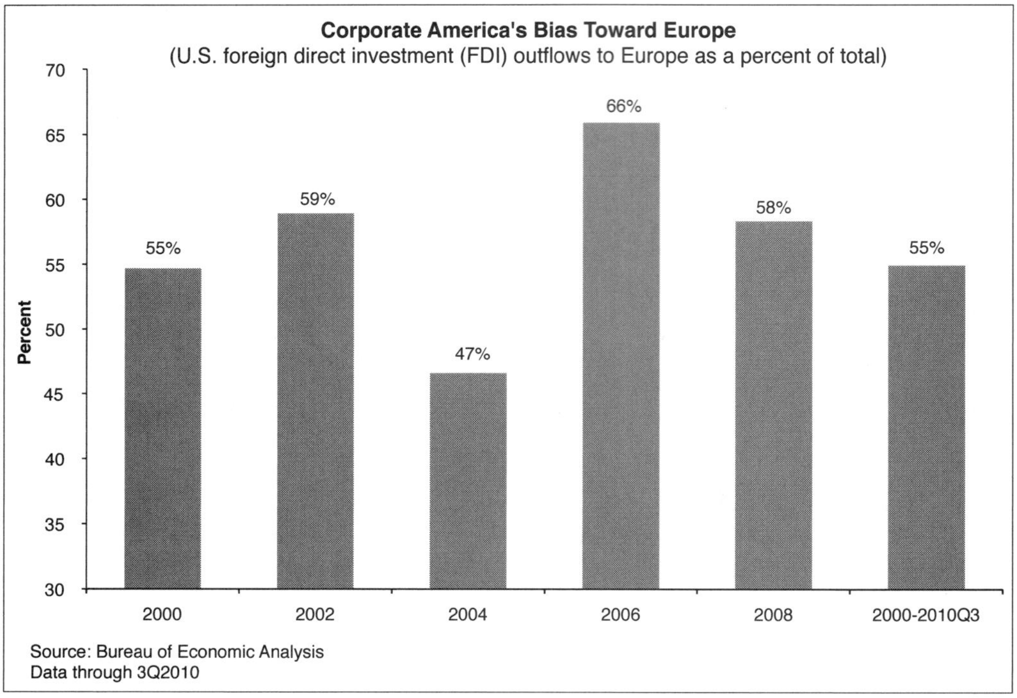

Mirroring the 2010 rebound in the U.S. economy, inbound foreign direct investment from Europe to the United States jumped sharply from the depressed levels of 2009. Based on the latest figures, European inflows totaled $106 billion in the first nine months of 2010, a 70% rise from the same period a year earlier. That equates to an annualized figure of around $140 billion—a marked improvement from 2009, yet a figure still well below the pre-crisis levels of 2008. The upturn in inflows from Europe was led by the Netherlands (+391%), the United Kingdom (+93%), Switzerland (+87%), Ireland (+85%), Germany (+53%) and France (+17%). Combined, these six countries accounted for nearly two-thirds of total EU investment in the first nine months of last year.

Trends in transatlantic trade were similar to trends in transatlantic investment and foreign affiliate income. For 2009, which our survey covers, U.S. exports to Europe were subdued. Indeed, only 5 states posted positive export growth to Europe in 2009, with the rest feeling the full brunt of the economic recession in Europe. In 2010, however, total U.S. exports to the EU rose 7.1% in the first eight months of the year versus the same period a year earlier.

Trends in transatlantic capital flows reflect many of the variables just mentioned. Europe remains a key provider of capital to the United States, the world's largest debtor country. Yet U.S. capital inflows from the European Union (excluding the global money center, the United Kingdom) tailed off significantly between 2007 and 2009. Worries over the strength of the U.S. economy, the sub-prime credit crunch, and the U.S. dollar converged in 2008/09 to produce sharp selling among European investors of U.S. securities. Inflows rebounded in 2009 but were below peak levels of a few years ago. As a footnote, capital flow figures in the above chart do not include capital from the United Kingdom, since a great

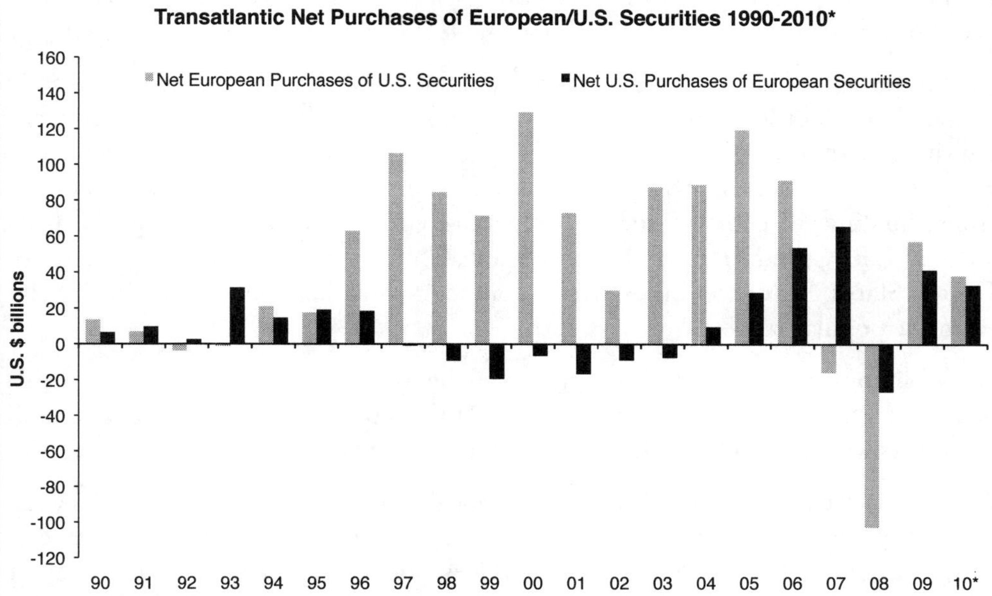

Excludes purchases to or from the United Kingdom
*Data through October 2010
Source: U.S. Department of the Treasury

deal of capital that flows from the United Kingdom originates elsewhere (Russia, the Middle East). The UK figures have been excluded from this analysis; the figures do include inflows from Norway and Switzerland.

U.S. portfolio outflows to the EU also declined over the crisis period. After outflows to the EU rose $54 billion and $66 billion in 2007, they turned negative in 2008. U.S. investors were net sellers of EU securities to the tune of $27 billion in that year, although purchases rebounded in 2009 and 2010.

Although European purchases overall are still down, in 2010 they revived, just when China's appetite for U.S. securities cooled. Chinese net purchases of U.S. securities totaled an estimated $20 billion. The slack was picked up amply by Europe, particularly the United Kingdom. Inflows from the UK totaled more than $360 billion in 2010, although these numbers need to be used with care.[4] Beyond the UK, it is interesting to note that French net purchases of U.S. securities were on par with China's in the first eleven months of last year, with French purchases totaling $19.7 billion versus China's total of $21 billion. Even Germany was not that far behind China, with net German purchases of roughly $14 billion in the first eleven months of last year. Greater purchases from both France and Germany,

[4] Treasury International Capital (TIC) data, U.S. Department of the Treasury. Chinese purchases are mostly foreign official accounts, whereas UK purchases are mostly private investors (retail and institutional) with accounts in London. Japan has a mix of both. Note that someone with an account in London is not necessarily British, he/she could be a French national residing in New York transacting through a London-based account. This is an unfortunate hazard of measuring cross-border flows, but does demonstrate the significance of London as a financial center.

we assume, were related to growing fears and risks over the sovereign debt problems of Greece and Ireland.

In terms of foreign holders of U.S. Treasuries, China and Japan rank number one and two, respectively; $896 billion was held by China, and $877 billion held by Japan. The UK ranked third, with holdings of $511 billion at the end of November 2010. Europe's total holdings of U.S. Treasuries, including by the UK, were in excess of $1 trillion—about 23% of foreign holdings of U.S. Treasuries, compared to 21% by China, 20% by Japan, 5% by members of OPEC, and 31% by others. In short, China is not the only critical creditor for the United States. Europe is an important source of capital as well, something rarely discussed in the popular media.

U.S. portfolio outflows to the EU declined over the past year. Indeed, after outflows to the EU soared in 2006 ($211 billion) and 2007 ($215 billion), they turned negative in 2008. U.S. investors were net sellers of EU securities to the tune of $40 billion in 2009 and 2010.

Finally, the services economies of the United States and Europe have never been as intertwined as they are today, notably in such activities as financial services, telecommunications, utilities, insurance, advertising, computer services, and other related activities. Regarding trade in services, five out of the top ten export markets for U.S. services in 2009 (the last year of available data) were in Europe. The United Kingdom ranked #1, followed by Ireland (4th), Germany (5th), Switzerland (7th) and France (8th).

U.S. services exports to the European Union more than doubled between 1997 and 2009, rising from around $100 billion to nearly $200 billion in 2009. Yet in 2009 U.S. services exports to Europe plunged by 11.5%, with a sharp decline in such activities such as travel, financial services, and consulting. U.S. services imports from Europe, meanwhile, also declined by nearly 10% in 2009. Services imports peaked at $162 billion in 2008, more than double the levels of 1999. The same five countries that ranked in the top ten U.S. export markets also ranked among the top ten service providers to the United States. On a regional basis, the European Union accounted for just over 41% of total U.S. services exports and for 43% of total U.S. services imports in 2009.

Beyond trade, there are the foreign affiliate sales of services, or the delivery of transatlantic services by U.S. and European foreign affiliates. Sales of affiliates have exploded on both sides of the Atlantic over the past decade. In fact, affiliate sales of services have not only supplemented trade in services to become a viable second channel of delivery for U.S. and European multinationals, they have become the overwhelming mode of delivery in a rather short period of time.

In sum, the United States and Europe remain each other's most important foreign commercial markets, a fact still not fully appreciated by opinion leaders on both sides of the transatlantic. Put simply, no other commercial artery in the world is as integrated and fused together as the transatlantic economy. Ties are particular thick in foreign direct investment, portfolio investment, banking claims, trade in goods and services, onshored jobs, and flows of ideas in terms of mutual R&D investment; patent cooperation; technology flows; and sales of knowledge-intensive services. These deep economic bonds have been critical to

The Potential of an Open Transatlantic Marketplace

Despite the rise of rapidly developing economies, the economic ties between the EU and the U.S. remain the core of the world economy. Their ties remain bigger, more prosperous, more tightly linked, more aligned in terms of free markets and open societies. The European think tank ECIPE estimates that a U.S.-EU zero-tariff agreement on trade in goods alone could boost annual EU GDP by up to .48% and 1.48% for the U.S.; generate welfare gains of up to $89 billion for the EU and $87 billion for the U.S.; and push EU exports to the U.S. up by 18% and U.S. exports to the EU up by 17%.[5]

Another source of new, secular growth: the transatlantic services economy, which we believe represents the sleeping giant of the transatlantic partnership. As we have discussed at length in other publications,[6] services sector reforms in such industries as capital markets, airlines, health care, telecom services and many others would provide an enormous economic boost to the transatlantic economy and enhance the global competitiveness of both sides of the Atlantic. According to a study conducted by the Dutch firm Ecorys, a 75% reduction of services tariffs would yield almost $13.9 billion annually for the EU and $5.6 billion for the U.S.[7]

Moreover, given that transatlantic trade tariffs are already quite low, the main obstacles to transatlantic commerce are not traditional "at the border" trade barriers but rather "behind the border" non-tariff barriers—different regulations, barriers to foreign investment, or different public preferences on issues such as product safety. The OECD estimates that reforms that included the elimination of tariffs on goods, reductions of regulations and barriers to mutual investment would permanently boost GDP per person by up to 3.5% on both sides of the Atlantic. This is the equivalent of giving every American and every European a year's extra salary over their working lifetimes. Even partial successes could have significant positive benefits for jobs, trade and investment. Ecorys estimates that aligning half of relevant non-tariff barriers and regulatory differences between the EU and U.S. would push EU GDP .7% higher in 2018, an annual potential gain of €122 billion; and boost U.S. GDP .3% a year in 2018, an annual potential gain of €41 billion. An average EU household would receive an additional €12,500 over a working lifetime, and an average U.S. household would receive an additional $8,300 over a working lifetime. U.S. exports would increase by 6.1% and EU exports by 2.1%.[8]

---

[5] Fredrik Erixon and Matthias Bauer, "A Transatlantic Zero Agreement: Estimating the Gains from Transatlantic Free Trade in Goods," ECIPE Occasional Paper No. 4/2010 (Brussels: ECIPE, 2010).

[6] Daniel S. Hamilton and Joseph P. Quinlan, *Sleeping Giant: Awakening the Transatlantic Services Economy* (Washington, DC: Center for Transatlantic Relations, 2008).

[7] Koen Berden, et. al, *The Impact of Free Trade Agreements in the OECD: The Impact of an EU-US FTA, EU-Japan FTA and EU-Australia/New Zealand FTA* (Rotterdam, Ecorys, 2009).

[8] Koen Berden, et. al, *Non-Tariff Measures in EU-US Trade and Investment: An Economic Analysis* (Rotterdam: Ecorys, 2009).

The Power Brokers of the Global Economy Compared

	Eurmerica	Asia	Chindia	Chimerica
GDP, PPP	42.1%	30.3%	18.1%	33.1%
GDP, Nominal	54.3%	24.3%	10.8%	33.0%
Market cap. (as of 1/25/2011)	$27.8 trillion	$17.0 trillion	$5.0 trillion	$19.3 trillion
Personal consumption exp. (as of 10/31/10)	58.4%	23.4%	7.4%	34.3%
M+A Sales	69.4%	24.3%	6.8%	20.4%
M+A Purchases	48.5%	25.7%	8.7%	18.1%
Inward FDI stock	62.9%	19.7%	3.6%	20.3%
Outward FDI stock	75.3%	16.0%	1.6%	23.9%
Inflows (2000-2009)	58.6%	21.6%	7.2%	21.5%
Outflows (2000-2009)	74.4%	15.4%	2.2%	19.1%
Exports* (Goods)	28.2%	30.6%	15.4%	25.4%
Imports* (Goods)	33.4%	27.6%	13.4%	27.7%
Military Spending**	$996.0 63.7%	$272.30 17.4%	$135.4 8.7%	$762.1 48.7%
Top 100 Global Brands (2010)	89 brands valued at $1.1 tr.	8 brands valued at $105 bil.	None	50 brands (all American) valued at $761.6 bil.

* Total does not inclu. Intra-EU27 + Norway, Switzerland, & Iceland trade
**U.S. $ billions at constant 2008 prices
Sources: IMF, Bloomberg, UNCTAD, SIPRI, Interbrand, EIU
All data for 2009 otherwise noted

prosperity on both sides of the Atlantic. Yet as both the EU and the United States struggle to recover from the economic and financial crisis, such ties can also amplify the challenges of slow growth.

Europe and the United States need to focus their search for future growth on each other as well as on satisfying demand from the rising middle classes of the emerging markets. The latter, no doubt, represent a secular growth dynamic for both the U.S. and Europe. But there are plenty of untapped growth streams available within the transatlantic economy itself, assuming forward-looking, enlightened policies from both parties. The notion that such policies have to be mutually exclusive in terms of investments and political energies is a false choice.

In this regard, the 2008/09 recession should be seized upon as an opportunity to deepen transatlantic economic linkages. Today, despite all the attention being paid to rising powers, trend lines and numerous metrics still point to a predominant role for the transatlantic economy. Investment, not trade, drives the transatlantic commercial ties, and investment flows between Europe and North America dwarf those between any other continents. Despite current difficulties, this is likely to remain the case in future.

While the concept of "Chimerica" has come into vogue in the past few years, "Eurmerica" is still the largest and most influential economic entity in the world. As the accompanying figure highlights, by virtually any measurement, the economic clout of "Eurmerica" surpasses that of "Chimerica," "Chindia," and Asia itself.

In this turbulent time, a key test of strategic U.S.-EU partnership will be the ability of the transatlantic partners to work with other key actors to restructure the world economy. There is still no substitute for transatlantic leadership, but in a G20 world this must be of a different kind—a more nuanced role that works to preserve the principles that have guided the remarkable global growth of the last few decades, addresses risky behaviors, and engages emerging economies as responsible stakeholders. They must resist those who see protectionism as the best way to safeguard national prosperity. They must take the lead in keeping the global economy open, starting by reducing the remaining barriers and obstacles between their own economic spaces, and inviting others to join. They must also be pathfinders to new forms of global economic governance that recognize the rights and responsibilities of the emerging economies while strengthening a rules-based open market global economy.[9]

Those who worry that ambitious transatlantic economic initiatives could threaten the multilateral system should consider that the opposite may be true. Europeans and Americans certainly share an interest in extending prosperity through multilateral trade liberalization. The Doha Round of multilateral trade negotiations is at the make-or-break point. But even a successful Doha agreement will not address such pressing issues affecting the European and American economies as competition policies, corporate governance, more effective regulatory cooperation, tax and other issues. Nor will it address cutting-edge issues raised by European and American scientists and entrepreneurs who are pushing the frontiers of human discovery in such fields as genetics and nanobiotechnology.

Transatlantic markets are the laboratory of globalization. Together the U.S. and Europe face issues that neither yet faces with others. That is why the "multilateral versus transatlantic" dichotomy is a false choice. The U.S. and EU should advance on both fronts simultaneously: push multilateral liberalization through Doha and press transatlantic market-opening initiatives in services, financial markets, telecommunications, energy, innovation policies and other areas not yet covered by multilateral agreements. The alternative is not drift; it is growing protectionism, U.S.-EU rivalry in third markets, and the triumph of lowest-common-denominator standards for the health and safety of Europeans and Americans.

The bottom line is that the transatlantic economy remains very strong on a secular and structural basis. We estimate that the transatlantic economy continues to generate close to $5 trillion in total commercial sales a year and employs up to 15 million workers in mutually "onshored" jobs on both sides of the Atlantic. These workers enjoy high wages and high labor and environmental standards. In addition, we continue to espouse the view that the transatlantic economy remains at the forefront of globalization—meaning that commercial ties between the U.S. and Europe are deeper and thicker than between any other two continents, and are presented with challenges and opportunities of deep integration that neither yet faces with others. This is evident from this survey, which paints a picture of continuing prosperity for both parties.

The transatlantic economy is on the mend, but its future health is not only dependent on the cyclical economic rebound underway. It also rests on more proactive, coordinated and forward-looking policy initiatives from policy makers and legislators on both sides of the Atlantic.

---

[9] For specific proposals, see Daniel S. Hamilton, ed., *Shoulder to Shoulder: Forging a Strategic U.S.-EU Partnership* (Washington, DC: Center for Transatlantic Relations, 2010); and *Transatlantic Leadership for a New Global Economy*, Report of the Atlantic Council Task Force co-chaired by Stuart E. Eizenstat and Grant D. Aldonas, of which the authors were members, with Frances G. Burwell as rapporteur. Policy Paper, Atlantic Council of the United States, April 2007.

Special Focus: The Dollar Reigns, the Euro Survives

The U.S.-led financial crisis, not surprisingly, has dulled the appetite of foreign central banks for U.S. dollars. That is the primary conclusion from the latest figures from the International Monetary Fund. Nonetheless, the greenback—by design and default—will continue its reign as the world's reserve currency for the foreseeable future.

A number of factors structurally underpin the dollar—notably America's capital markets, which are among the deepest, widest and most innovative in the world. The fact that a significant amount of the world's trade in goods and commodities is invoiced in dollars is another factor supporting the greenback's sway. Institutional inertia is another variable—despite all the talk about diversifying out of dollars, global circulation of greenbacks fuels the global financial system. America's military might, its favorable demographics and the U.S. economy's record of flexibility and resiliency are other key dynamics supportive of the dollar.

Moreover, where are the alternatives? The sun has set on the British pound sterling and the Japanese yen as core reserve currencies, although both continue to play a marginal role.

What about the prospect of China's currency, the renminbi, emerging as the world's number one currency? Our take: Don't hold your breath. It is going to be some time before the Middle Kingdom's currency challenges the dollar. International use of the renminbi is still marginal. Chinese authorities have started to allow certain investors to buy renminbi bonds issued in the domestic capital market. Some Asian central banks have started now to buy such instruments, and some Western multinationals are experimenting with using the renminbi in trade deals. But China maintains capital controls and does not seem keen on making its currency convertible, or free to trade in global capital markets. The IMF has resisted China's interest in including the renminbi in the IMF's basket of main currencies—so-called Special Drawing rights—because it does not pass the test of being "freely usable." Major questions remain regarding the rule of law and information flows with regard to Chinese financial transactions. And the Chinese financial industry remains relatively immature, quite opaque, and difficult for foreigners to access. All of these factors will limit the international use of the Chinese currency and ultimately constrain the international role of China's financial centers.[10]

In order for China's currency to be remotely competitive against the dollar, China has to modernize and open its financial sector, allowing for the build-out of efficient money and capital markets. The baby steps that have been taken recently are but a modest beginning. Not until the mainland fortifies and opens its capital account and strengthens its financial sector will the renminbi remotely challenge the greenback. The renminbi's trajectory to become a significant part of central bank foreign reserves will take years, yet could reshape

[10]For recent developments, see Patti Waldmeir, "Shanghai has some way to go to realise ambitions," *Financial Times*, October 27, 2010; Geoff Dyer, "Scramble to adjust to a new reality," *Financial Times*, October 27, 2010; Robert Cookson and Geoff Dyer, "Yuan direction," *Financial Times*, December 14, 2010.

global trade and finance. Initially, however, it is more likely to be used in China's trade with developing countries.

That leaves the euro. Despite its current woes, the euro has given Europe a global currency that is a legitimate and favorable alternative to the U.S. dollar. Despite the global financial crisis and the Greek and Irish dramas of 2010, the euro held its own. According to the IMF, the euro accounted for 26.5% of total allocated global foreign exchange holdings at mid-year 2010, significantly higher than its 18.3% share at the end of 2000. The pound sterling also increased its share, from 2.8% to 4.2%, while the dollar's share declined from 71.1% at the end of 2000 to 62.1% at mid- year 2010. The Japanese yen's share also declined during this period from 6.1% to 3.3%.

Among developing countries, demand for the euro is slightly higher—the euro accounted for 28.3% percent of allocated reserves by emerging and developing countries at mid-year 2010, compared with just 18.1% in 2000. The pound sterling also boosted its share from 2.6% to 6.3%. The dollar's share during this period declined from 74.8% to 58.4%; the yen's share also declined from 2.7% to 2.4%. Global claims in all other currencies amounted to only 3.9%.

This is a key point to consider since developing countries increasingly control a large share of the world's economic wealth, accounting for 64.5% of total central bank reserves in the third quarter of 2010. A decade earlier, they accounted for just 38% of the total. What's behind this trend: their fierce and unrelenting accumulation of reserves following the Asian financial crisis, a financial shock that turned one-time-deficit emerging markets into fanatical surplus countries. In other words, the foreign institutions that control the bulk of the world's capital (in terms of official central bank reserves) are becoming less and less enamored with the greenback, but remain relatively bullish on the euro.

The euro has allowed the EU to attract more of the word's excess savings. Europe's capital markets have deepened and become more globally competitive on account of the attractiveness of the euro as a world reserve currency. The result has been a more competitive financial sector in Europe, more low-cost capital available for capital investment and consumer spending within the region, and greater intra- and extra-euro area trade in goods and services. Enabling capital to flow from one member state to another without exchange rate risk is a key advantage of the euro.[11]

The bottom line: the dollar's reign is set to continue, although faint signs of a multi-currency world lie on the horizon, with the euro continuing to figure prominently if—a *big* if—European leaders are able to extract themselves from the mess they are in. The euro might be in even greater demand as a reserve currency today if not for its current travails. The euro area's Stability and Growth pact and no-bailout clause proved grossly inadequate during the single currency's first ten years. Its strictures on budget deficits were ignored by

---

[11]See Daniel S. Hamilton and Joseph P. Quinlan, *Globalization and Europe: Prospering in a New Whirled Order* (Washington, DC: Center for Transatlantic Relations, 2008); OECD, *Economic Globalisation Indicators 2010*, pp. 106-107, 111.

Germany, France and Greece, and proved irrelevant to Spain and Ireland, whose problems centered not on public finances but on private sector debt and asset bubbles.

The Greek crisis prompted lenders, especially from Germany, to call for more fiscal discipline by member states, leading to agreement among EU members to consider ways to rewrite parts of the EU treaties to ensure the euro's stability, by establishing permanent bailout procedures for future Greece-like crises to replace the current European Financial Stability Facility, a temporary €440 billion rescue fund, which expires in 2013. Yet this will take time, there is no agreement on how to pay for such a fund or whether private investors should bear more of the costs of future rescues, and the fundamental contradiction at the heart of the euro—the lack of a common economic policy to go with the common currency—remains unresolved. As Martin Wolf notes, the failings of the eurozone have not been fiscal irresponsibility, but rather macroeconomic divergence, financial irresponsibility, asset price bubbles, and shifts in competitiveness. If the eurozone is to function more effectively, it must manage these disorders.[12] Uncertainty about the euro, at a time of skyrocketing debts, deficits and sluggish growth, is something the EU simply cannot afford. And as the euro goes, so goes the EU itself.

[12]Martin Wolf, "The eurozone needs more than discipline from Germany," *Financial Times*, December 22, 2010.

Special Focus:
Trading with China—Advantage Who?

With so much of the media focused on China's exports, it is easy to forget that China is also the second largest importer in the world, trailing only the United States. Yes, China exports a great deal of goods—but the nation also consumes nearly 8% of world imports, a share greater than any country in Europe. Rising expenditures on infrastructure and the rapid emergence of a middle class have combined to boost Chinese imports dramatically to the benefit of many leading transatlantic firms.

In particular, benefitting from this little known fact are European exporters, who are way out in front of their U.S. counterparts when it comes to providing goods to the Middle Kingdom. Indeed, in 2009, firms from the EU15 even outdid Japan (albeit slightly), with Chinese imports from the EU15 totaling $110 billion versus $109 billion from Japan. The laggard: the United States. China's imports from the U.S. tallied just $70 billion in 2009, far below China's imports from Europe. While China has always imported more goods from the EU than the United States, the gap has widened over the past decade. Whereas Chinese imports of EU goods were 43% larger than U.S. imports in 2000, they were 57% larger in 2009.

In the first eight months of 2010, China's imports from the EU totaled $80 billion, a rise of 17.5% from the prior year, while imports from the U.S. tallied $56 billion, a jump of 35%. Imports from Japan rose at an even faster rate—43% in the first eight months of 2010.

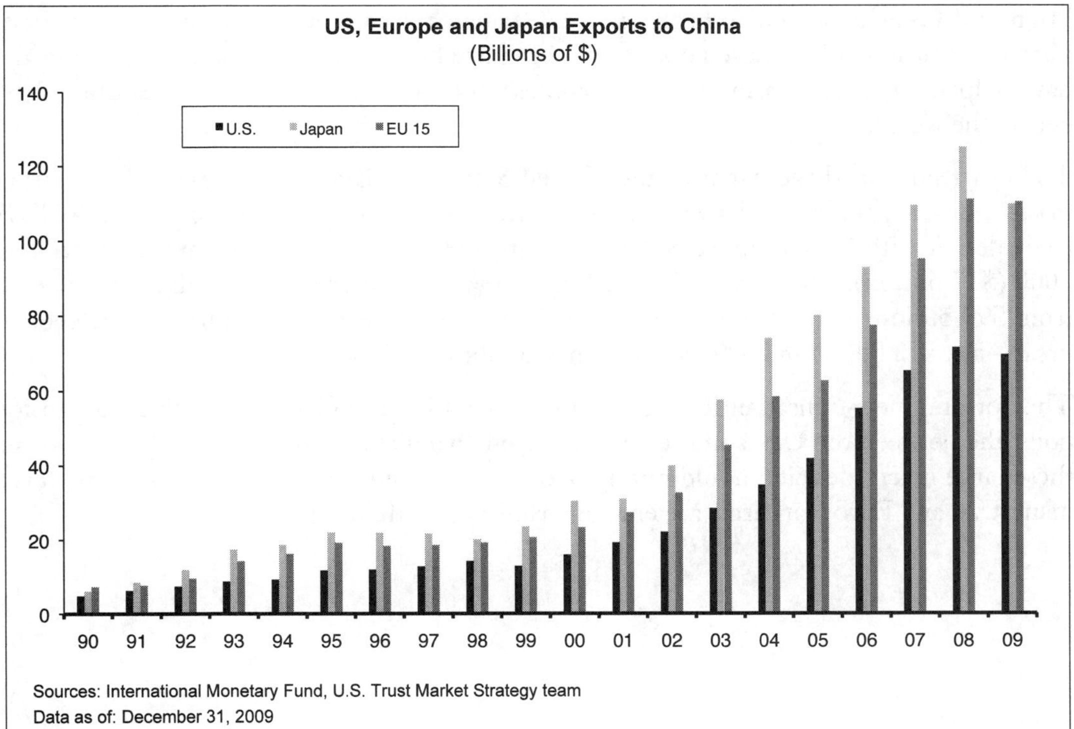

Sources: International Monetary Fund, U.S. Trust Market Strategy team
Data as of: December 31, 2009

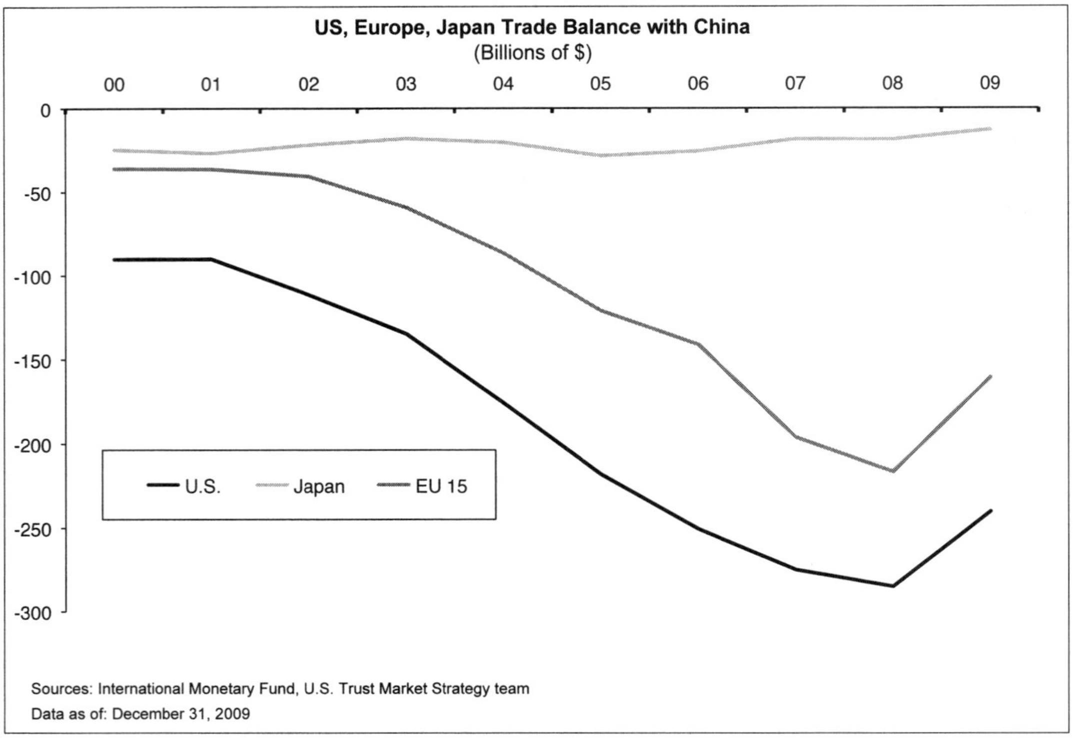

High-end French and Italian luxury items, German automobiles and capital goods, Swiss pharmaceuticals—all of these goods and more have become more attractive to China and have helped underwrite rising trading volumes with one of the largest and wealthiest markets in the world.

The downside: all three parties—the United States, the EU and Japan—still run either massive or large trade deficits with China. As the accompanying chart highlights, the EU's trade deficit with China topped $160 billion in 2009, a sizable jump from the shortfall in 2000 ($37 billion). The U.S. deficit with China was in excess of $240 billion in 2009, up from $90 billion at the start of the decade. Japan's imbalance with China has not been as great—just $12 billion in 2009, down from $25 billion in 2000.

The bottom line—transatlantic trade with China is still out of balance, a perennial tension point the between the U.S. and the EU on the one hand and China on the other. However, these large macro deficits should not mask or subsume the fact that at the corporate level, many U.S. and European firms are enjoying robust growth in exports to China.

Chapter 2

The Post-Crisis Transatlantic Economy: The Eight Ties that Still Bind

It is remarkable to consider today, as we enter the second decade of the 21st century, that cross-border trade is still considered to be the primary benchmark of global commerce. This measure, in our opinion, has been out of date for at least a half-century, and is now completely misleading in a world of extended production chains and dispersed economic dynamism. Why? Because trade is a limited form of international commerce. U.S. firms and their global counterparts in Europe, Japan and now even China prefer to deliver goods and services via foreign direct investment (foreign affiliates) rather than trade (exports).

One of the first U.S. companies to invest overseas, the Singer Sewing Company, opened a plant in the United Kingdom in the first decade of the 20th century. That is another way of saying that when it comes to investing overseas, U.S. firms have been at it for over a century. And in the past thirty years, the pace at which the global economy has become intertwined and integrated via foreign direct investment has only accelerated—and yet, strangely, trade alone remains the conventional yardstick by which many political leaders and most media measure and monitor international commercial interaction.

As we have highlighted in the past, it is foreign investment—the deepest form of global integration—that binds the transatlantic economy together, far more than trade. The latter, the cross-border movement of goods and services, is a shallow form of integration and often associated with the early phases or stages of bilateral commerce. In contrast, a relationship that rests on the foundation of foreign investment is one in which both parties are extensively embedded and entrenched in each other's economies. Such a relationship is more job-creating, income-producing, and wealth-generating for both parties than one based solely on trade. The transatlantic economy epitomizes this type of economic integration. As such, most American foreign affiliates in Europe are indistinguishable from local German, British, or Dutch firms, while European affiliates operating in the United States are barely distinguishable to U.S. consumers who enjoy European goods and services on a daily basis without much thought. Ubiquitous brands such as Trader Joe's, Jenny Craig, Sunglass Hut, Lenscrafters, AC Nielsen, Glidden Paint, Skippy Peanut Butter and Budweiser beer—all are as American as apple pie and all are European-owned companies.

We do not mean to downplay the importance of transatlantic trade, which remains considerable. North America, in fact, was the largest destination for EU goods exports (23%) among 12 world regions in 2009, according to Eurostat. EU goods exports to North America were about 7% more than to Wider Europe; 2½ times more than to Africa; 2.2 times more than to Rising Asia; about 3 times more than to China (U.S. share 2.4 times more than to China); almost 4 times more than to Russia; almost 7 times more than to Japan; almost 9 times more than to India. The EU exports about the same amount of goods to North America as to the entire Asia-Pacific region, with each region accounting for about 23% of EU exports.

North America was the #3 regional source of EU goods imports (15.9%) in 2009, behind Wider Europe and China. EU goods imports from North America were 87% of EU goods imports from China (U.S. share 70% of that coming from China) and 88% of EU goods imports from Wider Europe; 40% more than from Russia; 74% more than from Rising Asia; almost 2 times more than from Africa; over 3 times more than from Japan; and over 7 times more than from India.

In short, transatlantic trade is sizable and important to both economies. But one must add investment to the picture to get a true sense of the size and dynamism of the transatlantic economy, particularly compared to any other bilateral economic relationship either partner has in the world.

Companies invest abroad for various reasons. They may want to make a strategic investment, for instance to introduce a new product or service. They may seek resources, such as acquiring access to specialized knowledge or particular technologies. They may want to win share in new markets, or they may want to achieve greater efficiencies by gaining access to cheap factors of production. While much media and political attention focuses on the resource- or efficiency-seeking motivations behind such investments, particularly the need for cheap foreign labor, the reality is that the increasingly critical need for companies to position themselves within pan-continental markets, and to generate new sources of knowledge that they can turn into new sources of profit, drives a good deal of mutual investment across the Atlantic.

The U.S. and Europe are each other's primary source and destination for foreign direct investment. 38% of the EU's foreign direct investment (FDI) went to North America (32.5% to the U.S.) in 2008, the last year of comprehensive global data available from Eurostat. EU FDI outflows to the U.S. were more than the next 6 destinations combined, and 1.7 times more than in Wider Europe; 4½ times more than in Rising Asia; 5 times more than in Central and South America; over 9 times more than in Africa; over 13 times more than in Russia; 16 times more than in Japan; 18 times more than in the Middle East; over 26 times more than in China; and 65 times more than in India.

North America, in turn supplied almost half of all FDI coming into the EU. The U.S. remains the principal source (44.4%) of FDI in the EU; the EU is the top destination of U.S. global FDI. In 2008, the last year of comprehensive data, U.S. FDI in the EU totaled €1.05 trillion, more than the next 20 investors combined.

Moreover, these affiliates invest in local communities. European affiliates in the United States employ millions of American workers and are the largest source of onshored jobs in America. Similarly, U.S. corporate affiliates in Europe employ millions of European workers and are the largest source of onshored jobs in Britain, Ireland and across the continent.

The Transatlantic Economy in the World

There is no commercial artery in the world as large as the one binding the United States and Europe together. The transatlantic economy still accounts for over 54% of world GDP in terms of value and 42% in terms of purchasing power, is the largest and wealthiest market in the world, and is at the forefront of driving global foreign direct investment and global mergers and acquisitions activity. Even following the financial crisis, U.S. and EU financial markets continue to account for well over two-thirds of global banking assets; three-quarters of global financial services; 77% of equity-linked derivatives; more than 70% of all private and public debt securities; almost 80% of all interest-rate derivatives; almost 75% of all new international debt securities; 70% of all foreign exchange derivatives transactions; 65% of the top R&D companies and 56% of all global R&D; and 18 of the top 20 knowledge regions in the world. 92.8% of global foreign exchange holdings are either in dollars (62.1%), euros (26.5%) or sterling (4.2%).[1]

All told, by our estimate nearly $5 trillion in commerce takes place between U.S. and European companies and their affiliates each year.

Hence, when one half of the transatlantic partnership suffers or goes into recession, as the United States did in 2009, the other half suffers as well. The transatlantic economic recession has been deep and painful, and has yet to run its course. The economic outlook in Europe's periphery (Ireland, Greece, Portugal and Spain) remains problematic. The eurozone posted overall growth of nearly 2% in 2010, but growth was concentrated in Germany and the north, while Ireland and the south struggle to shore up their banks, adjust to new austerity measures and deal with soaring unemployment. While U.S. banks have avoided the financial fallout from Europe's debt crisis—at least thus far—U.S. firms and their affiliates in Ireland, Greece and other debt-laden nations have felt the full brunt of the trials and tribulations of many in Europe.

In the U.S., meanwhile, it is hardly "mission accomplished." The economy is showing signs of life, although a staple of the economy, the U.S. housing market, remains mired in one of the worse downturns in history. The federal budget deficit is expected to top $1 trillion again this fiscal year. State finances remain a mess and a U.S. unemployment rate above 9% speaks to the sluggish nature of domestic job growth. The U.S. continues to be overly reliant on spending and borrowing, rather than saving, investing and competing in the global marketplace.

U.S. economic challenges, in turn, have consequences for Europe, given that the U.S. is the top country export destination for EU goods and services, the EU's leading source and destination of both FDI and private portfolio investment, and a key innovation partner for European economies seeking to maintain their competitive position in knowledge-based activities.

In other words, the transatlantic economy has some heavy lifting to do over the next twelve months. Success or failure in one part of the relationship will affect the other since no two

---

[1] IMF; Bank for International Settlements; Steffen Kern, "Global financial centres after the crisis," DB Research, August 2, 2010; Transatlantic Business Dialogue (TABD), " EU-U.S. financial markets—need for cooperation in difficult times," Brussels and Washington, February 2010; World Knowledge Competitive Index, available at http://www.cforic.org/downloads.php.

regions of the global economy are as economically fused as the two parties straddling the Atlantic.

That said, it has long been our contention that one of the most dangerous deficits affecting the transatlantic partnership is not one of trade, values, or military capabilities but rather a deficit in understanding among opinion leaders of the vital stakes Americans and Europeans have developed in the success of each other's respective economies. Hence, transatlantic differences over financial sector reform, divergent fiscal and monetary policies, and other critical issues like global climate change are cause for concern. With so much attention devoted to the rise of the Chinese economy and shifting trade flows in both the United States and Europe, many on both sides of the Atlantic have forgotten about the importance of investment and the unappreciated, invisible and little understood activities of foreign affiliates, which represent the real backbone of the transatlantic economy.

This is illustrated in accompanying chart, which illustrates the weight of the transatlantic economy in the overall global economy. Taken together U.S. and European exports to the world accounted for only 28.2% of global exports in 2009; and combined U.S. and European imports accounted for 33.4% of global imports. But the U.S. and Europe together accounted for 62.9% of the inward stock of foreign direct investment (FDI), and a whopping 75.3% of outward stock of FDI. Moreover, each partner has built up the great majority of that stock in the other economy. In short, mutual investment in the North Atlantic space is very large, dwarfs trade, and has become essential to U.S. and European jobs and prosperity.

The Transatlantic Economy vs. The World

Share of World Total

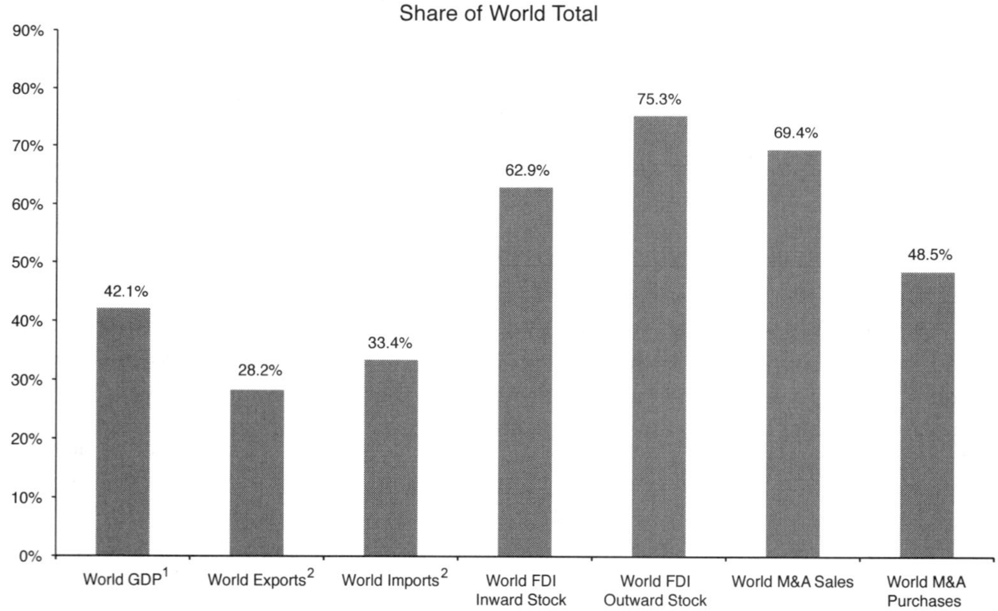

Source: UN, IMF, figures for 2009
1. Based on PPP estimates,
2. Excluding intra-EU, Norway, Switzerland and Iceland trade

In short, the transatlantic economy remains the dominant force in the global economy. Rising powers are resetting the global economy, but they haven't done so yet. Such a transformation is neither complete nor pre-ordained. And a different world economy is not necessarily a worse one for Americans and Europeans—if they use the coming decade to leverage global growth, human talent and innovation while tackling related challenges of deficits and debt, building on their own considerable strengths, and exploiting the full potential of the transatlantic economy.

Time is not standing still, however. Over the past decade, for instance, Asia's share of investment banking revenues has risen from 13% to more than 20%. The transatlantic share in global stock market capitalization has declined substantially from 78% to just over 50% today, and its share in stock trading has fallen from 86% to just over 70%. BRIC stock markets grew more than 40% per year in the past decade, while EU and U.S. markets contracted. The BRIC share of listed companies worldwide has jumped from just over 2% in 2000 to 22% today. More than half of the world's IPOs in 2009 were listed in China alone.[2]

Moreover, European and American financial and economic credibility was damaged considerably by the financial crisis. As Chinese Deputy Premier Wang Qishan reportedly noted, "the teachers now have some problems." As a result, the window is closing on the ability of the U.S. and Europe alone to set the rules and reap the benefits of an open global economy. Whereas much of the past decade was about the deep integration of the transatlantic economy, during the coming decade U.S. and European companies are likely to focus much more on positioning themselves for a global economy with multiple engines and sources of growth and innovation. In this year's survey, in addition to our basic review of the deep interlinkages binding the two sides of the North Atlantic, we explore specific areas in which rising economies are beginning to affect the dynamics of the transatlantic economy.

The Ties that Bind—Quantifying the Transatlantic Economy

Foreign affiliates on both sides of the Atlantic have constructed a formidable commercial infrastructure over the past half century. Remarkably, notwithstanding all the stress and strain on the transatlantic partnership over the past decade, this infrastructure remains solid and dynamic. Even in the face of the transatlantic recession of 2008/09, the transatlantic foundation remains firm. Indeed, if there is a common theme running through the narrative below, it is this: while many measures of economic performance declined sharply in 2009 due to the transatlantic recession, these same variables posted a sharp rebound in 2010 as the transatlantic economy stabilized and began to expand again.

[2] Figure includes Hong Kong SAR. See Steffen Kern, "China's financial markets—a future global force?" Deutsche Bank Research, Frankfurt am Main, 2009, p. 22; Kern (2010), op. cit.; "International Financial Markets in the UK," International Financial Services London, May 2010, p. 5; World Federation of Exchanges. For a detailed analysis of the role of U.S. and EU financial markets in the world economy, see Steffen Kern, "EU-U.S. financial market integration – work in progress," Deutsche Bank Research, Frankfurt, 2008; also TABD, op. cit.

Over the past few years we have suggested eight key indices that offer a clearer picture of the "deep integration" forces shaping the transatlantic economy. This chapter updates those indices with the latest available data. Each variable, in general, has grown in size and importance over the past decade. However, in the face of the transatlantic recession of 2008/09, many of the variables discussed below are in a state of flux and have contracted as part of the economic downturn. This was to be expected, and as the transatlantic economy regains momentum in 2011, so will many of the metrics below.

1. Gross Product of Foreign Affiliates

In their own right, U.S. affiliates in Europe and European affiliates in the United States are among the largest economic forces in the world. For instance, the total output of U.S. foreign affiliates in Europe ($638 billion in 2008) and of European affiliates in the U.S. ($423 billion) is greater than the total gross domestic output of most countries. Combined, transatlantic foreign affiliate output (roughly $1 trillion) was basically unchanged from the prior year. Putting that number into perspective, the combined output of transatlantic affiliates is equivalent to the total output of South Korea or Mexico. As a separate unit, and in terms of output, transatlantic affiliates rank among the top 20 economic producers of the world. Of particular note, U.S. affiliate output in Europe rose 5.1% in 2008, while European affiliate output in the U.S. fell 1.6%. That is not surprising—the U.S. led the world into recession, hurting European affiliates first, while Europe output rolled over some six months after the "Made in U.S." financial crisis.

America's Major Commercial Arteries

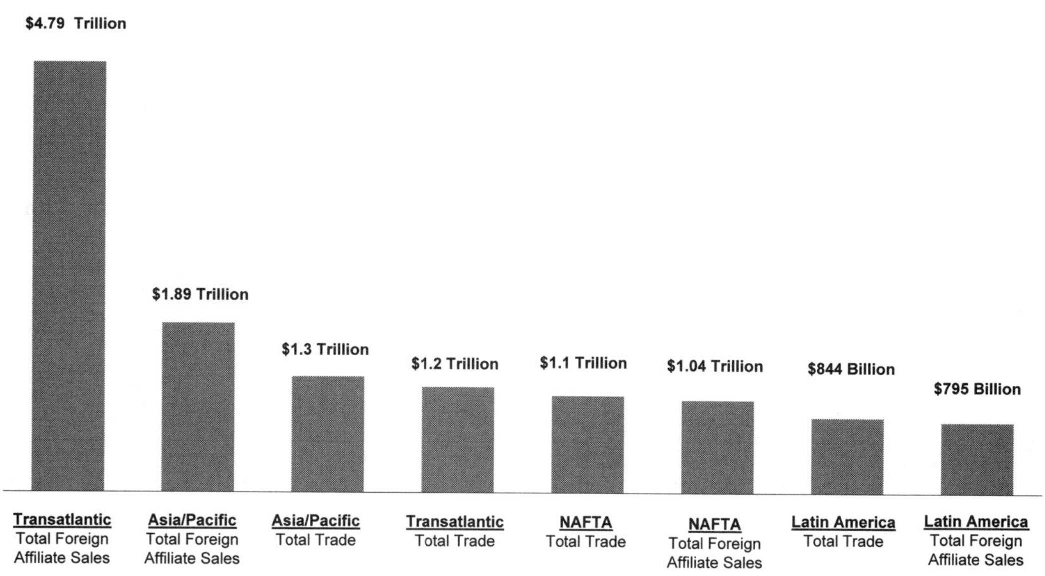

Foreign Affiliate Sales: Data for 2008 Total Trade: Data in goods & services, 2008
Source: Bureau of Economic Analysis

On a global basis, aggregate output of U.S. affiliates reached nearly $1.2 trillion in 2008, with Europe accounting for roughly 53% of the total. The latter figure was basically unchanged from the prior year. The United Kingdom, where U.S. investment ties are among the deepest, accounted for 26% of total affiliate output in Europe, followed by Germany (15%) and France (9%). These three countries accounted for roughly half of total U.S. affiliate output in Europe in 2008. By sector, output was almost evenly split between services and manufacturing.

The presence of U.S. affiliates in some European countries is particularly noteworthy. The gross output of American affiliates in Ireland, for instance, represented 21% of Ireland's total output in 2008, roughly unchanged from the prior year. This dynamic reflects, in part, the large U.S. investment base, notably among U.S. technology companies, in the "Celtic Tiger." It also underscores the point that the U.S. and Ireland are joined at the economic hip—for better in good times and for worse in bad times—and Ireland is experiencing some painful times now. Ireland quickly felt the effects of the U.S. downturn, hurting American affiliates, and then slipped into an even deeper recession last year due to its banking crisis. U.S. affiliates in Ireland are not only in the process of trimming their workforce and deferring additional capital spending; the country's banking sector remains burdened with massive amounts of non-performing loans. Deep in debt, Ireland's economic future is quite uncertain, and as key component of the economy, U.S. affiliates will not be spared the country's pain.

Elsewhere, U.S. affiliates accounted for 7.2% of Norway's aggregate output, 6.2% of the United Kingdom's aggregate output, 5.7% of Switzerland's aggregate output, and 4.5% of Belgium's total output. Regarding the latter, it is interesting to note that U.S. foreign affiliate output in Belgium in 2008 ($22.5 billion) was more than double U.S. foreign affiliate output in India ($9.2 billion) and Indonesia ($14.3 billion).

Slowly but surely, more U.S. firms are taking advantage of the EU's expanded Single Market and are incorporating central and eastern European member states, as well as such key non-EU countries as Turkey and Russia, into their European and global production networks. U.S. affiliate output in Poland, for instance, totaled $8.3 billion, exceeding U.S. output in more developed markets like Austria, Portugal, and Denmark. U.S. affiliate output in Hungary in 2008 ($5 billion) was larger than output in Greece ($4 billion); U.S. output in Russia ($8.3 billion) easily surpassed output in Portugal ($4.7 billion); and total output in Turkey ($8 billion) was nearly a quarter larger than output in Austria.

In the United States, European affiliates are major economic producers in their own right, with British firms of notable importance. Their U.S. output reached nearly $108 billion in 2008, or roughly a quarter of the European total. Output from German affiliates operating in the U.S. totaled $83 billion, or one-fifth of the total, while output from French affiliates accounted for 14% of the total. However, reflecting the onset of the U.S. recession, U.S. output of British, French and Germany affiliates declined 10%, 9.1%, and 5.8%, respectively in 2008. That is hardly surprising since the U.S. spent the entire year in recession. Beyond European affiliates, only Corporate Japan has any real economic presence in the United States—Japanese affiliate output totaling $87 billion in 2008, well below output from British affiliates but slightly above output from German affiliates. Overall, foreign affiliates contributed nearly $670 billion to U.S. aggregate production in 2008, with European affiliates accounting for nearly two-thirds of the total.

2. Assets of Foreign Affiliates

America's global commercial presence, in the form of foreign assets of corporate America, totaled over $11.4 trillion in 2008. That represents a 15% decline from the historic peak of 2007. The bulk of these assets—roughly 60%—were located in Europe, with the largest share, by far, in the United Kingdom. U.S. assets in the UK totaled $1.6 trillion in 2008, 14% of the global total, and an amount greater than total combined U.S. assets in Asia, South America, Africa and the Middle East.

U.S. assets in the Netherlands ($1.2 trillion) were the second largest in the world in 2008. America's sizable asset base in the Netherlands reflects the host country's strategic role as an export platform/distribution hub for U.S. firms doing business in the rest of the European Union. To this point, more than half of affiliate sales in the Netherlands are for export, namely within the EU. Meanwhile, America's asset base in Germany ($547 billion) was nearly double its asset base in all of South America in 2008. America's collective asset base in Poland, Hungary, and the Czech Republic (roughly $85 billion) was twice the size of corporate America's assets in India. As for Corporate America's in-country presence in Ireland, U.S. assets totaled $650 billion in 2008, more than total U.S. assets in either Germany or Switzerland. Ireland accounted for 9.5% of total U.S. assets in Europe in 2008.

As for foreign-owned assets in the United States, Europe's stakes are sizable yet declined to $8.6 trillion in 2008 from $9.3 trillion in 2007, a 7.5% decline. The United Kingdom ranked first as the largest holder of U.S. assets in 2008 ($2.1 trillion), followed by Swiss firms ($1.6 trillion). France and Germany ranked third and fourth, respectively, in 2008.

Global Engagement: Foreign Affiliate Sales vs. Trade

$ billions, 2008	U.S. Foreign Affiliate Sales vs. Trade
Global Sales of U.S.-owned Affiliates[1] (G&S)	5,202.2
Total U.S. Exports (G&S)	1,839.0
U.S. Sales of Foreign-owned Affiliates[2]	3,448.6
Total U.S. Imports (G&S)	2,537.8
European Sales of U.S.-owned Affiliates[1]	2,726.1
U.S. Exports to Europe (G&S)	558.4
U.S. Sales of European-owned Affiliates[2]	2,063.9
U.S. Imports from Europe (G&S)	624.9

Source: Bureau of Economic Analysis

[1] Majority-owned nonbank affiliates

[2] Majority-owned affiliates

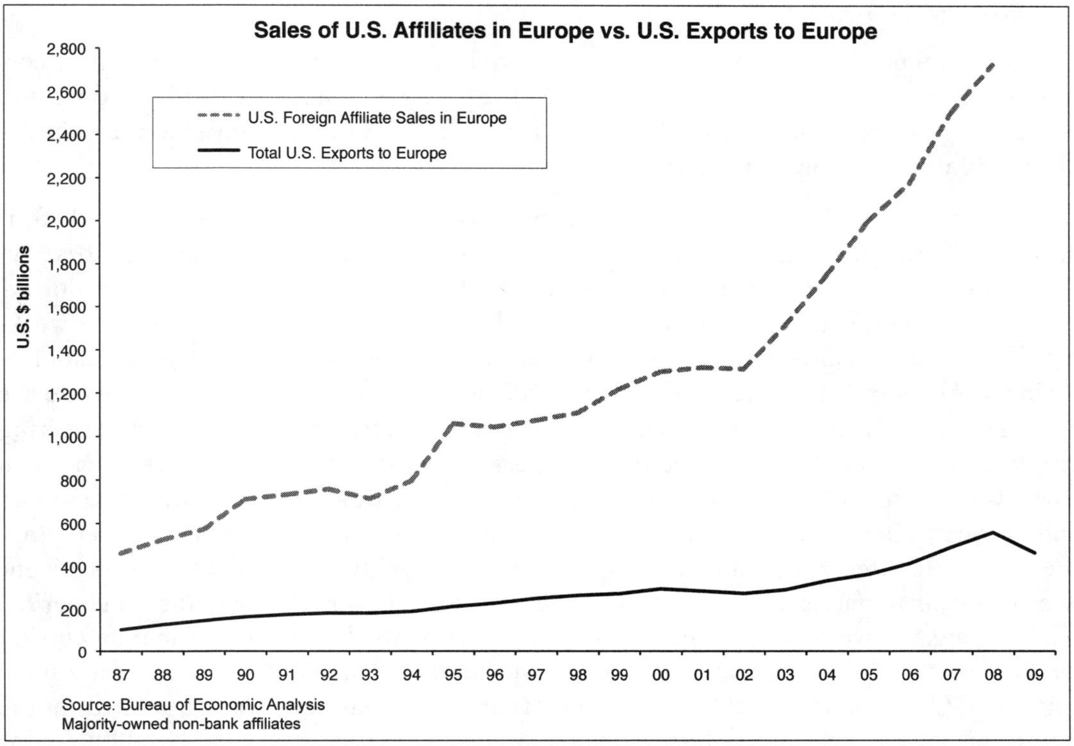
Sales of U.S. Affiliates in Europe vs. U.S. Exports to Europe
U.S. Foreign Affiliate Sales in Europe
Total U.S. Exports to Europe
U.S. $ billions
2,800
2,600
2,400
2,200
2,000
1,800
1,600
1,400
1,200
1,000
800
600
400
200
0
87 88 89 90 91 92 93 94 95 96 97 98 99 00 01 02 03 04 05 06 07 08 09
Source: Bureau of Economic Analysis
Majority-owned non-bank affiliates

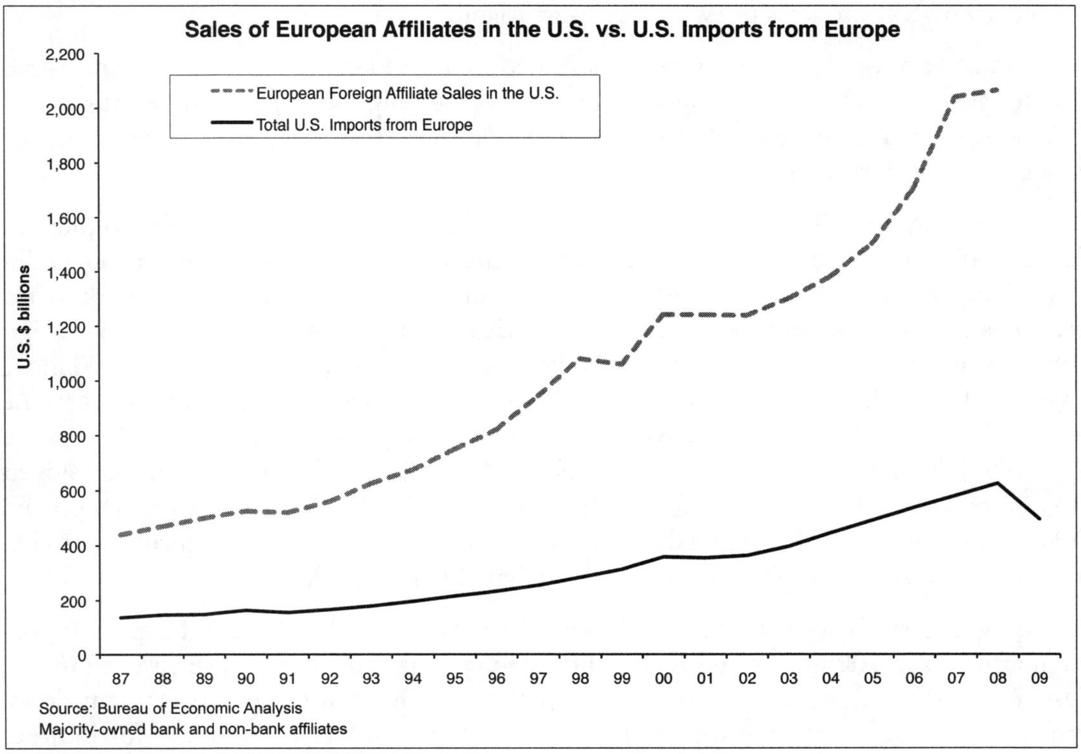
Sales of European Affiliates in the U.S. vs. U.S. Imports from Europe
European Foreign Affiliate Sales in the U.S.
Total U.S. Imports from Europe
U.S. $ billions
2,200
2,000
1,800
1,600
1,400
1,200
1,000
800
600
400
200
0
87 88 89 90 91 92 93 94 95 96 97 98 99 00 01 02 03 04 05 06 07 08 09
Source: Bureau of Economic Analysis
Majority-owned bank and non-bank affiliates

3. Affiliate Employment

The common perspective is that when it comes to hiring workers overseas, the bulk of corporate America's overseas work forces toils in the developing nations. Reality is different. Most foreign workers on the payrolls of U.S. foreign affiliates are employed in the industrialized countries, notably in Europe.

Out of a global overseas workforce of 10.1 million in 2008 by U.S. majority-owned affiliates in 2008, roughly 42% were located in Europe. The bulk of these workers were based in the United Kingdom, Germany and France. The European workforce of U.S. majority-owned foreign affiliates was almost evenly split between manufacturing and service workers. That said, it is interesting to note that U.S. affiliates employed just as many manufacturing workers in Europe (1.9 million) in 2008 as they did in 1990. However, while the aggregate number has stayed the same, the geographic distribution of U.S. manufacturing employment in Europe has shifted over the past fifty years. In general, the shift has been towards lower cost locations like Ireland and Spain, at the expense of the United Kingdom and Germany. Between 1990 and 2008, for instance, U.S. affiliate manufacturing employment in the United Kingdom and Germany fell by roughly 34% and 14%, respectively. Meanwhile, manufacturing employment in Ireland soared over 27% over the same period, while rising by over 18% in Spain. However, even with the decline of manufacturing employment in Germany, the manufacturing workforce of U.S. affiliates in Germany alone totaled 387,000 workers in 2008—15,000 more than the year before and not far from the number of manufactured workers employed in China by U.S. affiliates (410,000). As for Ireland, U.S. affiliates employed nearly 90,000 workers in 2008, a larger number than those employed by U.S. affiliates in Sweden or Switzerland.

The transportation equipment sector continued to be the largest source of manufactured employment in Europe; wholesale employment was among the largest sources of service-related employment, which includes employment in such areas as logistics, trade, insurance and other service-related activities.

When it comes to affiliate employment, trends in the United States are similar to those in Europe. In other words, despite stories on the continent about local European companies decamping for cheap labor markets in central Europe or Asia, most foreigners working for European companies outside the EU are Americans. European majority-owned foreign affiliates directly employed roughly 3.6 million U.S. workers in 2008—over 100,000 more workers than U.S. affiliates employed in Europe. The top five European employers in the U.S. were firms from the United Kingdom (957,000), Germany (614,000), France (550,000), Switzerland (394,000) and the Netherlands (371,000). French firms employed 34,000 more people in the U.S. in 2008 than in 2007, while German firms employed 39,000 less and Dutch firms 20,000 less. European firms employed two-thirds of all U.S. workers on the payrolls of majority-owned foreign affiliates in 2008.

In the aggregate, the transatlantic workforce directly employed by U.S. and European foreign affiliates in 2008 was roughly 8 million strong. That said, as we have stressed in our last survey, these figures understate the employment effects of mutual investment flows, since these numbers are limited to direct employment, and do not account for indirect

The U.S. - European Employment Balance
Thousands of employees, 2008

Country	European Affiliates[1] of U.S. Companies	U.S. Affiliates[2] of European Companies	Employment Balance
Austria	44.0	14.4	-29.6
Belgium	129.0	179.3	+50.3
Denmark	38.9	26.8	-12.1
Finland	23.8	31.5	+7.7
France	604.4	550.2	-54.2
Germany	621.3	614.2	-7.1
Ireland	89.0	66.2	-22.8
Italy	232.9	86.5	-146.4
Luxembourg	13.6	35.5	+21.9
Netherlands	228.8	371.5	+142.7
Norway	33.7	8.0	-25.7
Spain	188.1	66.8	-121.3
Switzerland	81.5	394.4	+312.9
United Kingdom	1,174.2	957.4	-216.8
Europe	3,503.2	3,402.7	-100.5

Note: Employment balance "+" favors the United States
Source: Bureau of Economic Analysis

[1] Majority-owned non-bank affiliates
[2] Majority-owned bank and non-bank affiliates

employment effects of nonequity arrangements such as strategic alliances, joint ventures and other deals. Moreover, affiliate employment figures do not include jobs supported by transatlantic trade flows. Trade-related employment is substantial in many U.S. states and many European regions.

In total, and adding in indirect employment, we estimate that the transatlantic work force numbers some 13-15 million workers. Europe is by far the most important source of "onshored" jobs in America, and the U.S. is by far the most important source of "onshored" jobs in Europe.

4. Research and Development (R&D) of Foreign Affiliates

While most multinationals still tend to cluster their R&D expenditures and activities in their home country, foreign affiliate R&D has become more prominent over the past decade as firms seek to share development costs, spread risks and tap into the intellectual talent of other nations. Alliances, cross-licensing of intellectual property, mergers and acquisitions and other forms of cooperation have become more prevalent characteristics of the transatlantic economy in the past decade. The internet, in particular, has powered greater transatlantic R&D. The complexity of scientific and technological innovation is leading innovators to partner to share costs, find complementary expertise, gain access to different technologies and knowledge quickly, and collaborate as part of "open" innovation networks. Cross-border collaboration with foreign partners can range from a simple one-way transmission of information to highly interactive and formal arrangements. Collabora-

Geographic Origin of R&D Expenditure by Foreign-Controlled Affiliates, 1997 and 2007

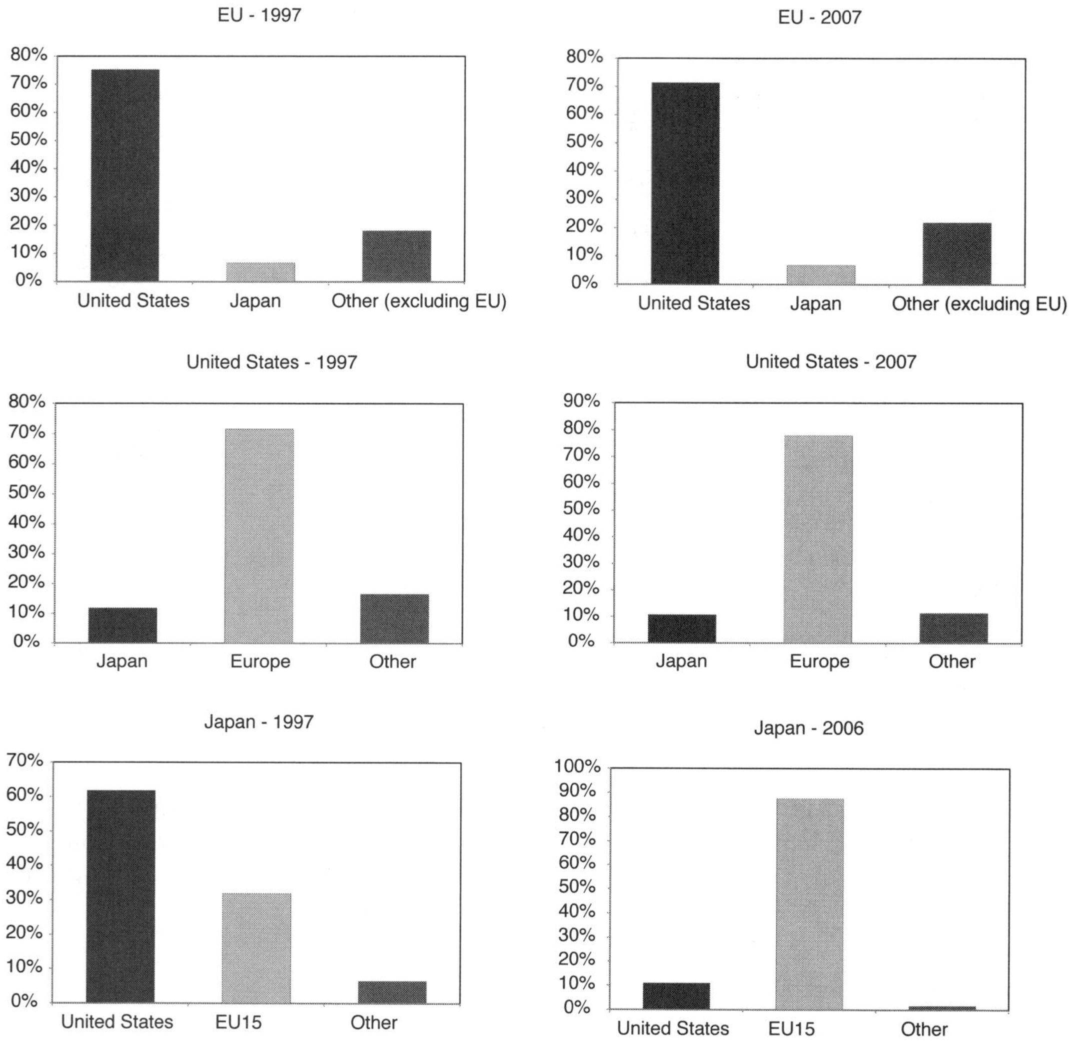

tion with foreign customers and/or suppliers helps firms develop new products, processes or other innovations.[3]

Bilateral U.S.-EU flows in research, development and innovation are the most intense between any two international partners. In 2008, U.S. affiliates sunk $24 billion on research and development in Europe, or nearly 65% of total R&D expenditures of total global R&D by U.S. foreign affiliates of $37 billion. R&D expenditures by U.S. affiliates were greatest

[3] OECD, *Science and Technology Indicators 2009*,op. cit.

in the United Kingdom, Germany, France, Sweden and Ireland. These five countries accounted for nearly three-fourths of U.S. global spending on R&D in 2008.

In the United States, meanwhile, expenditures on R&D performed by majority-owned foreign affiliates totaled nearly $40.5 billion in 2008, relatively unchanged from the prior year and a figure amounting to around 15% of total R&D spending in the U.S. A significant share emanated from world-class leaders from Europe, given their interests in America's highly skilled labor force and first-class university infrastructure. Most of this investment took place among European firms in such research-intensive sectors as energy, chemicals, telecommunications, and automobiles.

By country, British-owned affiliates were the largest foreign source of R&D in the United States in 2008. British R&D in the U.S. totaled $7.4 billion in 2008, yet that was down by nearly one-quarter from the prior year. UK firms accounted for 18% of total affiliate R&D in the United States. Swiss-owned affiliates accounted for the second largest percentage of affiliate R&D expenditures, with a 17% share in 2008, followed by France with a 15% share. The R&D of German affiliates totaled $5.5 billion, and was mainly concentrated in transportation equipment, pharmaceuticals and machinery. Given recessionary conditions in the U.S., German investment fell 5.1% in 2008, while French and Swiss R&D investment rose 7% and 7.8%, respectively.

Despite all of the above, the research and development capabilities of other countries, notably China, have attracted a great deal of attention. The topic is the subject of our "Special Focus: Innovation Goes Global," at the end of this chapter.

5. Intra-Firm Trade of Foreign Affiliates

While we have frequently highlighted the fact that cross-border trade is a secondary means of delivering goods and services across the Atlantic, the modes of delivery—affiliate sales and trade—should not be viewed independently. They are more complements than substitutes, since foreign investment and affiliate sales increasingly drive cross-border trade flows. Indeed, a substantial share of transatlantic trade is considered intra-firm trade or related-party trade, which is cross-border trade that stays within the ambit of the company.

Intra-firm or related-party trade occurs when BMW or Mercedes of Germany send parts to BMW of South Carolina or Mercedes of Alabama; when Lafarge or Michelin send intermediate components to their plants in the Greater Cincinnati area, or when 3M ships components for its office products or communications sectors from St. Paul to affiliates in Germany or the UK. The tight linkages between European parent companies and their U.S. affiliates are reflected in the fact roughly 61% of U.S. imports from the European Union consisted of related-party trade in 2009. The percentage was even higher in the case of Ireland (85%) and Germany (65%). Meanwhile, roughly 31% of U.S. exports to Europe in 2009 represented related-party trade, but the percentage is higher for some countries. For instance, over half of total U.S. exports to the Netherlands in 2009 was classified as related-party trade.

Related Party Trade, 2009

	US Imports: "Related Party Trade," as % of Total	US Exports: "Related Party Trade," as % of Total
European Union	60.7	30.6
Germany	64.5	29.6
France	55.9	27.7
Ireland	84.7	30.4
Netherlands	64.4	54.1
United Kingdom	59.4	23.6

Source: U.S. Census Bureau

6. *Foreign Affiliate Sales*

U.S. foreign affiliate sales (goods and services) hit a record $5.2 trillion in 2008, well in excess of U.S. exports of $1.6 trillion. Europe accounted for half of total global foreign affiliate sales, with sales totaling a record high of $2.8 trillion in 2008, an 8% rise from the prior year. Reflecting just how important Europe is to Corporate America, sales of U.S. affiliates in Europe were roughly double comparable sales in the entire Asia/Pacific region. Affiliate sales in the United Kingdom ($622 billion) exceeded aggregate sales in Latin America. While U.S. affiliate sales in China have soared over the past decade, they do so from a low base, and still remain well below comparable sales in Europe. For instance, U.S. affiliate sales of $131 billion in China in 2008 were slightly above Italy's ($129 billion) but well below those in Germany ($347 billion) or France ($232 billion). U.S. foreign affiliate sales in Ireland ranked fourth in Europe at nearly $250 billion in 2008, more than sales in France or the Netherlands.

Affiliate sales are also the primary means by which European firms deliver goods and services to consumers in the United States. In 2008, for instance, majority-owned European affiliates sales in the U.S. ($2 trillion) were more than four times larger than U.S. imports from Europe (roughly $500 billion). Affiliate sales in 2008 were basically unchanged from the previous year. That figure, however, masks the divergent trends of affiliates. For instance, sales of French affiliates in the U.S. rose 5% in 2008, while sales among German affiliates dropped sharply, by 12.3%. Swiss affiliates also posted a decline of 6% in 2008 from the prior year; British firms fared better, with affiliate sales rising 6.5% in 2008. For virtually all countries in Europe, foreign affiliate sales were easily in excess of their U.S. imports in 2008.

7. *Foreign Affiliate Profits*

The transatlantic economy enjoyed a profits boom between 2002 and 2007, although the tide turned in the second half of the year and into 2008. Looking just at 2008, U.S. affiliates in Europe earned $192 billion, up nearly 10% from the prior year. In the first half of 2008, U.S. affiliate income from Europe rose 9% from the same period a year earlier but then the bottom fell out in the final quarter of the year—affiliate income plunged along with the economic downturn in late 2008. The profits picture was hardly any better in 2009—

Source: Bureau of Economic Analysis
* Data through 3Q2010, Data annualized for full year estiamte

indeed, affiliate income dipped 10%, dropping back to the levels of 2007, with steep declines registered in most major markets. Affiliate income in the United Kingdom declined 17% in 2009, while affiliates in Germany, France and Italy posted annual losses in income of 30%, 54%, and 31%, respectively.

However, affiliate income rebounded quite strongly in 2010, totaling roughly $147 billion in the first nine months of the year, a 17% rise from the same period a year earlier. Better than expected growth from the European Union, notably from such large markets as Germany and Poland, have fueled the rebound. For the year, affiliate income is expected to have approached $200 billion, a potential record total. Even if affiliate profits fall short of previous peak levels, the fact remains that on a global basis, Europe remains the most profitable region of the world for U.S. multinationals. Even in recession year 2009 Europe accounted for just over 53% of total global affiliate earnings for U.S. companies. Since 2000, the region has accounted for nearly 57% of the total.

On a comparative basis, U.S. affiliate income from Europe was more than 40% more than total earnings from Latin America and Asia. It is interesting to note that combined U.S. affiliate income from China and India in 2009 ($8.7 billion) was a fraction earned in the Netherlands ($53 billion). Affiliates earned nearly three times in Ireland in 2008 than India and China combined, although past is not prologue: affiliate income in Ireland is expected to have declined in 2010.

Similarly, the United States remains the most important market in the world in terms of earnings for many European multinationals. Profits of European foreign affiliates in the United States actually rose by roughly 10% in 2008, but plunged 11% in 2009. However, as the U.S. economy improved over the course of 2010, so did the incomes of European foreign affiliates. In the first nine months of 2010, for instance, affiliate income surged 54% from the depressed levels of the year before. Strong gains were reported by various countries, with French affiliate income in the first nine months of last year soaring 344% from the dismal levels of 2009. Affiliate income among German, British and Dutch affiliates rose 83%, 23%, and 33%, respectively.

8. Transatlantic Service Linkages

As we have remarked in the past, services are the sleeping giant of the transatlantic economy, or the one key area where significant opportunities exist to strengthen and deepen transatlantic commercial ties.[4]

The United States and Europe are the two leading services economies in the world. According to the World Trade Organization, the U.S. is the largest single country trader in services, while the EU is the largest trader in services among all world regions. While the U.S. remains the world's top national exporter of commercial services, with a global export share of 14.1% in 2009, the U.K. ranks second (7%), followed by Germany (6.8%) and France (4.3%).

Europe registered 10% annual average growth in commercial services exports between 2000 and 2009, 1% more than the global average, 1% less than Asia, but 4% more than North America. The EU15 almost quadrupled their services trade balance over the past decade; the EU in 2009 had a trade surplus in services with every world region except North America and the Caribbean. 18 EU member states ranked among the top 40 exporters of services in 2009, accounting for 43.4% of world market share.

The EU has sustained or expanded its share of world trade in most broad service categories except transport services, in contrast to developments in the United States. Regarding services exports, the EU ranked #1 in the world in 8 of 11 categories of services exports, and in fact boosted its position between 2005 and 2008 in communications, telecommunications, construction, computer and information services. The U.S. has the lead in three categories: royalties and license fees; personal, cultural and recreational services; and audiovisual services.

The U.S. and Europe are also each other's most important commercial partners when it comes to services trade and investment. North America was the largest destination for extra-EU services exports (29.6%) and the largest source of extra-EU services imports (36.9%) even in recession year 2009 (down from 32% of exports and 39% of exports in 2008).

EU services exports to North America were in 2009 were 31% higher than to Wider Europe; over 3.5 times more than to Rising Asia and Latin America; 4 times more than to

[4] For a closer examination of the transatlantic services economy, see Daniel S. Hamilton and Joseph P. Quinlan, eds., *Sleeping Giant: Awakening the Transatlantic Services Economy* (Washington, DC: Center for Transatlantic Relations, 2007).

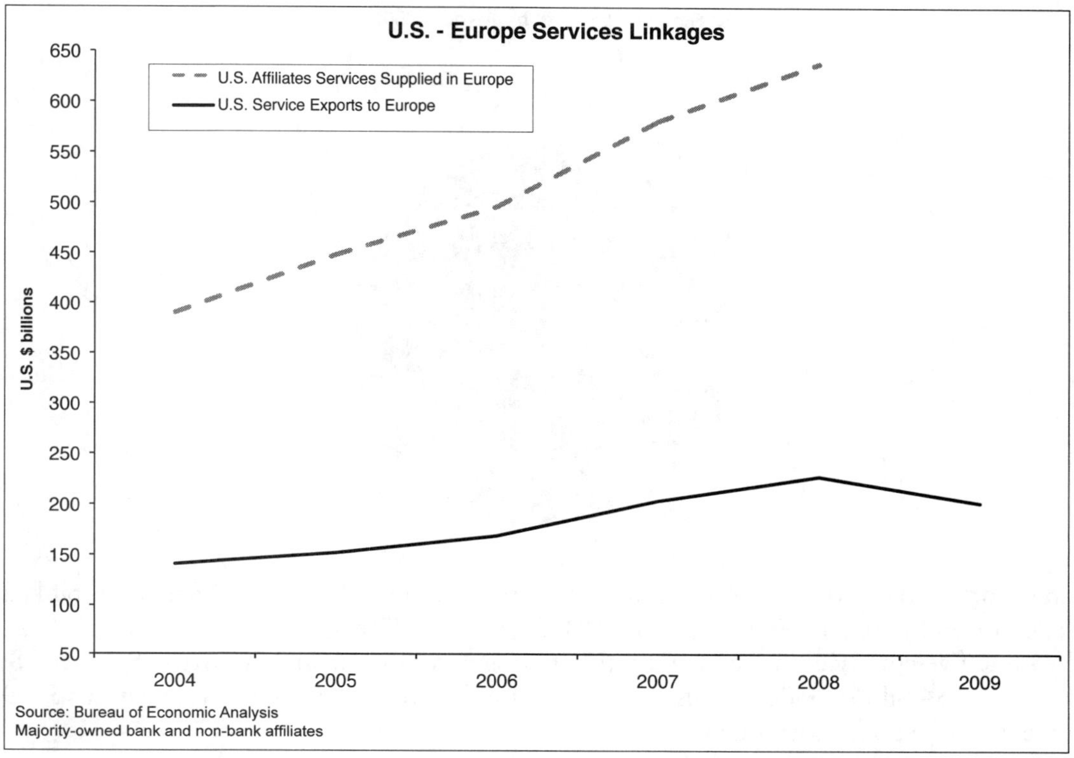

the Middle East and to Africa; almost 5 times more than to Oceania; over 7 times more to Russia, China and Japan; almost 15 times more than to India; and 29 times more than to the Caribbean.

EU services imports from North America in 2009 were 43% more than from Wider Europe; over 4.5 times from Rising Asia; over 5 times from Africa; over 6 times from the Middle East; over 9 times more than from Oceania, China and Latin America; over 12 times more than from Japan and Russia; over 18 times more than from India; and 37 times more than from the Caribbean.

While transatlantic services trade figures are impressive, the more important services linkages are actually in mutual flows of foreign direct investment. The services economies of the United States and Europe have become even more intertwined over the past year, with cross-border trade in services and sales through affiliates posting strong gains. By sectors, transatlantic linkages continue to deepen in financial services, insurance, education, telecommunications, utilities, advertising, and computer services. Other sectors such as aviation are slowly being liberalized and deregulated.

On a regional basis, Europe accounted for 41% of total U.S. services exports and for 43% of total U.S. services imports in 2009.[5] Starting with trade in services, five out of the top

---

[5] Bureau of Economic Analysis, U.S. International Services, Cross-Border Services Exports and Imports by Type and Country, 2009; Eurostat.

EU Services Exports by Region, 2009

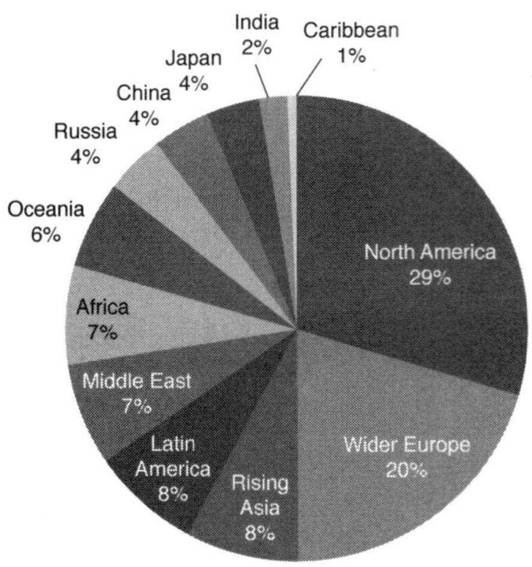

Source: Eurostat.

ten export markets for U.S. services in 2009 were in Europe. The United Kingdom ranked #1, followed by Ireland (4th), Germany (5th), Switzerland (7thh) and France (8th). Similarly, the same five countries ranked among the top ten services providers to the U.S. The U.S. enjoyed a $54 billion trade surplus in services with Europe in 2009, compared with its $120 trade deficit in goods with Europe.

Thanks to a variety of factors—stronger growth, the weaker dollar, EU enlargement, industry reform and deregulation—U.S. services exports to the European Union more than dou-

EU Services Exports by Region, 2004–2009

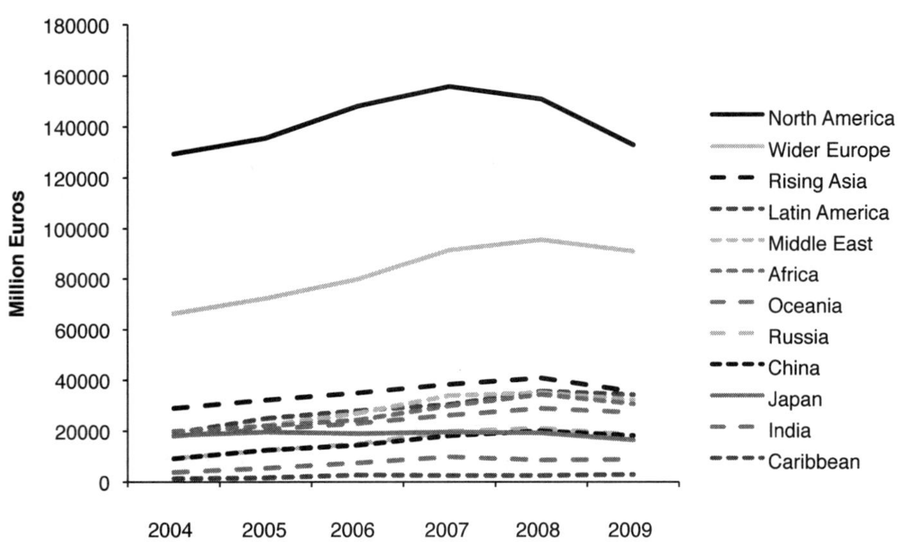

Source: Eurostat.

EU Services Imports by Region, 2009

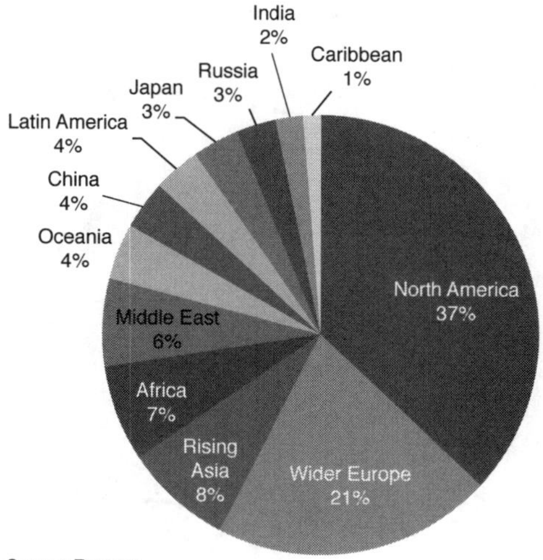

Source: Eurostat.

bled between 1997 and 2009, rising from around $100 billion to nearly $200 billion in 2009. Yet in 2009 U.S. services exports to Europe plunged by 11.5%, with sharp declines in such activities as travel, financial services, and consulting leading the downturn. Gains were reported among exports of "other private services," or in such value-added activities as computer processing, engineering, advertising and related activities. In this category, the U.S. posted a $24 billion trade surplus in 2009.

U.S. services imports from Europe, meanwhile, also declined by nearly 10% in 2009. Services imports peaked at $162 billion in 2008, more than double the levels of 1999. The same five

EU Services Imports by Region, 2004–2009

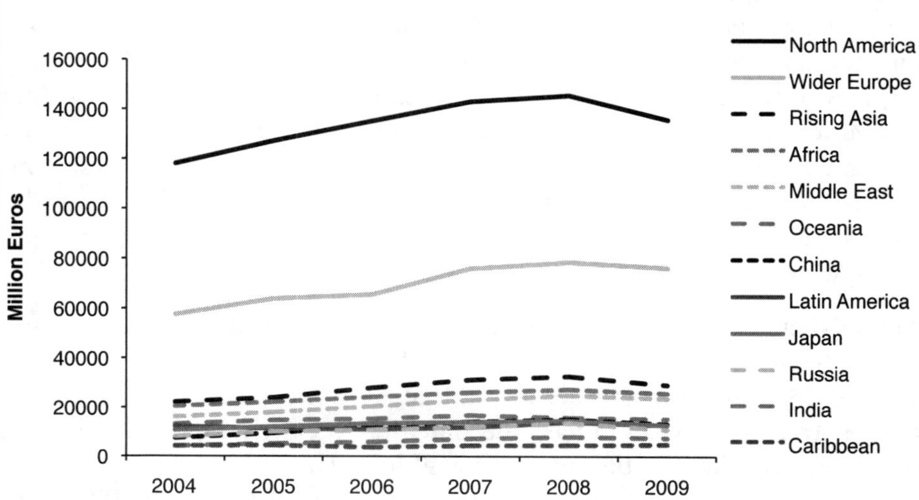

Source: Eurostat.

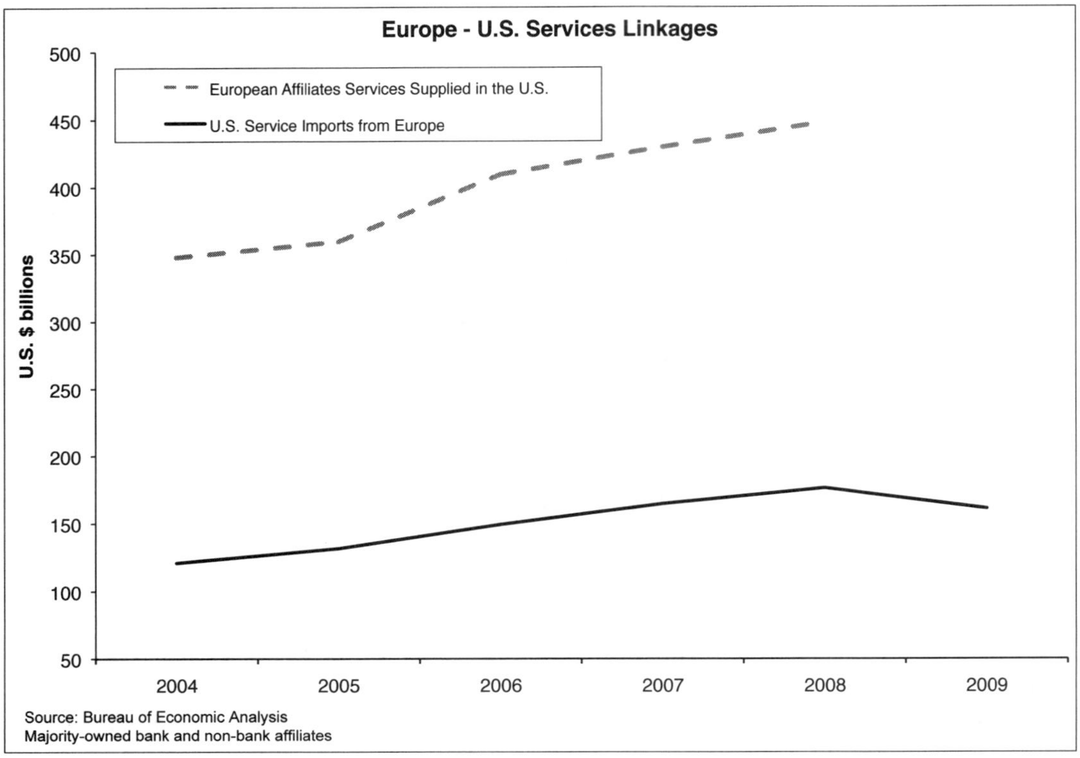

countries that ranked in the top ten U.S. services export markets also ranked among the top ten services providers to the U.S. On a regional basis, the European Union accounted for just over 41% total U.S. services exports and for 43% of total U.S. services imports in 2009.

Meanwhile, while the U.S. recorded a $73 billion deficit in goods exports with Europe in 2009, a sizable amount of the deficit in goods was offset by America's $54.1 billion surplus in services. That was down from a surplus of $64 billion in 2008. The U.S. enjoys a sizable surplus in many activities, including financial services, telecommunications and in particular in "other private services," notably in activities associated with "business, professional and technical services." The latter surplus was roughly $15 billion in 2009. By activity, the U.S. registered a surplus in computer and information services, management consulting, legal services, construction engineering, and operational leasing with Europe in 2009. Top U.S. business services exports to Europe included management, consulting, and public relation services, with U.S. receipts (or exports) totaling nearly $17 billion in 2009.

Beyond trade, there are the foreign affiliate sales of services, or the delivery of transatlantic services by U.S. and European foreign affiliates. Sales of affiliates have exploded on both sides of the Atlantic over the past decade; indeed, affiliate sales of services have not only supplemented trade in services but also become the overwhelming mode of delivery in a rather short period of time. To the latter point, affiliate sales of U.S. services rose more than 10-fold between 1990 and 2009, topping $1 trillion for the first time in 2007. In the same year, U.S. services exports were roughly the level of affiliate sales of services.

America's FDI Roots in Europe
(Billions of $)

Industry	US FDI to Europe	% of Industry Total
European Total	1,976	56%
Mining	47	28%
Manufacturing	285	53%
Food	26	57%
Chemicals	78	60%
Primary and fabricated metals	13	55%
Machinery	28	65%
Computers and electronic products	26	39%
Electrical equipment, appliances, and components	17	68%
Transportation equipment	24	52%
Wholesale trade	102	51%
Information	104	69%
Depository institutions	78	68%
Finance (except depository institutions) and insurance	364	49%
Professional, scientific, and technical services	49	63%
Other industries	123	54%

Europe's FDI Roots in the US
(Billions of $)

Industry	US FDI from Europe	% of Industry Total
Total from Europe	1,685	73%
Manufacturing	609	77%
Food	16	79%
Chemicals	169	83%
Primary and fabricated metals	40	82%
Machinery	89	93%
Computers and electronic products	29	52%
Electrical equipment, appliances, and components	23	94%
Transportation equipment	37	38%
Wholesale trade	171	52%
Retail trade	32	72%
Information	142	97%
Depository institutions	57	51%
Finance (except depository institutions) and insurance	243	83%
Real estate and rental and leasing	26	47%
Professional, scientific, and technical services	31	67%
Other industries	374	74%

Note: Historic-cost basis, 2009
Source: Bureau of Economic Analysis

Sales of services of U.S. foreign affiliates in the European Union rose again in 2008, the last year of available data. Sales rose to a record $638 billion, more than double the level of 2000; meanwhile affiliate sales of services were nearly triple U.S. services exports to EU in the same year. The United Kingdom accounted for around 36% of all U.S. affiliate sales in the EU; UK services sales ($229 billion in 2009) were not that far behind total affiliate sales of services to all of Asia ($268 billion). On a global basis, Europe accounted for nearly 57% of total U.S. services sales.

U.S. affiliate sales of services in the EU continue to exceed sales of services by U.S. affiliates of European firms. The latter totaled $447 billion in 2008, the former some $638 billion.

However, on a country-by-country basis, French, German, and Dutch affiliates sold more services in the U.S. in 2008 than American affiliates sold in France, Germany, and Switzerland. Of particular note, European affiliate sales of services were more than two and a half times larger than U.S. services imports—a fact that underscores the ever-widening presence of European services leaders in the U.S. economy.

In fact, the U.S. and EU each owe a good part of their competitive position in services globally to deep transatlantic connections in services industries provided by mutual investment flows. A good share of U.S. services exports to the world are generated by European companies based in the United States, just as a good share of EU services exports to the world are generated by U.S. companies based in Europe.

In the end, these eight indices convey a more complete and complex picture of global engagement than simple tallies of exports and imports. Foreign direct investment and foreign affiliate sales, not trade, represent the backbone of the transatlantic economy. The eight variables just highlighted underscore the depth and breadth of the transatlantic commercial relationship.

Special Focus: Innovation Goes Global

Innovation is a key driver of improved living standards and has emerged as the key wealth-creating asset in most industrial economies.[6] Nobel laureate economist Joseph Stiglitz argues that of all the intercontinental connections engendered by globalization, "at the top of the list is globalization of knowledge, the free flow of ideas that has followed the lowering of communication costs and the closer integration of societies. The transfer of that knowledge, which globalization has facilitated, is likely to prove one of the strongest forces for growth."[7]

OECD research and McKinsey studies indicate that firms now invest as much in intangible assets related to innovation (R&D, software, skills, organizational know-how and branding) as they invest in traditional capital such as machinery, equipment and buildings.[8] Leading-edge industries in advanced economies—microelectronics, telecommunications, computer software, biology, nanotechnology—rely heavily on the production and use of advanced knowledge as a key source of their value-added. Yet knowledge is also critical to many traditional sectors of the economy as well. The knowledge component of the output of manufacturing goods is estimated to have risen from 20% in the 1950s to more than 75% today.[9] According to the 2010 Global Manufacturing Competitiveness Index, talent-driven innovation remains the top driver of manufacturing competitiveness across all global regions.[10] Workers in all of these industries increasingly need to understand, process and generate advanced knowledge.

Since the United States and most EU countries are knowledge economies, a substantial portion of the goods they produce, the services they provide, and the jobs they generate are tied to their ability to provide their people with good education and skills, create and commercialize new knowledge, and to tap innovation and absorb knowledge generated elsewhere.

The advanced industrial countries remain the leaders in terms of global share of R&D. Overall, according to the OECD, U.S.-based companies account for 34.3% and EU-based

---

6 See, for instance, Thomas A. Stewart, *Intellectual Capital* (New York: Doubleday/Currency Publishers, 1997); Daniel S. Hamilton, *Europe 2020: Competitive or Complacent?* (Washington, DC: Center for Transatlantic Relations, 2011), Chapter 6; "How can Europe create jobs?" European Parliament Directorate- General for Internal Policies, Policy Department A: Economic and Scientific Policy, European Parliament's Special Committee on the Financial, Economic and Social Crisis, April 2010.

7 Joseph E. Stiglitz, "Globalization and growth in emerging markets," *Journal of Policy Modelling* 26(4), 2004, pp. 465-84.

8 OECD, "Fostering Innovation to Strengthen Growth and Address Global and Social Challenges: Executive Summary and Key Findings," www.oecd.org/innovation/strategy, p. 8; McKinsey Global Institute, "Beyond austerity," op. cit.

9 Stewart, op. cit.; Robert Huggins and Hiro Izushi, *Competing for Knowledge: Creating, Connecting, and Growing* (London: Routledge, 2009).

10 Deloitte Touche Tohmatsu and U.S. Council on Competitiveness, *2010 Global Manufacturing Competitiveness Index*, June 2010.

The Innovation Top 20

Rank		R & D Spending			
2009	Company	2009 $ US Millions	Change from 2008	Headquarters Location	Industry
1	Roche Holding	9,120	11.6%	Europe	Healthcare
2	Microsoft	9,010	10.4%	North America	Software and Internet
3	Nokia	8,240	-1.0%	Europe	Computing and Electronics
4	Toyota	7,822	-19.8%	Japan	Auto
5	Pfizer	7,739	-2.6%	North America	Healthcare
6	Novartis	7,469	3.5%	Europe	Healthcare
7	Johnson & Johnson	6,986	-7.8%	North America	Healthcare
8	Sanofi - Aventis	6,391	0.2%	Europe	Healthcare
9	GlaxoSmithKline	6,187	12.7%	Europe	Healthcare
10	Samsung	6,002	7.9%	South Korea	Computing and Electronics
11	General Motors	6,000	-25.0%	North America	Auto
12	IBM	5,820	-8.2%	North America	Computing and Electronics
13	Intel	5,653	-1.2%	North America	Computing and Electronics
14	Merck	5,613	16.8%	North America	Healthcare
15	Volkswagen	5,359	3.6%	Europe	Auto
16	Siemens	5,285	3.1%	Europe	Industrials
17	Cisco Systems	5,208	1.1%	North America	Computing and Electronics
18	Panasonic	5,143	-7.9%	Japan	Computing and Electronics
19	Honda	4,996	-17.7%	Japan	Auto
20	Ford	4,900	-32.9%	North America	Auto
	Top 20 Total	**128,943**	**3.7%**		

Source: Booz & Company

companies for 30.6% of the top R&D companies in the world, with Japan accounting for an additional 22%. As the accompanying "Innovation Top 20" chart highlights, the corporations that spend the most on innovation are still almost exclusively based in the transatlantic economy. Of the twenty firms listed, nine are domiciled in the United States, while seven are headquartered in Europe. Note that according to data from Booz & Company, European pharmaceutical manufacturer Roche Holding was #1 in the world in R&D spending in 2009, sinking over $9 billion in research and development. Microsoft was not far behind, followed by Finnish giant Nokia. Only one company made the list from the emerging markets—Samsung from South Korea.

The 2010 EU Industrial R&D Investment Scoreboard presents information on the 1400 leading R&D companies in the world. It contains data drawn from the latest available companies' accounts, i.e. for fiscal year 2009.[11] Despite the global economic downturn, the world's R&D landscape has maintained its characteristic sector composition, with the U.S. dominating in high R&D intensive sectors and the EU in medium-high ones.

The most R&D intensive sectors account for 69% of total R&D by U.S. companies, 37.8% by Japanese companies and 34.9% for EU companies. EU companies account for 48% of all R&D in medium-high sectors, and for a larger share of low R&D intensive sectors compared to U.S. companies. Among the top 15 sectors, the R&D intensity of EU companies is larger than that of the U.S. and Japan in 6 sectors, including software and computers, services, technology, hardware & equipment, and automobiles and parts. Japanese companies show higher R&D intensity than the EU and the U.S. in 7 sectors, including pharmaceuti-

[11]The complete dataset is available at: http://iri.jrc.ec.europa.eu/.

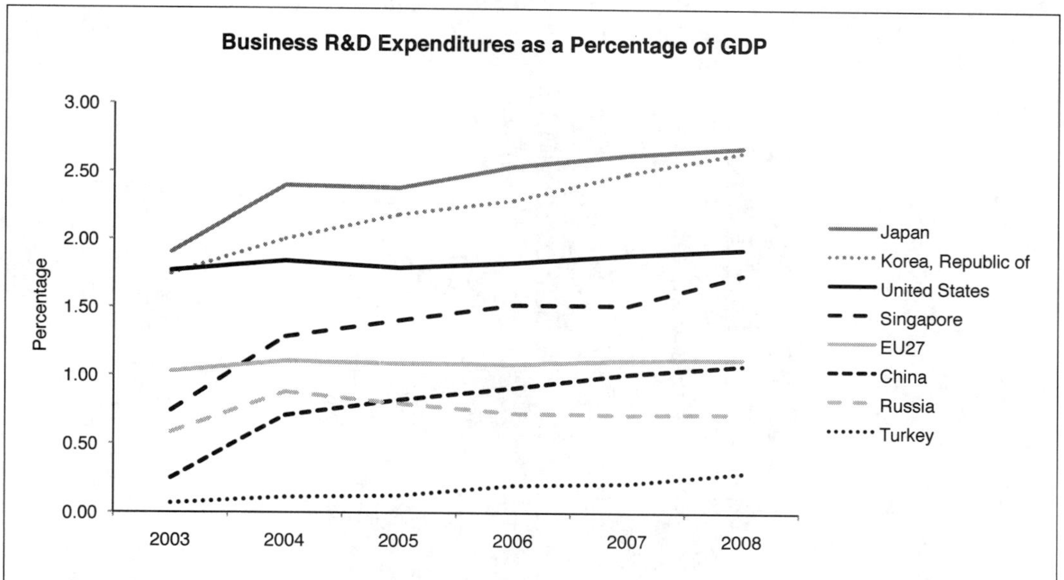

Source: The 2010 EU Industrial R&D Investment Scoreboard European Commission, JRC/DG RTD.

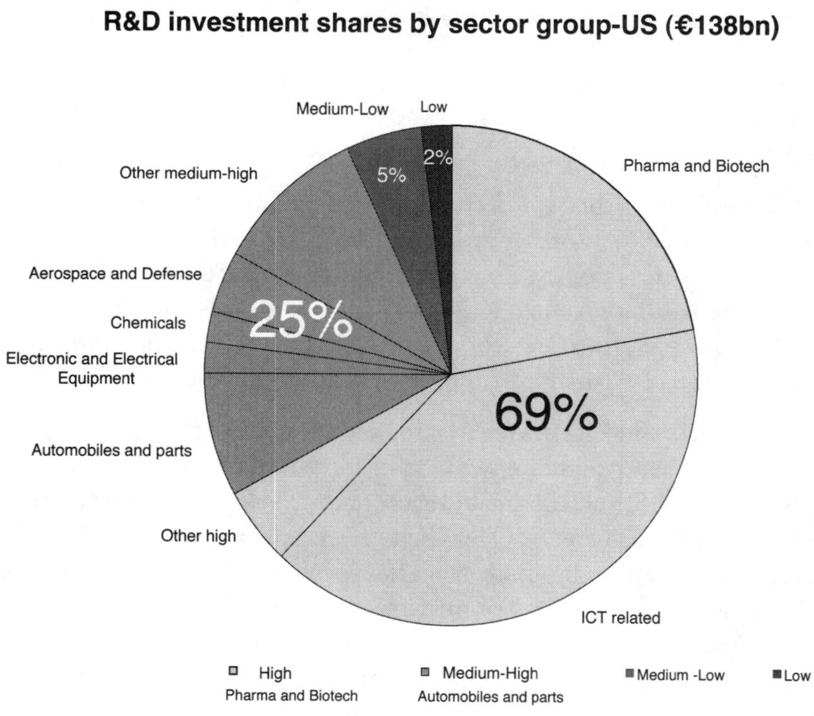

Source: The 2010 EU Industrial R&D Investment Scoreboard European Commission, JRC/DG RTD.

R&D investment shares by sector group-EU (€123bn)

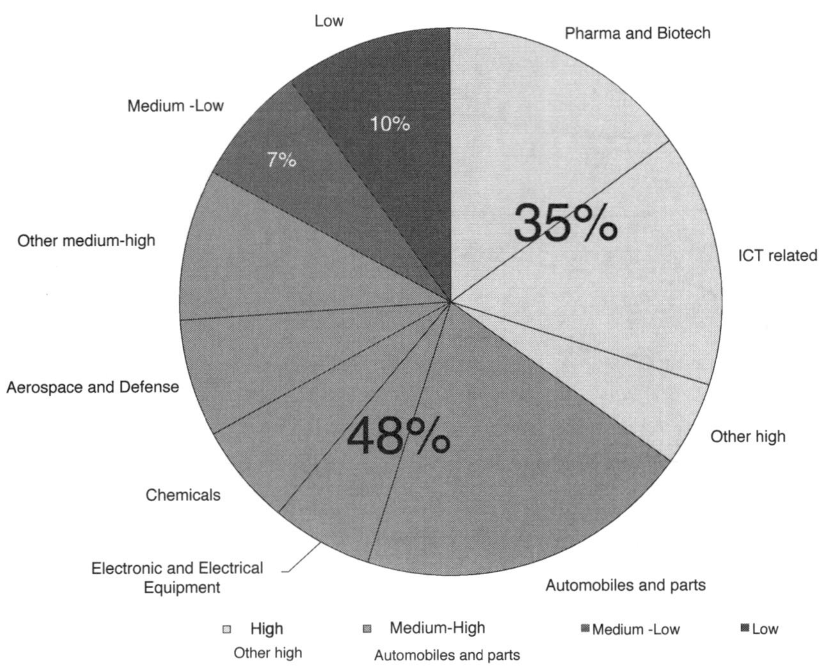

Source: The 2010 EU Industrial R&D Investment Scoreboard European Commission, JRC/DG RTD.

cals & biotechnology, electronic and electrical equipment and chemicals. The R&D intensity of U.S. companies is higher than that of the EU and Japan in leisure goods and health care equipment and services.

The major R&D regions of the world consistently exhibit different characteristics. EU companies contribute 43.5% of total automotive R&D and 40.3% of R&D in chemicals. In these same sectors, Japanese companies contribute 36.3% and 34.4%, respectively. U.S. companies contribute a different mix: 43.2% of pharmaceuticals R&D; 48.0% of IT hardware R&D; and 74.6% of software & computer services R&D. Companies from all other countries contribute 34.1% to the electronic & electric equipment sector.

R&D is an important competitiveness factor for such leading-edge sectors as semiconductors, biotechnology and nanotechnology, which in turn have the potential to deliver hugely significant economic benefits across the entire economy, just as electricity, computers and mobile phones have done in the past. Over the next decade, annual growth rates of 30% in biotech products and 20% in nanomaterials are expected. EU companies lag behind U.S counterparts in these sectors in terms of growth, number and ranking of companies, even though they outpace other regions. According to McKinsey, U.S. companies invested nearly five times more than EU companies in semiconductors, four times more in software and eight times more in biotechnology.[12]

[12]Charles Roxburgh, et al., *Beyond austerity: a path to economic growth and renewal in Europe* (London: McKinsey Global Institute, 2010), p. 3.

The EU, the U.S. and Japan also lead in internationalization of patents. The EU is the most important host country for U.S. overseas patents by far, as is the U.S. for the EU. The U.S. accounts for 60% of all overseas patents applied for by EU entities at the European Patent Office. This share is virtually unchanging over time.[13]

A related measure of research prowess comes from looking at the world's major research universities, which serve as critical hubs in knowledge economies. The world's leading centers for university research are still overwhelmingly located in North America and Europe. The U.S. hosts the top four centers, but London (5th), Paris (7th), and Zurich (8th) all rank ahead of San Jose/Silicon Valley (9th). Cambridge, England is 10th, Munich 12th, Stockholm 15th, and Oxford 16th. Such clusters in North America and the EU still enjoy a commanding lead in research and knowledge-generation, indicating that efforts to upgrade research universities, attract top scientific talent, and build world-class research environments in China, India, the Middle East, and other parts of the world still face significant uphill battles—provided that the U.S. and European countries continue to provide world-class support to their world-class research centers.[14]

Continued high levels of innovation will be essential to the ability of the U.S. and Europe to recover from the economic crisis and to prosper in today's highly competitive and connected global economy. The prosperity of Americans and Europeans alike will also be increasingly dependent on the strength of their knowledge links to each other and to other global hubs of innovation and ideas. Growing global connections have meant that the knowledge base of many advanced economies, and sub-regions within those economies, are no longer simply locally rooted but positioned within broader regional and intercontinental knowledge networks.[15] The OECD, which has conducted extensive research into global competitiveness, concludes that "the critical issue for the emerging economic geography of the twenty-first century is the location and spatial distribution of knowledge-assets."[16] Translation: the better connected you are to innovation networks, the more competitive you are.

While the transatlantic economy remains the primary source of global innovation, the international landscape for innovation is changing. As a result of the recession, for instance, private R&D spending in 2009 declined by 11% in Japan, 3.8% in the U.S. and 0.2% in Europe. Total R&D spending by the "Innovation Top 20" declined by 3.7% in 2009, with very steep declines among battered automobile manufacturers like General Motors and Ford, whose spending plunged 25% and 33%, respectively.

In contrast, combined private R&D spending soared 41% in India and China, albeit the rise was from a low base. As the accompanying chart highlighting global R&D by region makes clear, Asia's twin emerging giants account for only 1% of global private sector R&D spending, versus a 38% share for the United States and 31% share for Europe. China's real

---

[13]European Commission, *European Competitiveness Report 2010*, pp. 118-119.

[14]Academic Ranking of World Universities 2010, available at http://www.arwu.org/ARWU2010.jsp; Richard Florida, "Where the World's Brains Are," *Atlantic*, October 18, 2010.

[15]Huggins and Izushi, op. cit., p. 96.

[16]OECD, *Globalisation and Regional Economies: Can OECD Regions Compete in Global Industries?* (Paris: OECD, 2007).

Global Private Sector R&D by Region
(percent of global total)

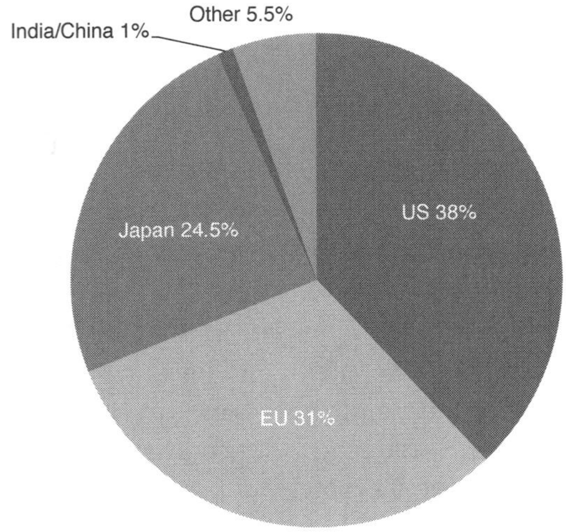

Source: Bloomberg, Booz & Company

source of R&D funding, of course, is the public sector, which has set ambitious targets for coming years.

As innovation becomes more international, it is also becoming both more competitive and more collaborative.

China is already the third largest R&D investor in the world, sinking at least $100 billion into R&D, according to latest figures from Goldman Sachs.[17] In terms of R&D investment as a share of GDP, China has doubled its share to 1.5% since 1999, and plans to boost its percentage to 2.5% by 2020. Goldman Sachs notes that while R&D investment in the G7 has grown by 3.2% on an average annual basis over the past decade, the comparable figures in China and South Korea were 20% and 8%, respectively. In both countries, and in other markets like Brazil, Turkey and India, more capital is being pumped into new patents and productivity-enhancing processes that will ultimately make corporations across the developing countries more competitive in the future.

Asian companies have increased their share of high- and medium-high R&D intensive sectors. U.S. and EU R&D companies will face growing competitive pressure from these new players in such medium-high R&D intensity sectors as automobiles and parts. South Korean and Japanese automotive companies have already proved themselves to be formidable competitors, and new companies from China and India are ready to follow suit. China surpassed the United States as the world's largest exporter of IT goods in 2004, and the share of technology-driven industries in EU imports from China is higher than in intra-EU imports—bearing in mind that a good share of these imports is produced or assembled

[17]Goldman Sachs, *The New Geography of Global Innovation*, Douglas Gilman, September 20, 2010.

by European and other foreign companies in China: "Made in China" does not necessarily mean "Made by China."[18]

Nonetheless, the share of transatlantic patents attributed to either the U.S. or Europe now stands at 62%, down from 70% in 1999. Six non-U.S. firms (all from Asia) now rank among the top ten private sector recipients of U.S. patents.

While U.S. and European research publications remain highly regarded and continue to lead the world in terms of scholarly work, according to the OECD leading scientific articles from China have increased more than six-fold since the mid-1990s, rising from 9,000 to 57,000 articles per year. The EU accounted for slightly more than 25% of scientific publications in 2007, the highest share of any region, yet less than its share of about 28% in 1997. The United States accounted for about 18%, considerably lower than its 25% share in 1997. China boosted its share considerably over that ten-year span, registering a 12% share of scientific publications, compared with only about 2.5% in 1997. Japan's share has fallen from about 7% to 5%. India, Russia and Brazil each account for less than 3%.

The U.S. and European education sectors still lead the world in attractiveness. The OECD reports that in 2007, the last year of available data, one out of every two tertiary-level students studying in another country went to only four countries: the U.S. (19.7% of all foreign students worldwide); UK (11.6%); Germany (8.6%); and France (8.2%). Yet other countries continue to develop. Goldman Sachs notes that China awards four times as many engineering doctorates each year than the average G7 nation. Science and engineering degrees now represent nearly 40% of all new university degrees in China and South Korea, compared to 24% in the G7 and 15% in the United States. Both the United States and Europe are home to roughly 13% of total university-enrolled students in the world, behind China with a 15% global share. The Middle Kingdom is now the largest source of new university graduates in the world.

Post-secondary education in Brazil has more than doubled since 2000 to 30%. That figure is relatively low but highlights the fact that education is becoming more of a strategic imperative of emerging markets at precisely the moment when schools are either being closed or underfunded in the United States and educational performance levels in many EU member states have declined.

All of the above serves to highlight the competitive challenge before the transatlantic economy. The days are past when innovation was a monopoly of the West. Innovation has gone global, a strategic dynamic that will produce winners and losers in the United States and Europe.

In this regard, Europe seems to have more catching-up to do: globally, EU research networks are less thick or productive than U.S. networks. In Canada, China, India, Israel, Korea, Mexico and Taiwan, for instance, the share of patents co-invented with the U.S. is at least twice as high as the share co-invented with the EU. According to the *European Com-*

---

[18]Luc Soete, "The costs of a non-innovative Europe: the challenges ahead," September 21, 2010, available at http://ec.europa.eu/research /social- sciences/pdf/demeter-costs-non-innovative-europe_en.pdf; *European Competitiveness Report 2009.*

petitiveness Report, the U.S. performs better than the EU in 11 of 17 indicators of innovation performance and the R&D intensity of U.S. companies is larger than that of EU companies in 9 of 15 sectors. Younger EU companies also tend to be less R&D intensive than their U.S. counterparts, a difference that accounts for over half of the EU-U.S. R&D intensity gap. Moreover, the EU has failed to increase R&D investments as a share of GDP to catch up with the U.S., has fallen behind other key countries, and now could be eclipsed by China. On the other hand, Paul Zagame estimates that if the EU would meet its target of boosting R&D investment to 3% of GDP from its 2008 level of 1.87%, it could create 3.75 million jobs and increase annual EU GDP by up to €795 billion by 2025.[19]

[19]P. Zagame, (2010) *The cost of a non-innovative Europe*, http://ec.europa.eu/research/social- sciences/policybriefs-research- achievements_en.html.

Chapter 3

European Commerce and the 50 States: A State-by-State Comparison

Corporate Europe's capital stock in the United States remains quite extensive and expansive, and the improving U.S. economic situation sparked a sharp revival in European investment flows into the U.S. in 2010. Based on the latest figures, European inflows totaled $106 billion in the first nine months of 2010, a 70% rise from the same period the year before. That equates to an annualized figure of around $140 billion—a marked improvement from 2009, when inflows from Europe to the United States plunged to just $84 billion, yet still well below the pre-crisis levels of 2008, when inflows totaled $202 billion.

As the accompanying chart highlights, the 2010 upturn in inflows from Europe to the U.S. was led by the Netherlands (+391%), the United Kingdom (+93%), Switzerland (87%), Ireland (+85%), Germany (+53%) and France (+17%). Combined, these six countries accounted for nearly two-thirds of total European investment in the U.S. during the first nine months of 2010.

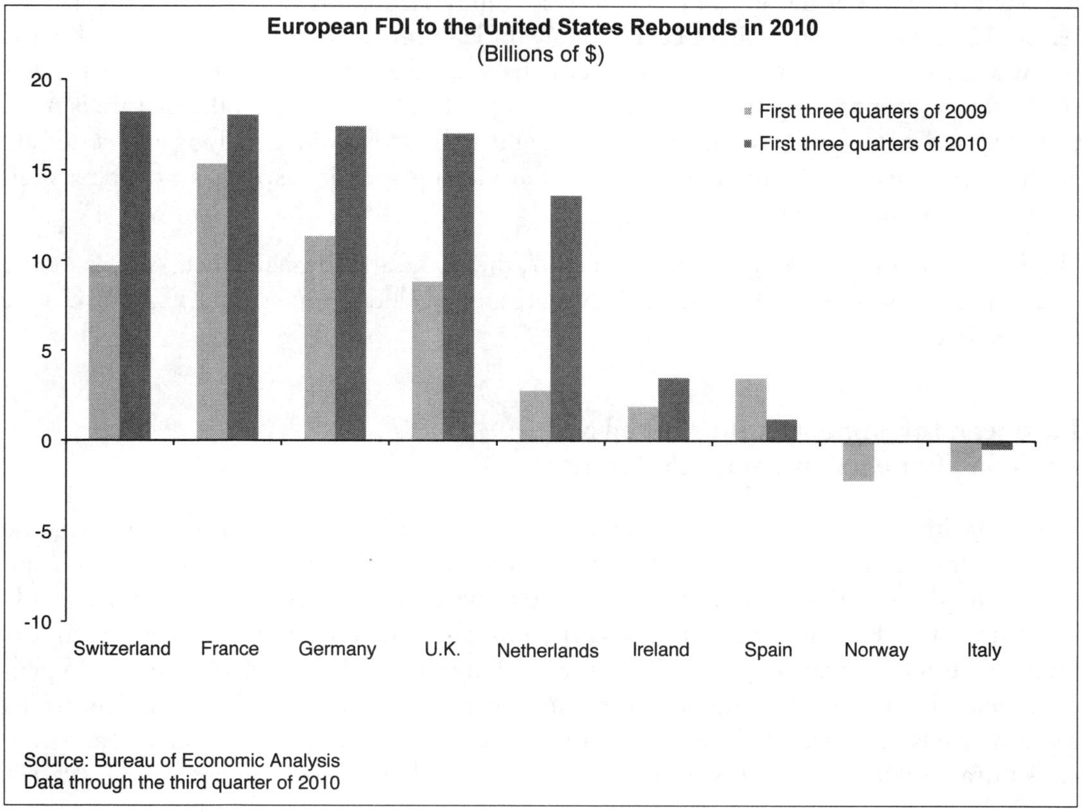

European investment in the U.S. (measured as the stock of gross property, plant and equipment owned by European foreign affiliates in the United States) is in excess of $600 billion. The latter figure mainly captures foreign investment in manufacturing activities. Another variable that measures Europe's investment stock in the U.S. is foreign investment based on a historic cost basis. According to this measure, Europe's investment stock in the U.S. is even larger. In recession year 2009, for instance, Europe's investment stakes in the U.S. totaled a record $1.7 trillion, a 13% rise from 2008 and more than triple the level of a decade earlier. Corporate Europe accounted for 74% of total foreign direct investment in the U.S. in 2009 ($2.3 trillion).

Put another way, no other region of the world has invested as much in the United States as Corporate Europe, a state of affairs we don't expect to change any time soon. On a historic cost basis, the largest foreign investors in the United States are companies from the United Kingdom, followed by Japan, the Netherlands, Canada, and Germany. Such investments are a primary source of "onshored" American jobs and are an integral part of the U.S. economy.

That said, at the regional and state level, Europe's investment stock in the U.S. continues to ebb and flow. Corporate Europe's investment position in the U.S. is in constant flux, reflecting general U.S. economic conditions and industry- and company-specific dynamics. Not unexpectedly, as the U.S. recession unfolded in 2008 and 2009, various European firms with operations in the United States had to adjust quickly to a much more difficult operating environment. For instance, Florida, Nevada, and Arizona—three states at the epic center of U.S. boom and bust—have been notably difficult markets for foreign-owned affiliates in the U.S. When economic circumstances change, so too do the strategies of firms. As such, while European investment overall is rising in the United States, the picture is more nuanced and not as uniform at the regional and state level. Some regions and states are gaining European investments while others are losing such investments or seeing their stock of investment decline.

While some of our figures are only up to 2007, the last year of available data, we have little doubt that Europe's investment at the U.S. state and local level underwent dramatic change over the last few years.

European Investment in the United States: Regional, Industry and State Preferences

European investment can be found in all fifty U.S. states. Yet at the regional level, and based on the last available data, the bias remains towards the American Southeast and Mid-Atlantic regions of the United States. Together, these two regions accounted for roughly one-third of all EU investment in the United States. The Southeast's share of European investment in 2007 was roughly 17% of the total, up slightly from the year before. In general, the region remains among one of the most attractive in the U.S. for investment owing to attractive land costs, relatively low unit labor costs, nominal union participation, a first-class infrastructure and aggressive state incentives (including tax holidays in many cases).

European* Foreign Investment in the U.S.
By geographic region, 2007

Region	U.S. $ billions	% of Total European* Investment	% of Total in the Region
Southeast	106.7	17.1%	56.6%
Mid-Atlantic	101.7	16.2%	55.9%
Great Lakes	70.7	11.3%	54.1%
Southwest	65.6	10.5%	41.9%
Far West	61.9	9.9%	32.5%
New England	28.9	4.6%	49.0%
Plains	20.3	3.3%	56.1%
Rocky Mountains	10.5	1.7%	45.5%

Source: Bureau of Economic Analysis
*European investment includes France, Germany, Netherlands, Switzerland, and the United Kingdom
Due to a need to align resources with current funding levels, the Bureau of Economic Analysis has reduced its coverage to major investing countries.

The Mid-Atlantic region also registered an increase in its share of European investment in 2007, with the region attracting 16.2% of total European investment versus a share of 14.4% the year before. The Mid-Atlantic is particularly attractive for financial services, pharmaceuticals, and R&D-intensive investment.

Reflecting past trends, British, French, German, Dutch and Swiss foreign investors remain the largest and most prominent European investors in the United States. On a state-by-state basis, the United Kingdom was the top foreign investor in terms of employment in 23 U.S. states based on the latest available data; Germany and the Netherlands ranked number one in three states, while France was the number one foreign employer in two states.

British, French and German investors each had their favored geographic location of the United States in the latest survey. For instance, the Southeast was the favored location of French and German firms in 2007, while the Mid-Atlantic slightly outranked the Southeast as the top geographic investment destination for British firms.

British affiliates operating in the U.S. increased their American payrolls by only 1% in 2008, although employment gains were higher for the year in the Mid-Atlantic (+2.7%) and Southeast (+3.6%). French affiliates recorded a 6.6% rise in U.S. payrolls in 2008, while employment levels fell among German affiliates by 6.5%. As a footnote, the data we are highlighting are for 2008; and given the U.S. recession of 2008/09, we highly suspect that most foreign affiliates in the United States pared their American workforces during the subsequent year. The U.S. recession started in December 2007 and ended in June 2009—it will be remembered as a painful period of employment cuts and pared jobs among U.S. companies and foreign affiliates operating in the United States.

At the state level, Texas, California and New York maintained their rank as the top three destinations for European foreign investment. These three states represent roughly one-fourth of the U.S. population yet account for over one-third of total European investment in the United States. This should not be surprising, given that each ranks among some of the largest and wealthiest states in America. In addition, each state has its own particular appeal to European investors—Texas is a magnet for energy investment from Europe and

Gross Property, Plant, and Equipment of French Affiliates* in U.S. Regions, 2007
(Millions of $, % of total in region)

Southeast	18,218	10%
Mideast	15,630	9%
Southwest	12,653	8%
Great Lakes	8,175	6%
Far West	7,764	4%
Plains	3,638	10%
New England	2,867	5%
Rocky Mountains	1,558	7%
Total	73,926	6%

Source: Bureau of Economic Analysis

Overall Direct Employment of French Affiliates* in U.S. Regions, 2008
(Thousands of employees, % of total in region)

Mideast	123.0	12%
Southeast	119.8	9%
Great Lakes	88.1	10%
Far West	81.2	10%
Southwest	59.2	10%
New England	33.7	8%
Plains	28.0	8%
Rocky Mountains	16.3	11%
Total	550.2	10%

Source: Bureau of Economic Analysis

Manufacturing Employment of French Affiliates* in U.S. Regions, 2007
(Thousands of employees, % of total in region)

Southeast	46.5	10%
Great Lakes	25.9	7%
Mideast	21.0	10%
Far West	20.1	11%
Southwest	14.0	12%
New England	9.8	11%
Plains	8.5	7%
Rocky Mountains	2.6	9%
Total	148.6	9%

Source: Bureau of Economic Analysis
* All Majority-owned affiliates

Gross Property, Plant, and Equipment of German Affiliates* in U.S. Regions, 2007
(Millions of $, % of total in region)

Southeast	44,518	24%
Mideast	32,820	18%
Great Lakes	23,025	18%
Southwest	17,412	11%
Far West	16,206	9%
Plains	7,103	20%
New England	3,984	7%
Rocky Mountains	1,027	4%
Total	201,889	16%

Source: Bureau of Economic Analysis

Overall Direct Employment of German Affiliates* in U.S. Regions, 2008
(Thousands of employees, % of total in region)

Southeast	154.2	11%
Mideast	115.4	11%
Great Lakes	120.5	14%
Far West	88.9	11%
Southwest	51.5	9%
New England	36.7	9%
Plains	31.2	9%
Rocky Mountains	12.9	8%
Total	614.2	11%

Source: Bureau of Economic Analysis

Manufacturing Employment of German Affiliates* in U.S. Regions, 2007
(Thousands of employees, % of total in region)

Great Lakes	83.5	23%
Southeast	74.3	16%
Mideast	27.2	13%
New England	15.2	17%
Far West	14.2	8%
Plains	13.2	11%
Southwest	8.5	7%
Rocky Mountains	2.3	8%
Total	242.3	15%

Source: Bureau of Economic Analysis

Gross Property, Plant, and Equipment of British Affiliates* in U.S. Regions, 2007
(Millions of $, % of total in region)

Mideast	32,314	18%
Great Lakes	31,020	24%
Southeast	25,683	14%
Southwest	21,384	14%
Far West	18,978	10%
New England	12,835	22%
Plains	4,658	13%
Rocky Mountains	4,370	19%
Total	222,308	17%

Source: Bureau of Economic Analysis

Overall Direct Employment of British Affiliates* in U.S. Regions, 2008
(Thousands of employees, % of total in region)

Mideast	223.5	21%
Southeast	203.6	15%
Great Lakes	160.2	18%
Far West	119.7	15%
Southwest	91.7	16%
New England	76.7	19%
Plains	50.8	15%
Rocky Mountains	27.2	18%
Total	957.4	17%

Source: Bureau of Economic Analysis

Manufacturing Employment of British Affiliates* in U.S. Regions, 2007
(Thousands of employees, % of total in region)

Great Lakes	55.4	15%
Southeast	43.3	9%
Mideast	33.2	16%
Far West	25.3	14%
Southwest	19.3	16%
New England	17.7	20%
Plains	11.7	10%
Rocky Mountains	4.3	14%
Total	211.2	13%

Source: Bureau of Economic Analysis

Ranking of U.S. States Benefiting from European* Investment

Ranking of States by European* Direct Investment
(Billions of $, 2007)

U.S. State	European Direct Investment (FDI)
Texas	58.2
California	46.8
New York	43.4
New Jersey	25.0
Illinois	21.6
Pennsylvania	21.3
Indiana	17.9
Ohio	17.4
Massachusetts	17.1
South Carolina	14.2
Florida	13.3
North Carolina	13.0
Virginia	12.3
Alabama	11.8
Kentucky	11.6
Georgia	11.1
Washington	9.3
Michigan	8.7
Colorado	8.4
Connecticut	8.4
Missouri	8.2
Louisiana	8.0
Maryland	7.8
Tennessee	6.1
Arizona	5.4
Wisconsin	5.1
Minnesota	3.9
Iowa	3.8
Kansas	3.3
Oregon	2.6
New Hampshire	2.5
Arkansas	2.4
Delaware	2.3
Nevada	2.3
Mississippi	1.7
Oklahoma	1.7
West Virginia	1.3
Utah	1.1
Hawaii	1.0
Idaho	0.8
Nebraska	0.8
Maine	0.4
New Mexico	0.4
Rhode Island	0.4
Montana	0.2
North Dakota	0.1
South Dakota	0.1
Vermont	0.1
Wyoming	0.1
Alaska	0.0

Ranking of States by Jobs Supported Directly by European* Investment
(Thousands of employees, 2008)

U.S. State	Employees
California	287.0
New York	255.3
Texas	212.2
Pennsylvania	164.4
Illinois	152.7
New Jersey	145.5
Massachusetts	116.4
Florida	116.2
Ohio	114.0
North Carolina	95.1
Georgia	93.1
Indiana	75.5
Michigan	74.7
Virginia	74.0
Connecticut	68.6
Maryland	65.0
South Carolina	59.5
Tennessee	57.1
Missouri	47.0
Washington	45.8
Wisconsin	41.5
Minnesota	41.0
Arizona	40.0
Kentucky	39.0
Colorado	34.7
Alabama	33.8
Louisiana	26.1
Oregon	26.0
Iowa	24.6
Kansas	23.2
New Hampshire	22.7
Delaware	19.4
Utah	19.3
Nevada	17.9
Oklahoma	17.4
Arkansas	15.8
Rhode Island	15.4
West Virginia	11.0
Mississippi	10.9
Idaho	10.1
Hawaii	9.2
Nebraska	9.0
New Mexico	8.6
Maine	6.9
Alaska	5.1
Vermont	5.0
Wyoming	4.8
South Dakota	3.3
Montana	3.0
North Dakota	1.9

Source: Bureau of Economic Analysis

*European investment includes France, Germany, Netherlands, Switzerland, and the United Kingdom

Due to a need to align resources with current funding levels, the Bureau of Economic Analysis has reduced its coverage to major investing countries. We estimate that this statistical change underestimates the number of U.S. jobs directly generated by European FDI by at least 300,000.

Special Focus:

The BRICs Set their Sights on the U.S. and Europe

Cross-border wheeling and dealing, long an exclusive sport of the West, is rapidly becoming popular in the corporate board rooms of Moscow, Mumbai, Beijing and San Paulo, adding a whole new dimension to global mergers and acquisitions.

Since the rough and tumble days of the East India Trading Company, global mergers and acquisitions have been the domain of multinationals from the developed nations. Well-endowed with capital and possessing superior brands and extensive logistics networks, Western multinationals have long been the global hunters, or the commercial entities with the wherewithal to purchase foreign assets or companies via cross-border mergers and acquisitions. For decades global M&A was largely a corporate strategy deployed by Western multinationals with the deep pockets, the technological capabilities and the managerial expertise to venture far from home.

Conversely, for decades, firms from developing countries were no match for the hunters since they lacked the capital, the management expertise, the brands and other core competencies to effectively compete beyond their home market. Times, however, have changed. Global deal-making is no longer a monopoly of the West. Aspiring multinationals from the BRIC countries are not only becoming more aggressive bidders for assets in other emerging markets, thereby crowding out Western multinationals from acquiring oil fields in central Asia, telecommunication companies in Africa, or banks in Argentina. These same firms have boldly set their strategic sites on assets and popular brands in the United States and Europe, creating, in the process, a whole new competitive landscape for many Western firms.

In other words, emerging global giants have joined the fray in hunting for global assets, with BRIC companies spending nearly a combined $60 billion on cross-border mergers and acquisitions in the United States ($14.4 billion in 2010) and particularly in developed Europe ($44 billion). That compares to just $1 billion in acquisitions in 2001. Primary sectors of interest include mining, energy, financial services, transportation and technology. Where cross-border M&A deals initiated by developing countries have traditionally been directed at other developing countries, the transatlantic economy is increasingly the focus of corporate entities from Russia, Brazil and a host of other countries. The appeal of the developed markets is manifold—access to global brands, cutting edge technology, wealthy consumers, and distribution channels are all key variables driving more M&A deals from the Rest to the West. And these same variables are also spurring on many emerging market corporations to invest directly in the United States and Europe.

For many U.S. states and local communities, that means more new jobs, new tax revenues and more economic growth. At the national level, however, the risk is that rising investment from the developing countries—notably from state-owned companies—

will ignite a backlash in the U.S. and Europe. Despite these risks, we expect the BRICs to continue to eye U.S. and EU investment opportunities for no other reason than when it comes to having an in-country presence in the transatlantic economy, still one of the wealthiest markets in the world, most globally-inspired companies from the developing countries are woefully unrepresented. In the end, the corporate giants of the BRICs are coming. They are no longer content to just trade anymore with the West, they are intent on investing and competing locally in Los Angeles, Houston, Detroit, Boston, Spartanburg, Lyon, Barcelona, Munich, London, Athens and elsewhere.

Nonetheless, while this new trend is noticeable, it begins from a low base. FDI by the BRICs in the EU is miniscule, accounting only 3.5% of EU FDI inflows 2002-2007—about the same as Norwegian FDI in the EU, and only about 9% of U.S. FDI in the EU.

Wall Street is a focus of many European banks and financial institutions. Silicon Valley in California has long been a main attraction for European technology firms, and as we reported last year, European investments account for almost half of all foreign-owned and -affiliated business establishments in Los Angeles County, more than Asian parent companies.[1] Moreover, the energy patch, Wall Street and the technology sector were key sectors leading the U.S. economy out of recession, which is likely to support the long-term foreign investment attractiveness of each state.

European affiliates directly employed the most U.S. workers in California (287,000), New York (255,300) and Texas (212,200).

Trade Linkages: European Multinationals and American States

Virtually every U.S. state maintains cross-border trade ties with Europe. In fact, the U.S. remains the #1 country market for EU exports of goods, accounting for 20% of total EU goods exports outside the EU in 2009. The U.S. also imports most services from the EU—43% of all U.S. services imports in 2009.

Europe is also a key export market in goods and services for many U.S. states, a role that grants even more economic benefits to states, ranging from income growth to the creation of jobs. For recession year 2009, which our survey covers, U.S. exports to Europe were subdued. Indeed, only 4 states and Puerto Rico posted positive export growth to Europe in 2009, with the rest feeling the full brunt of the economic recession in Europe. In 2010, however, total U.S. exports to the EU rose 7.1% in the first eight months of the year versus the same period a year earlier. But U.S. exports to the world rose by over 22% over the same time frame, making Europe a relative laggard in terms of U.S. export growth in 2010.

[1] See Daniel S. Hamilton and Joseph P. Quinlan, *The Transatlantic Economy 2010* (Washington, DC: Center for Transatlantic Relations, 2010)

Ranking of U.S. States Total Exports to Europe, by Value, 2009
(Billions of $)

U.S. State	2000	2009	% Change from 2008	% Change from 2000
California	27.9	25.2	-22%	-10%
Texas	12.3	24.2	-23%	97%
New York	15.3	19.7	-35%	29%
Puerto Rico	5.6	15.3	17%	171%
Massachusetts	8.0	11.1	-15%	39%
Washington	13.1	10.0	10%	-24%
Illinois	7.3	9.5	-26%	30%
Florida	3.9	8.8	-5%	127%
New Jersey	6.4	8.8	-41%	38%
Pennsylvania	4.7	7.5	-20%	61%
Ohio	5.0	7.3	-15%	45%
Indiana	3.1	7.0	-8%	122%
South Carolina	2.8	6.6	-26%	136%
Georgia	4.0	6.5	-22%	63%
Kentucky	3.1	6.0	-2%	96%
Connecticut	3.5	5.9	-11%	69%
North Carolina	4.6	5.8	-7%	26%
Utah	1.3	5.3	6%	296%
Virginia	3.8	5.3	-28%	37%
Louisiana	3.3	5.1	-40%	54%
Tennessee	2.7	4.6	-15%	71%
Minnesota	3.3	4.4	-21%	36%
Alabama	2.5	4.2	-31%	70%
Michigan	5.0	4.1	-28%	-18%
Wisconsin	2.4	3.7	-19%	53%
Nevada	0.3	3.4	-3%	1068%
Arizona	2.9	3.0	-30%	2%
Maryland	1.8	2.8	-29%	55%
Kansas	1.1	2.1	-37%	95%
West Virginia	0.7	2.0	-2%	177%
Oregon	1.9	1.8	-26%	-2%
Missouri	1.5	1.8	-22%	21%
Iowa	1.2	1.7	-37%	47%
Delaware	0.5	1.6	-23%	208%
Arkansas	0.6	1.4	-8%	120%
Mississippi	0.8	1.3	-14%	67%
Colorado	2.3	1.2	-35%	-49%
New Hampshire	0.9	0.8	-29%	-10%
Oklahoma	0.6	0.7	-20%	19%
Alaska	0.2	0.7	-9%	198%
Nebraska	0.4	0.6	-29%	56%
Rhode Island	0.3	0.4	-49%	16%
Maine	0.3	0.4	-12%	24%
Idaho	0.9	0.4	-27%	-60%
North Dakota	0.2	0.3	-52%	68%
Vermont	0.9	0.3	-26%	-67%
New Mexico	0.2	0.2	-28%	15%
Montana	0.1	0.2	-22%	66%
South Dakota	0.2	0.1	-28%	-36%
Wyoming	0.0	0.1	23%	275%
Hawaii	0.0	0.1	75%	583%
Unallocated	11.2	6.1	-28%	-46%
U.S. Total	187.4	258.1	-21%	38%

Source: Foreign Trade Division, U.S. Census Bureau

Ranking of U.S. States Total Exports to Europe, by Percentage Change, 2000-2009
(Billions of $)

U.S. State	2000	2008	2009	% Change from 2008	% Change from 2000
Nevada	0.3	3.5	3.4	-3%	1068%
Hawaii	0.0	0.1	0.1	75%	583%
Utah	1.3	5.0	5.3	6%	296%
Wyoming	0.0	0.1	0.1	23%	275%
Delaware	0.5	2.1	1.6	-23%	208%
Alaska	0.2	0.8	0.7	-9%	198%
West Virginia	0.7	2.0	2.0	-2%	177%
Puerto Rico	5.6	13.1	15.3	17%	171%
South Carolina	2.8	8.9	6.6	-26%	136%
Florida	3.9	9.2	8.8	-5%	127%
Indiana	3.1	7.6	7.0	-8%	122%
Arkansas	0.6	1.5	1.4	-8%	120%
Texas	12.3	31.4	24.2	-23%	97%
Kentucky	3.1	6.1	6.0	-2%	96%
Kansas	1.1	3.4	2.1	-37%	95%
Tennessee	2.7	5.4	4.6	-15%	71%
Alabama	2.5	6.1	4.2	-31%	70%
Connecticut	3.5	6.6	5.9	-11%	69%
North Dakota	0.2	0.7	0.3	-52%	68%
Mississippi	0.8	1.5	1.3	-14%	67%
Montana	0.1	0.2	0.2	-22%	66%
Georgia	4.0	8.3	6.5	-22%	63%
Pennsylvania	4.7	9.4	7.5	-20%	61%
Nebraska	0.4	0.9	0.6	-29%	56%
Maryland	1.8	3.9	2.8	-29%	55%
Louisiana	3.3	8.5	5.1	-40%	54%
Wisconsin	2.4	4.6	3.7	-19%	53%
Iowa	1.2	2.7	1.7	-37%	47%
Ohio	5.0	8.5	7.3	-15%	45%
Massachusetts	8.0	13.1	11.1	-15%	39%
New Jersey	6.4	14.9	8.8	-41%	38%
U.S. Total	187.4	325.0	258.1	-21%	38%
Virginia	3.8	7.3	5.3	-28%	37%
Minnesota	3.3	5.6	4.4	-21%	36%
Illinois	7.3	12.8	9.5	-26%	30%
New York	15.3	30.3	19.7	-35%	29%
North Carolina	4.6	6.3	5.8	-7%	26%
Maine	0.3	0.4	0.4	-12%	24%
Missouri	1.5	2.3	1.8	-22%	21%
Oklahoma	0.6	0.9	0.7	-20%	19%
Rhode Island	0.3	0.8	0.4	-49%	16%
New Mexico	0.2	0.3	0.2	-28%	15%
Arizona	2.9	4.3	3.0	-30%	2%
Oregon	1.9	2.5	1.8	-26%	-2%
New Hampshire	0.9	1.2	0.8	-29%	-10%
California	27.9	32.3	25.2	-22%	-10%
Michigan	5.0	5.7	4.1	-28%	-18%
Washington	13.1	9.0	10.0	10%	-24%
South Dakota	0.2	0.2	0.1	-28%	-36%
Unallocated	11.2	8.4	6.1	-28%	-46%
Colorado	2.3	1.8	1.2	-35%	-49%
Idaho	0.9	0.5	0.4	-27%	-60%
Vermont	0.9	0.4	0.3	-26%	-67%

Source: Foreign Trade Division, U.S. Census Bureau

The EU's Economic Links to Canada and Mexico

EU economic ties with Canada are also significant. The EU is Canada's second largest investment partner after the U.S., and Canada is the fourth largest country investment partner for the EU. The EU is Canada's second most important trading partner, after the U.S., with a 10.5% share of its total external trade. Canada is currently the EU's 11th most important trading partner, accounting for 1.8% of the EU's total external trade in 2009. The EU and Canada hope to conclude by 2012 a comprehensive trade and economic agreement that promises significant returns for both parties. Liberalizing trade in goods and services could boost EU exports to Canada by 24.3% or €17 billion and Canadian exports to the EU by 20.6% or €8.6 billion by 2014. The annual real income gain by the year 2014 would be approximately €11.6 billion for the EU (0.08% of EU GDP), and approximately €8.2 billion for Canada (0.77% of Canadian GDP). About half of the gains would come from liberalization of trade in services; more limited but still significant gains would derive from the elimination of tariffs on goods (25% of the total for the EU and 33.3% for Canada). The remaining gains are projected to result from a reduction in the trade costs of non-tariff barriers. While Canada would benefit relatively more from such an ambitious agreement (which is natural given the greater size of the EU's economy compared to Canada's), there will be notable gains to both economies.[2]

The EU signed a comprehensive free trade agreement with Mexico in 1997, with trade provisions entering into force in 2000 and 2001. The agreement has been of undoubted benefit to both parties: trade flows within the FTA have grown by over 25%, with Mexican exports to the EU growing by some 20% and EU exports to Mexico growing by close to 30%. Trade in industrial goods is fully liberalized, and agricultural products will be substantially liberalized by 2010. The FTA also foresees future negotiations on the liberalization of services trade.[3]

[2] *Assessing the costs and benefits of a closer EU- Canada economic partnership: A Joint Study by the European Commission and the Government of Canada*, 2008, available at http://www.international.gc.ca /trade-agreementsaccords-commerciaux/assets/pdfs/EU-CanadaJointStudy-en.pdf.

[3] Ibid.; European Commission, "EU launches major new trade relationship with Latin America," May 18, 2010. EU goods exports to Mexico 2009: €15.9 billion. EU goods imports from Mexico 2009: €9.9 billion. EU investment stock in the Mexico 2008: €49.0 billion.

The U.S. still enjoys a strong position as an exporter of services to Europe and to the world; as we outlined in Chapter 2, U.S. services exports to Europe more than doubled over the past decade. In 2009 Europe accounted for 41% of all U.S. services exports.

The U.S. is faring less well in exports of goods to Europe, particularly when compared to China, which has become the most important source of goods imported by the EU. Between 2000 and 2009, China's share of EU goods imports grew to 18.2% from 7.7%, while North America's entire share shrank to 15.9% from 23.9%. In this regard, President Obama's call to double U.S. exports over coming years is encouraging.

Not surprisingly, U.S. exports to crisis-stricken Ireland and Greece declined over the period, with U.S. goods exports to Greece plunging 43% in the first eight months of 2010. The decline in exports to Ireland was not as steep (3.3%), although U.S. goods shipments to Ireland are not expected to recover any time soon. Reflecting weaker growth in France, U.S. exports to one of Europe's largest and wealthiest markets declined 2% in the January-August 2010 period. Fortunately, demand elsewhere for U.S. exports was quite strong last year; to this point, U.S. exports to Germany rose 11.2% in the first eight months of last year, while U.S. exports to Switzerland, Italy, and Spain rose 11.2%, 15.6%, and 7.6%, respectively. Each accounted for roughly one-fifth of total U.S. exports to Europe in 2010. The United Kingdom and Germany were far and away the largest markets in the EU for U.S. goods.

At the state level, California, the largest exporter among U.S. states, exported roughly $25 billion in goods to Europe in 2009. The EU represents one of the largest markets in the world for information technology, and firms in California and other states like New York, Colorado and Oregon have seen exports of computers and related parts to Europe expand sharply over the past few years. Texas and New York are also sizable exporters to Europe. Texas' exports to Europe totaled $24.2 billion in 2009, almost double those in 2000. Exports from New York to Europe totaled nearly $20 billion in 2009, a significant decline from the more than the $30 billion the state exported to Europe in 2008. The composition of U.S. exports to Europe runs the gamut—from machinery to chemicals to pulp and paper.

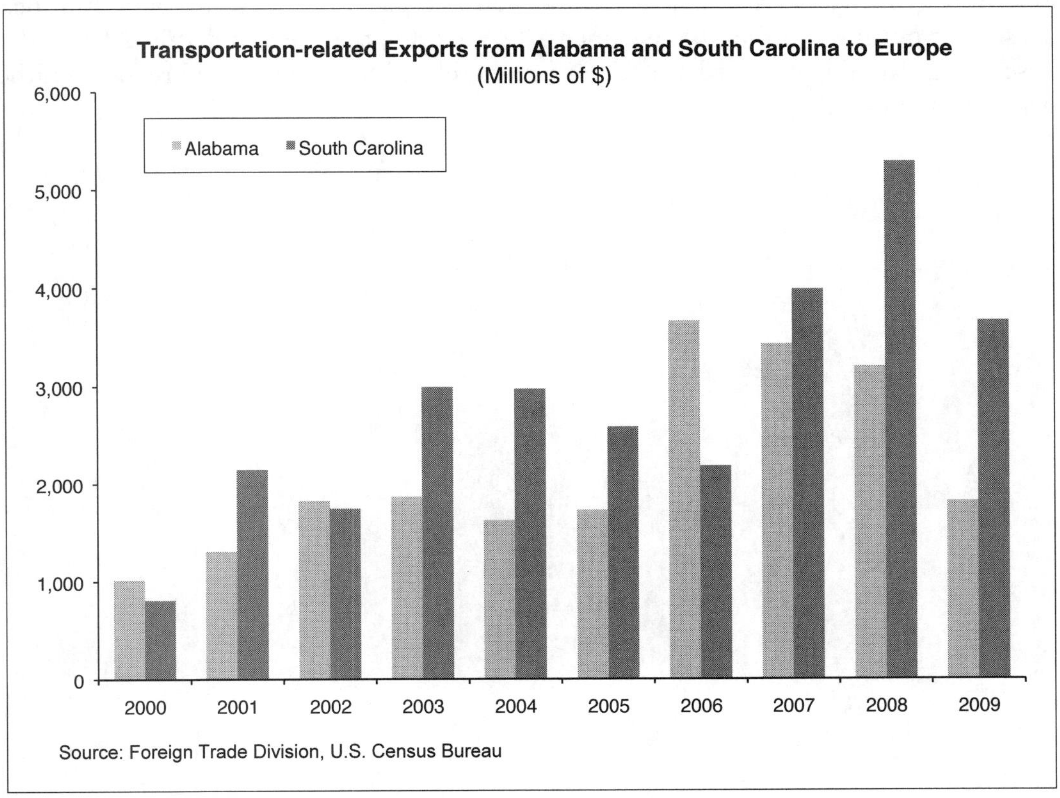

The United Kingdom was the top European export market for 15 U.S. states in 2009. Germany was second, the top European export market for 13 states, including Michigan and California. In general, Europe is one of the largest markets in the world for a host of U.S. goods, ranging from agricultural products to high-tech goods. By commodity, sharp increases were recorded for such exports as chemicals, transportation equipment, computers, processed foods and paper products.

The deep transatlantic linkages forged by investment and trade flows are underscored by the important ties such states as Alabama, Michigan and South Carolina have with European automobile manufacturers. Volkswagen's major new investment in Chattanooga, Tennessee is another prominent example. In many cases, trade flows represent "related party" trade, which are trade flows that stay within the ambit of the company. In this respect, European affiliates in the U.S. are significant exporters in their own right.

These figures about investment flows and exports may be abstract, but they translate into real jobs for American workers. For all the talk about "offshored" American jobs, European investments create "onshored" jobs in U.S. state and local economies. Moreover, those investments also tend to generate U.S. exports, opening additional markets to U.S. workers. Similarly, when European investments decline, this means job losses for American workers. The United States as a whole, and a substantial number of U.S. states and localities in particular, have developed a real stake in healthy, two-way transatlantic commerce.

European investment in many U.S. regions and states will continue to play a key role in promoting growth and creating jobs in American states and localities. Although European investment outflows to the U.S. declined 50% in 2009, they rebounded in 2010 and so these swings should be viewed as cyclical factors related to recession and recovery rather than as a structural shift.

Special Focus
European FDI Abroad: The U.S. versus the Rest of the World

While our previous surveys have focused just on Europe's investment in the United States in isolation, this special focus section compares this investment to the EU's foreign direct investment position on a global basis.

In terms of FDI flows and outward stock, the United States remains the primary destination of EU investment outside the EU itself. Based on data from Eurostat, the U.S. was the top recipient of extra-EU FDI outflows in 2009, which is the last year of available data. Outflows to the U.S. totaled €75 billion (down from €121 billion in 2008), 27% of the extra-EU27 total, followed by Switzerland (14%), Brazil (3%) and Argentina (2%). In terms of capital stock, the EU's investment stock in the United States rose by 51% between 2000 and 2009, with the U.S. accounting for nearly one-third of extra-EU27 FDI stock abroad.

Of particular interest is the spread between European FDI in the United States on the one hand versus EU FDI in China and India on the other. Simply put, there is no comparison: in 2009, EU FDI in the U.S. totaled €1.1 trillion, versus total combined investment of €85.5 billion in China and India. EU FDI in China totaled €58.3 billion in 2009, up from €47.2 billion in 2008, while EU FDI in India tallied just €27.2 billion in 2009, up from only €19.3 billion in 2008.

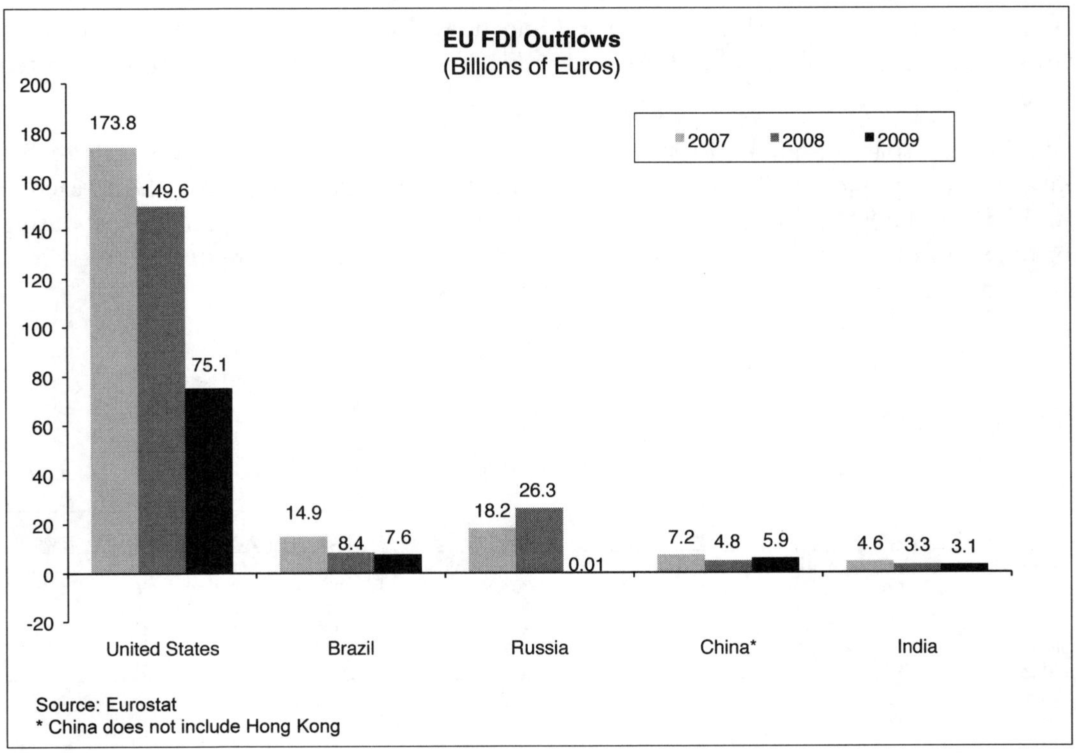

If one makes a global comparison, then in 2008—the last year of comparable global data—the amount of EU FDI flowing to the U.S. was more than to the next 6 destinations combined. Switzerland ranked 2nd, registering about 43% of the amount going to the United States. Canada was 3rd and Mexico 12th, bolstering the importance of North America as the EU's preferred FDI destination. Of the BRICs, Brazil ranked 4th, Russia 5th, China 13th and India 19th. EU FDI in the United States in 2008 was 9 times more than in Brazil, 11 times more than in Russia, 22 times more than in China and 55 times more than in India. EU FDI to Russia increased 12.5 times between 2001 and 2008, but still accounted for only 2.8% of the total. EU FDI to China tripled between 2000 and 2008, but still only accounted for little more than 1% of overall EU FDI.

As we highlight in the next chapter, however, both U.S. and European firms are gradually increasing their exposure to emerging markets. That's hardly surprising given the growth differential between the slow-growth, mature economies of the West versus the fast-growth, emerging markets of Asia, Latin America, the Middle East and Africa.

A related item of interest: although EU FDI in North America was considerably more than to other world regions (38%), the 2008 levels were 14% lower than in 2001, whereas FDI in all other regions except Central and South America increased. 22.5% went to other parts of Europe outside the EU—about 6% more than in 2001.

What is particularly striking from the latest three years of data is that EU FDI outflows to the BRICs are focused primarily on Russia, and then Brazil, rather than China or India. While EU FDI outflows to Russia dropped off to only €9 million in 2009, flows to Russia in 2007, 2008 and 2009 totaled €45 billion, nearly one-and-a-half times EU FDI to Brazil, two-and-a-half times EU FDI to China and four times EU FDI to India. Yet EU FDI outflows to Russia in 2007-2009 represented only 11% of EU FDI outflows to the United States in this period.

Although the share of EU FDI going to the BRICs still remains small—and has increased only moderately since 2002—overall the EU is the largest single provider of FDI to each of the BRICs. The EU is by far Russia's major commercial partner, for example, accounting for over half of its overall trade turnover. It is also by far the most important investor in Russia, accounting for up to 75% of FDI stocks in Russia.

EU FDI Assets
Billions of Euros

	2000	2001	2002	2003	2004	2005	2006	2007	2008	2009
United States	752	915	760	748	732	845	949	1,027	1,076	1,134
Brazil	75	73	44	59	70	74	92	108	108	132
Russia	7	11	10	15	21	33	51	72	83	89
China*	15	19	20	19	21	28	33	41	52	58
India	6	6	6	7	8	11	12	16	17	27
BRICs	104	110	81	99	121	145	188	236	261	307

Source: Eurostat
*China does not include Hong Kong

Nonetheless, in terms of EU FDI assets in each country, the gap between EU investment assets in the U.S. and the BRICs remains huge. EU investment assets in the U.S. are 31% of extra-EU27 investment stock and 3 times the size of EU investment assets in the BRICs.

Of the BRICs, EU investment assets are greatest in Brazil, with 4% of extra-EU27 investment. The value of that investment, however, was only one-tenth of that in the United States in 2009. EU investment assets in Russia were about 8% of those in the U.S. In China, the comparable figure was 5% of EU investment stock in the United States.

Despite considerable discussion about India's rapid development, EU FDI links to India are particularly thin. India accounted for less than 1% of extra-EU27 investment stock in 2009. In 2008, the last year of comparable global data, the EU total of €19 billion in FDI in India was 40% of its FDI in China; 28% of its FDI in the Middle East; 25% of its FDI in Japan; about 20% of its FDI in Russia; 14% of its FDI in Africa; 8% of its FDI in Latin America and 8% of its FDI in the Caribbean; 7% of its FDI in Rising Asia; less than 3% of its FDI in Wider Europe; and less than 2% of its FDI in North America.

According to the 2009 European Competitiveness Report, Germany and the United Kingdom are the EU's main FDI investors in the BRICs, followed by France and the Netherlands. In terms of amounts invested, Spain also ranks among the top five investors. The strong presence of EU firms in Brazil mainly reflects FDI from Spain and Germany. When looking at the number of projects, Italy also emerges as an important investor for the BRICs. Portugal, the former colonial power in Brazil, is not a major investor in terms of value, but has the highest number of investment projects. In addition to the activities of the top EU investors, Austrian, Belgian and Swedish companies also are responsible for relatively significant FDI in Russia.

Despite low overall FDI in the BRICS, for some EU firms FDI can be an important mode of entry and vehicle for production in BRIC markets. In fact, for several EU member states, sales by foreign affiliates of manufacturing firms in some BrIC markets already surpass their exports. For example, the sales of German manufacturing affiliates in Brazil are almost four times German merchandise exports to Brazil.

As with the EU's overall outward FDI, EU FDI stocks owned in the BRICs are skewed to the services sector. Services account for about 60% of EU projects and accumulated FDI stocks in the BRICS, compared to about 33% for manufacturing. EU FDI in manufacturing plays more of a role in China and India. The dominance of services over manufacturing is in line with the structure of the EU economy, but in stark contrast with the relative importance of these two broad sectors in international trade, confirming the importance of direct investment in the internationalization of services. Indeed, as services are typically more difficult to trade across borders, settling in BRICs through FDI is the main means for EU service companies to get access to BRIC markets.[4]

U.S. and European FDI in the BRICs and other emerging markets would be higher than it is today if not for continuing barriers to such investment in the emerging markets them-

[4] *European Competitiveness Report 2009.*

EU FDI Assets
Percent of extra-EU27 total

	2004	2005	2006	2007	2008	2009
United States	36.2%	34.8%	34.6%	31.8%	32.4%	30.9%
Brazil	3.5%	3.1%	3.4%	3.3%	3.3%	3.6%
Russia	1.0%	1.4%	1.8%	2.2%	2.5%	2.4%
China	1.1%	1.1%	1.2%	1.3%	1.6%	1.6%
India	0.4%	0.4%	0.5%	0.5%	0.5%	0.7%
BRICs	6.0%	6.0%	6.8%	7.3%	7.9%	8.4%

Source: Eurostat

selves. Inefficient bureaucracy and a poorly developed infrastructure figure among the most important barriers for FDI in India, for example. In China, investor concerns about property rights, intellectual property and remaining restrictions and caps on foreign ownership in the services sectors limit U.S. and EU investment.[5]

EU-U.S. FDI Outflows to the BRICs[1] 2001-2009
(Percent of total[2])

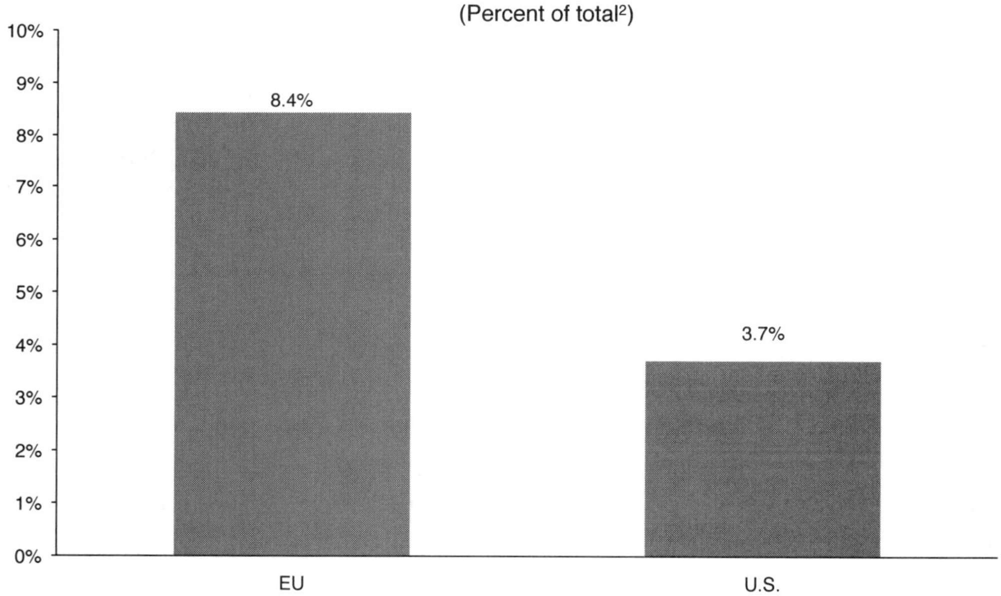

Source: Eurostat, Bureau of Economic Analysis
[1]China does not include Hong Kong
[2]Percent of Extra-EU27 outflows

[5] See European Chamber of Commerce in China, "European Business in China 2010/2011 Position Paper," http://www.europeanchamber.com.cn/images/documents/marketing_department/beijing/publications/2010/executive_summary.pdf; United States Trade Representative, "National Trade Estimate Report on Foreign Trade Barriers," May 17, 2010; Keith Bradsher, "China Sets Rules and Wins Wind Power Game," *The New York Times*, December 15, 2010; Pilling, op. cit.; Jamil Anderlini, "Pie is growing, but foreigners share is shrinking," *Financial Times*, October 27, 2010; "Train Makers Rail Against China's High-Speed Designs, *The Wall Street Journal*, September 28, 2010.

The bottom line is that U.S. and European companies continue to show a strong preference for each other's market when it comes to investing overseas. The notion that the U.S. and Europe are decamping from each other's markets for the low-cost destinations of China and India is wide of the mark. It ignores many other considerations besides cheap labor that drive investment decisions, and neglects the considerable barriers to investment still in place in emerging markets. Between 2001 and 2009 EU FDI outflows to the BRICS represented only 8.4% of global EU FDI outflows outside the EU27, and most of that was to Brazil and Russia, not China and India. U.S. FDI outflows to the BRICS during this same period accounted for only 3.7% of global U.S. FDI outflows.

Alabama and Europe

Employment, Investment, and Trade Linkages

Employment

European* investment in Alabama supported 33,800 jobs in 2008.

Sources of Employment within Alabama, 2008	
Country	**Employment**
Japan	13,600
Germany	11,300
United Kingdom	10,400
France	8,000
Canada	7,400

Investment

Of the $22.9 billion invested in Alabama in 2007, 52%, or $11.8 billion came from Europe*.

Trade

In 2009, Europe purchased $4.2 billion worth of goods from Alabama.
Over 43% of total exports represented transportation equipment, reflecting the state's linkages with European auto manufacturers.

Top European Export Markets, 2009	
Country	**Exports ($ Millions)**
Germany	1,810
United Kingdom	460
France	302
Netherlands	212
Italy	165

Top Ten Exports to Europe ($ Millions)

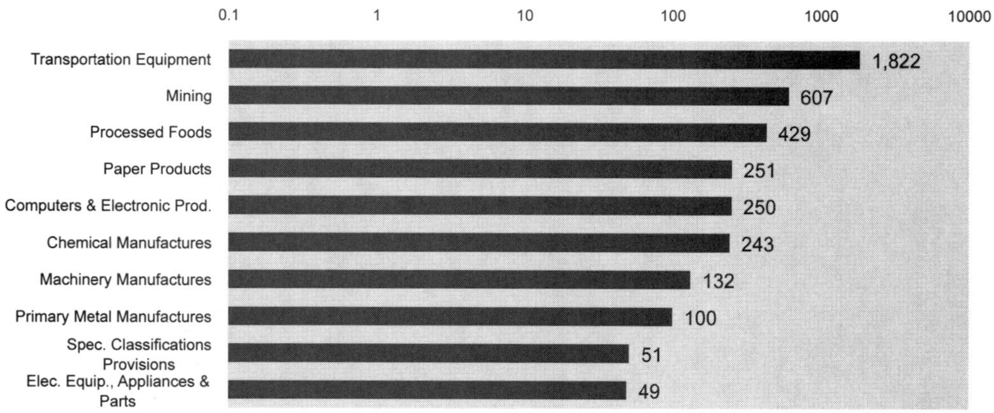

Source: Bureau of Economic Anlaysis, Foreign Trade Division, U.S. Census Bureau
*European investment includes France, Germany, Netherlands, Switzerland, and the United Kingdom
Due to a need to align resources with current funding levels, the Bureau of Economic Analysis has reduced its coverage to major investing countries.

Alaska and Europe

Employment, Investment, and Trade Linkages

Employment

European* investment in Alaska supported 5,100 jobs in 2008.

Sources of Employment within Alaska, 2008	
Country	**Employment**
United Kingdom	3,500
Canada	1,800
Japan	1,800
France	900
Switzerland	300

Investment

Alaska received $34.5 billion of investment in 2007, the amount from Europe* is not available.

Trade

In 2009, Europe purchased $723 million worth of goods from Alaska.
The bulk of exports consist of primary commodities.

Top European Export Markets, 2009	
Country	**Exports ($ Millions)**
Switzerland	150
Spain	138
Germany	126
Netherlands	88
Italy	46

Top Ten Exports to Europe ($ Millions)

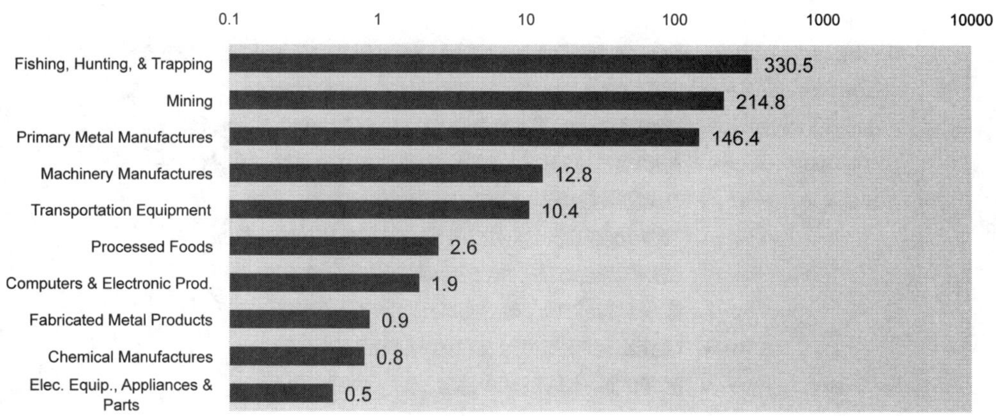

Source: Bureau of Economic Anlaysis, Foreign Trade Division, U.S. Census Bureau

*European investment includes France, Germany, Netherlands, Switzerland, and the United Kingdom

Due to a need to align resources with current funding levels, the Bureau of Economic Analysis has reduced its coverage to major investing countries.

Arizona and Europe

Employment, Investment, and Trade Linkages

Employment

European* investment in Arizona supported 40,000 jobs in 2008.

Sources of Employment within Arizona, 2008	
Country	**Employment**
Canada	13,500
United Kingdom	12,500
Germany	8,600
France	7,400
Switzerland	7,300

Investment

Of the $13 billion invested in Arizona in 2007, 42%, or $5.4 billion came from Europe*.

Trade

In 2009, Europe purchased $3 billion worth of goods from Arizona.
Nearly one third of the state's exports consist of transportation equipment.

Top European Export Markets, 2009	
Country	**Exports ($ Millions)**
United Kingdom	597
Germany	587
France	494
Italy	239
Netherlands	226

Top Ten Exports to Europe ($ Millions)

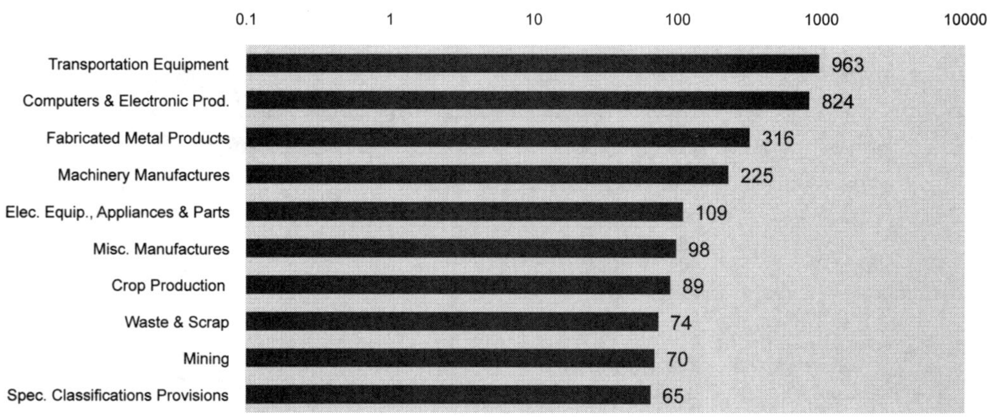

Source: Bureau of Economic Anlaysis, Foreign Trade Division, U.S. Census Bureau
*European investment includes France, Germany, Netherlands, Switzerland, and the United Kingdom
Due to a need to align resources with current funding levels, the Bureau of Economic Analysis has reduced its coverage to major investing countries.

Arkansas and Europe

Employment, Investment, and Trade Linkages

Employment

European* investment in Arkansas supported 15,800 jobs in 2008.

Sources of Employment within Arkansas, 2008	
Country	**Employment**
France	6,000
Japan	4,300
United Kingdom	3,800
Canada	2,400
Switzerland	2,200

Investment

Of the $4.9 billion invested in Arkansas in 2007, 49%, or $2.4 billion came from Europe*.

Trade

In 2009, Europe purchased $1.4 billion worth of goods from Arkansas.
Transportation equipment was the top export to Europe.

Top European Export Markets, 2009	
Country	**Exports ($ Millions)**
France	306
United Kingdom	233
Belgium	132
Germany	112
Luxembourg	103

Top Ten Exports to Europe ($ Millions)

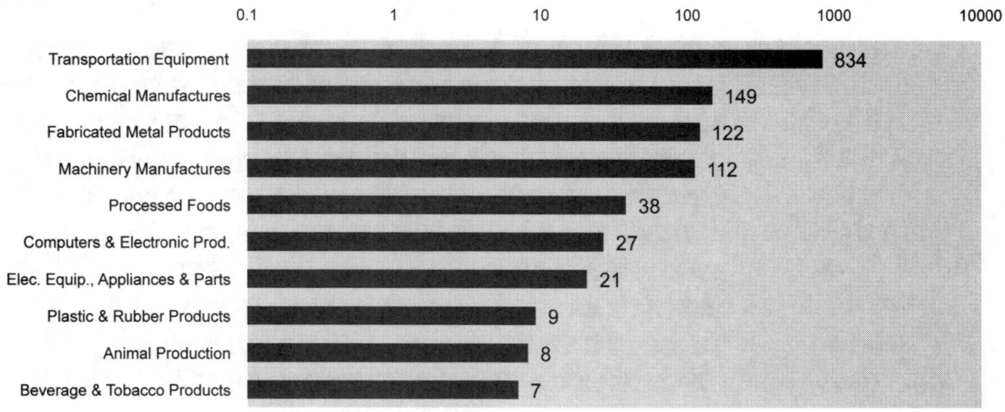

Source: Bureau of Economic Anlaysis, Foreign Trade Division, U.S. Census Bureau
*European investment includes France, Germany, Netherlands, Switzerland, and the United Kingdom
Due to a need to align resources with current funding levels, the Bureau of Economic Analysis has reduced its coverage to major investing countries.

California and Europe

Employment, Investment, and Trade Linkages

Employment

European* investment in California supported 287,000 jobs in 2008.

Sources of Employment within California, 2008	
Country	**Employment**
Japan	118,600
United Kingdom	84,900
France	61,000
Germany	60,700
Switzerland	57,500

Investment

Of the $108.6 billion invested in California in 2007, 43%, or $46.8 billion came from Europe*.

Trade

In 2009, Europe purchased $25.2 billion worth of goods from California.
Over 32% of Californian exports to Europe consist of high-tech goods.

Top European Export Markets, 2009	
Country	**Exports ($ Millions)**
Germany	4,441
United Kingdom	3,916
Netherlands	3,566
France	2,316
Belgium	1,983

Top Ten Exports to Europe ($ Millions)

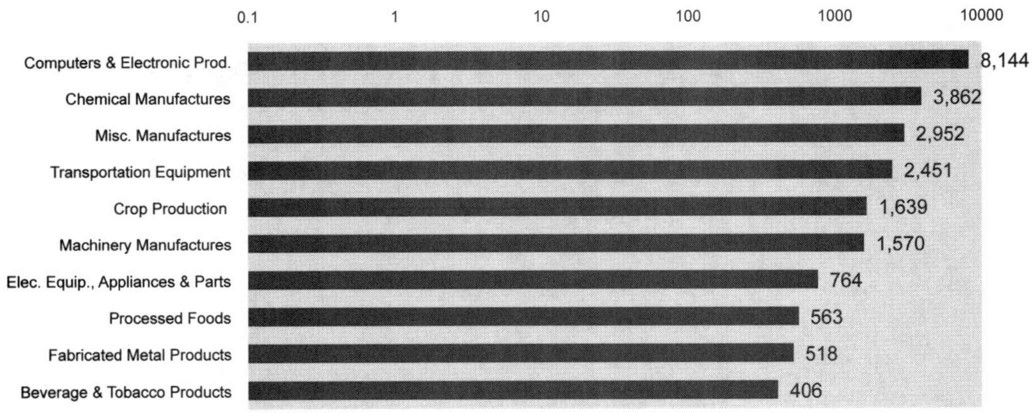

Source: Bureau of Economic Anlaysis, Foreign Trade Division, U.S. Census Bureau
*European investment includes France, Germany, Netherlands, Switzerland, and the United Kingdom
Due to a need to align resources with current funding levels, the Bureau of Economic Analysis has reduced its coverage to major investing countries.

Colorado and Europe
Employment, Investment, and Trade Linkages

Employment
European* investment in Colorado supported 34,700 jobs in 2008.

Sources of Employment within Colorado, 2008	
Country	**Employment**
United Kingdom	13,600
Canada	12,600
France	7,000
Germany	5,800
Switzerland	5,100

Investment
Of the investment in Colorado in 2007, $8.4 billion came from Europe*.

Trade
In 2009, Europe purchased $1.2 billion worth of goods from Colorado.
Almost 34% of the state's exports consist of high-tech goods like computers and electronic products.

Top European Export Markets, 2009	
Country	**Exports ($ Millions)**
Germany	220
Netherlands	175
Switzerland	159
Belgium	146
United Kingdom	142

Top Ten Exports to Europe ($ Millions)

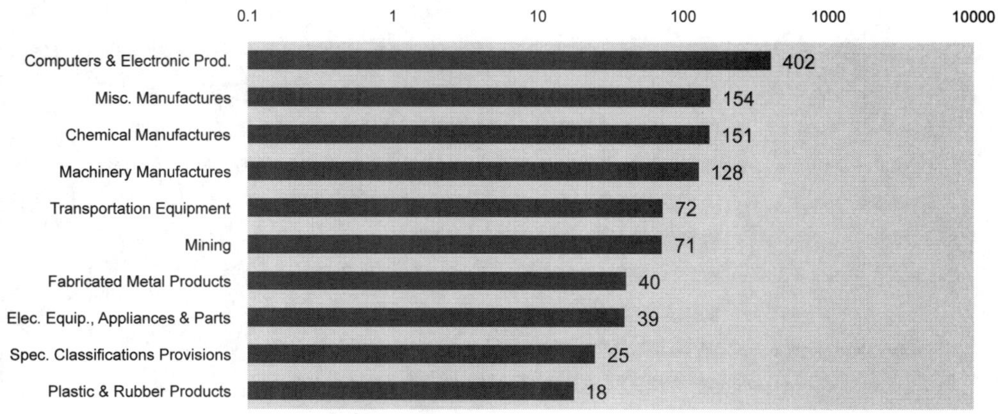

Source: Bureau of Economic Anlaysis, Foreign Trade Division, U.S. Census Bureau
*European investment includes France, Germany, Netherlands, Switzerland, and the United Kingdom
Due to a need to align resources with current funding levels, the Bureau of Economic Analysis has reduced its coverage to major investing countries.

Connecticut and Europe

Employment, Investment, and Trade Linkages

Employment

European* investment in Connecticut supported 68,600 jobs in 2008.

Sources of Employment within Connecticut, 2008	
Country	**Employment**
Netherlands	22,000
United Kingdom	16,600
Germany	12,400
Switzerland	9,500
France	8,100

Investment

Of the $13.4 billion invested in Connecticut in 2007, 63%, or $8.4 billion came from Europe*.

Trade

In 2009, Europe purchased $5.9 billion worth of goods from Connecticut.
Exports are heavily skewed towards transportation equipment.

Top European Export Markets, 2009	
Country	**Exports ($ Millions)**
France	2,217
Germany	1,306
United Kingdom	648
Belgium	235
Netherlands	234

Top Ten Exports to Europe ($ Millions)

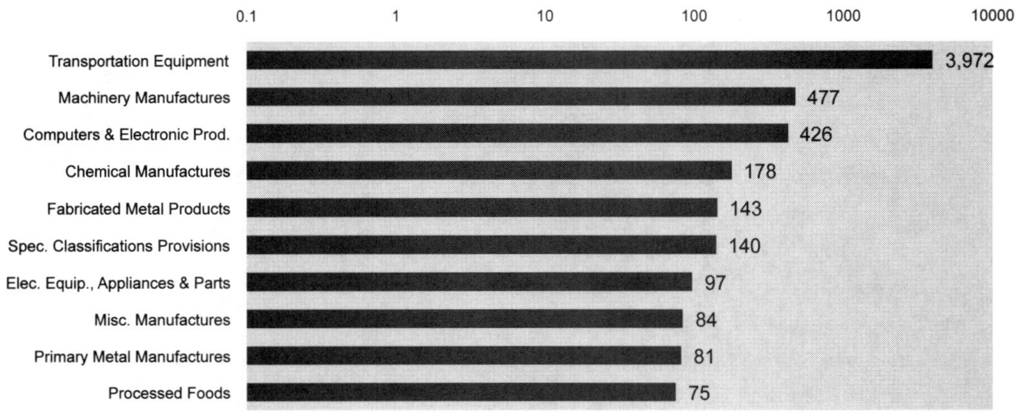

Source: Bureau of Economic Anlaysis, Foreign Trade Division, U.S. Census Bureau
*European investment includes France, Germany, Netherlands, Switzerland, and the United Kingdom
Due to a need to align resources with current funding levels, the Bureau of Economic Analysis has reduced its coverage to major investing countries.

Delaware and Europe

Employment, Investment, and Trade Linkages

Employment

European* investment in Delaware supported 19,400 jobs in 2008.

Sources of Employment within Delaware, 2008	
Country	**Employment**
United Kingdom	10,900
Canada	4,800
Netherlands	2,500
Germany	2,400
Switzerland	1,900

Investment

Of the $4.5 billion invested in Delaware in 2007, 51%, or $2.3 billion came from Europe.

Trade

In 2009, Europe purchased $1.6 billion worth of goods from Delaware.
Chemical exports are Delaware's primary export to Europe.

Top European Export Markets, 2009	
Country	**Exports ($ Millions)**
United Kingdom	866
Germany	352
Netherlands	78
Austria	66
Belgium	61

Top Ten Exports to Europe ($ Millions)

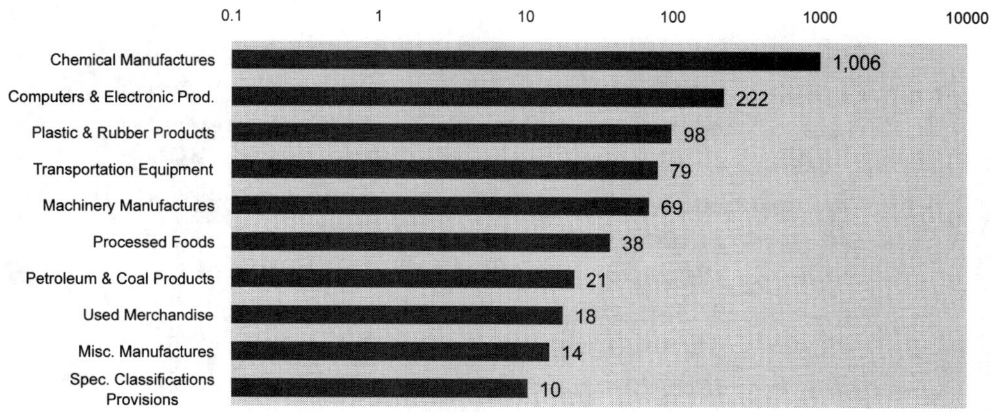

Source: Bureau of Economic Anlaysis, Foreign Trade Division, U.S. Census Bureau

*European investment includes France, Germany, Netherlands, Switzerland, and the United Kingdom

Due to a need to align resources with current funding levels, the Bureau of Economic Analysis has reduced its coverage to major investing countries.

Florida and Europe

Employment, Investment, and Trade Linkages

Employment

European* investment in Florida supported 116,200 jobs in 2008.

Sources of Employment within Florida, 2008	
Country	**Employment**
United Kingdom	44,000
Canada	24,100
Germany	22,400
Japan	21,700
France	19,000

Investment

Of the $35.1 billion invested in Florida in 2007, 38%, or $13.3 billion came from Europe*.

Trade

In 2009, Europe purchased $8.8 billion worth of goods from Florida.
Waste and scrap exports account for over 35% of total exports to Europe.

Top European Export Markets, 2009	
Country	**Exports ($ Millions)**
Switzerland	3,244
United Kingdom	1,000
Germany	985
Netherlands	679
France	509

Top Ten Exports to Europe ($ Millions)

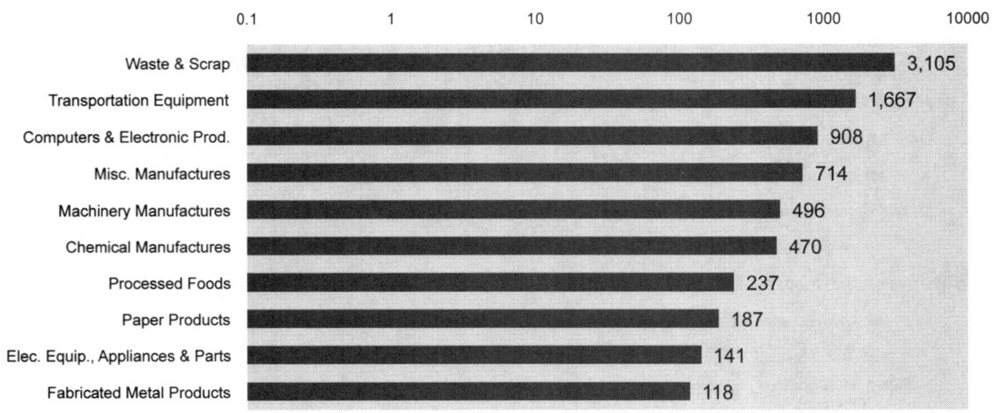

Source: Bureau of Economic Anlaysis, Foreign Trade Division, U.S. Census Bureau
*European investment includes France, Germany, Netherlands, Switzerland, and the United Kingdom
Due to a need to align resources with current funding levels, the Bureau of Economic Analysis has reduced its coverage to major investing countries.

Georgia and Europe

Employment, Investment, and Trade Linkages

Employment

European* investment in Georgia supported 93,100 jobs in 2008.

Sources of Employment within Georgia, 2008	
Country	**Employment**
United Kingdom	29,000
Japan	27,400
Germany	20,500
Netherlands	18,100
France	15,500

Investment

Of the investment in Georgia in 2007, $11.1 billion came from Europe*.

Trade

In 2009, Europe purchased $6.5 billion worth of goods from Georgia. Exports are broadly diversified among such exports as transportation equipment, machinery & chemical manufactures.

Top European Export Markets, 2009	
Country	**Exports ($ Millions)**
United Kingdom	1,216
Germany	1,015
Netherlands	662
Belgium	577
Italy	484

Top Ten Exports to Europe ($ Millions)

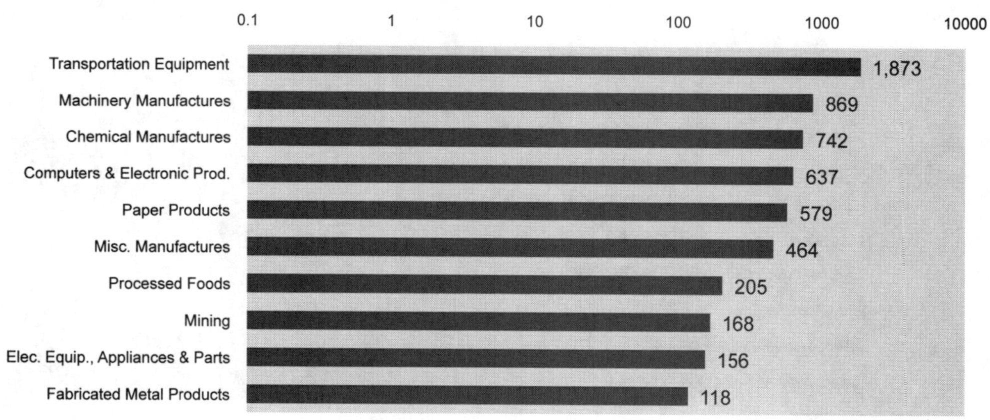

Source: Bureau of Economic Anlaysis, Foreign Trade Division, U.S. Census Bureau

*European investment includes France, Germany, Netherlands, Switzerland, and the United Kingdom

Due to a need to align resources with current funding levels, the Bureau of Economic Analysis has reduced its coverage to major investing countries.

Hawaii and Europe

Employment, Investment, and Trade Linkages

Employment

European* investment in Hawaii supported 9,200 jobs in 2008.

Sources of Employment within Hawaii, 2008	
Country	**Employment**
Japan	15,600
France	4,200
United Kingdom	3,100
Canada	900
Switzerland	900

Investment

Of the $6.2 billion invested in Hawaii in 2007, 16%, or $1 billion came from Europe*.

Trade

In 2009, Europe purchased $103 million worth of goods from Hawaii.
Transportation equipment accounts for nearly 80% of total exports.

Top European Export Markets, 2009	
Country	**Exports ($ Millions)**
Netherlands	66
Germany	23
France	5
United Kingdom	4
Sweden	2

Top Ten Exports to Europe ($ Millions)

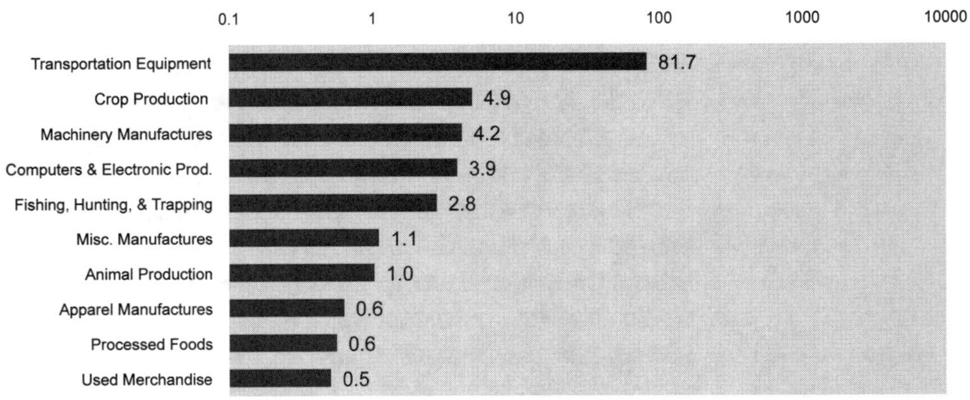

Source: Bureau of Economic Anlaysis, Foreign Trade Division, U.S. Census Bureau

*European investment includes France, Germany, Netherlands, Switzerland, and the United Kingdom

Due to a need to align resources with current funding levels, the Bureau of Economic Analysis has reduced its coverage to major investing countries.

Idaho and Europe

Employment, Investment, and Trade Linkages

Employment

European* investment in Idaho supported 10,100 jobs in 2008.

Sources of Employment within Idaho, 2008	
Country	**Employment**
Canada	3,900
Germany	3,000
France	2,800
United Kingdom	2,600
Switzerland	1,500

Investment

Of the $2 billion invested in Idaho in 2007, 40%, or $0.8 billion came from Europe*.

Trade

In 2009, Europe purchased $359 million worth of goods from Idaho.
Exports are mostly concentrated in computers and electronic products.

Top European Export Markets, 2009	
Country	**Exports ($ Millions)**
France	107
United Kingdom	90
Netherlands	44
Germany	26
Italy	24

Top Ten Exports to Europe ($ Millions)

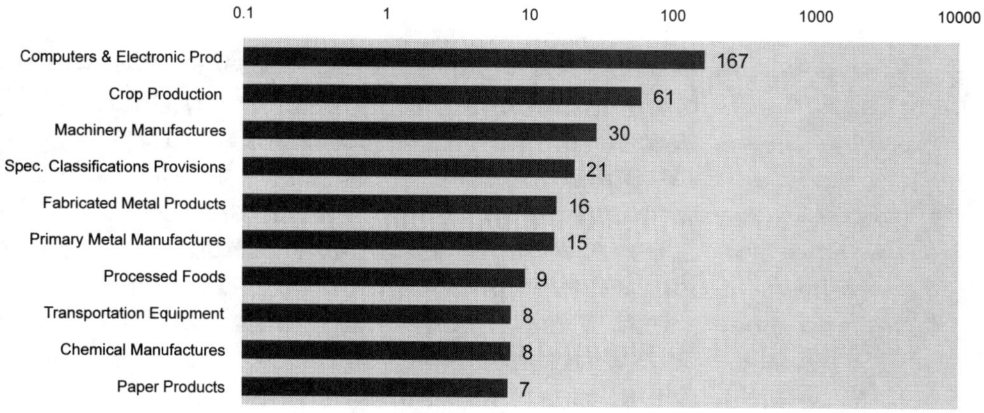

Source: Bureau of Economic Anlaysis, Foreign Trade Division, U.S. Census Bureau
*European investment includes France, Germany, Netherlands, Switzerland, and the United Kingdom
Due to a need to align resources with current funding levels, the Bureau of Economic Analysis has reduced its coverage to major investing countries.

Illinois and Europe

Employment, Investment, and Trade Linkages

Employment
European* investment in Illinois supported 152,700 jobs in 2008.

Sources of Employment within Illinois, 2008	
Country	**Employment**
United Kingdom	55,700
Japan	36,700
Germany	36,000
France	30,100
Canada	23,000

Investment
Of the $48.6 billion invested in Illinois in 2007, 44%, or $21.6 billion came from Europe*.

Trade
In 2009, Europe purchased $9.5 billion worth of goods from Illinois.
Cemicals are a key export, followed by machinery and computers.

Top European Export Markets, 2009	
Country	**Exports ($ Millions)**
Germany	2,009
United Kingdom	1,991
France	1,132
Netherlands	974
Belgium	929

Top Ten Exports to Europe ($ Millions)

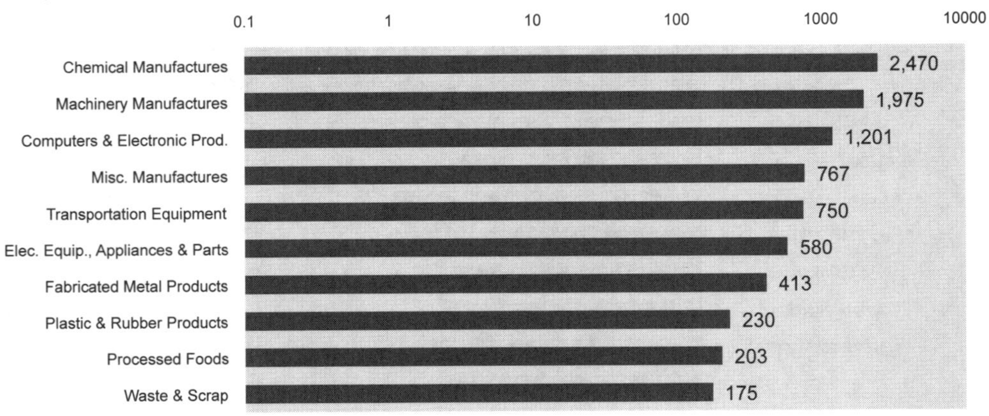

Source: Bureau of Economic Anlaysis, Foreign Trade Division, U.S. Census Bureau
*European investment includes France, Germany, Netherlands, Switzerland, and the United Kingdom
Due to a need to align resources with current funding levels, the Bureau of Economic Analysis has reduced its coverage to major investing countries.

Indiana and Europe

Employment, Investment, and Trade Linkages

Employment

European* investment in Indiana supported 75,500 jobs in 2008.

Sources of Employment within Indiana, 2008	
Country	**Employment**
Japan	36,100
United Kingdom	30,400
France	17,900
Germany	14,600
Canada	10,600

Investment

Of the investment in Indiana in 2007, $17.9 billion came from Europe*.

Trade

In 2009, Europe purchased $7 billion worth of goods from Indiana.
Exports are heavily skewed toward chemicals.

Top European Export Markets, 2009	
Country	**Exports ($ Millions)**
United Kingdom	1,627
France	1,291
Germany	1,249
Netherlands	520
Spain	458

Top Ten Exports to Europe ($ Millions)

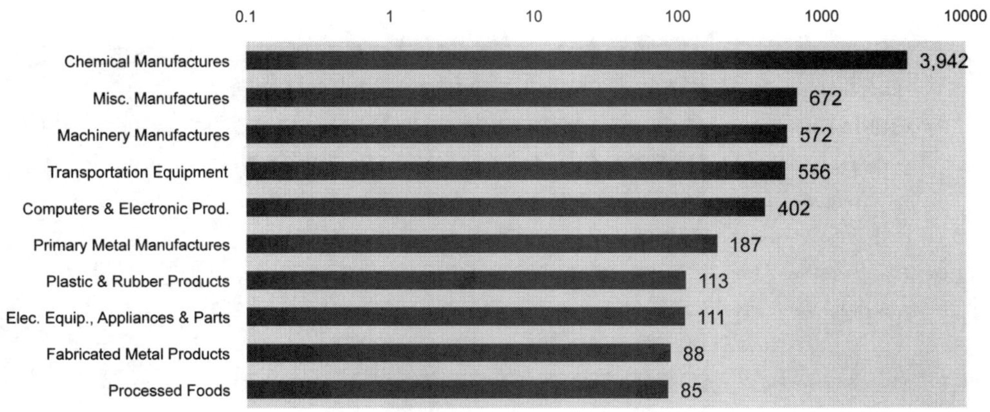

Source: Bureau of Economic Anlaysis, Foreign Trade Division, U.S. Census Bureau

*European investment includes France, Germany, Netherlands, Switzerland, and the United Kingdom

Due to a need to align resources with current funding levels, the Bureau of Economic Analysis has reduced its coverage to major investing countries.

Iowa and Europe

Employment, Investment, and Trade Linkages

Employment

European* investment in Iowa supported 24,600 jobs in 2008.

Sources of Employment within Iowa, 2008	
Country	**Employment**
United Kingdom	7,600
Netherlands	5,700
Japan	4,900
Germany	4,600
Canada	4,300

Investment

Of the $9.5 billion invested in Iowa in 2007, 40%, or $3.8 billion came from Europe*.

Trade

In 2009, Europe purchased $1.7 billion worth of goods from Iowa.
Machinery Manufactures account for roughly 37% of total exports.

Top European Export Markets, 2009	
Country	**Exports ($ Millions)**
Germany	452
France	285
United Kingdom	256
Netherlands	119
Italy	64

Top Ten Exports to Europe ($ Millions)

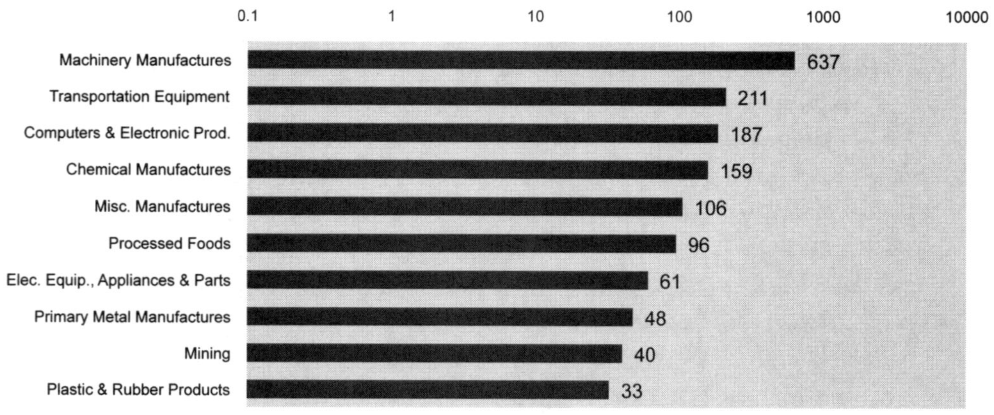

Source: Bureau of Economic Anlaysis, Foreign Trade Division, U.S. Census Bureau
*European investment includes France, Germany, Netherlands, Switzerland, and the United Kingdom
Due to a need to align resources with current funding levels, the Bureau of Economic Analysis has reduced its coverage to major investing countries.

Kansas and Europe

Employment, Investment, and Trade Linkages

Employment

European* investment in Kansas supported 23,200 jobs in 2008.

Sources of Employment within Kansas, 2008	
Country	**Employment**
Canada	16,400
United Kingdom	7,100
Germany	5,800
Switzerland	4,100
France	3,900

Investment

Of the $7.9 billion invested in Kansas in 2007, 42%, or $3.3 billion came from Europe*.

Trade

In 2009, Europe purchased $2.1 billion worth of goods from Kansas.
Nearly 58% of the state's exports consists of transportation equipment.

Top European Export Markets, 2009	
Country	**Exports ($ Millions)**
Germany	380
United Kingdom	359
Belgium	198
France	185
Turkey	159

Top Ten Exports to Europe ($ Millions)

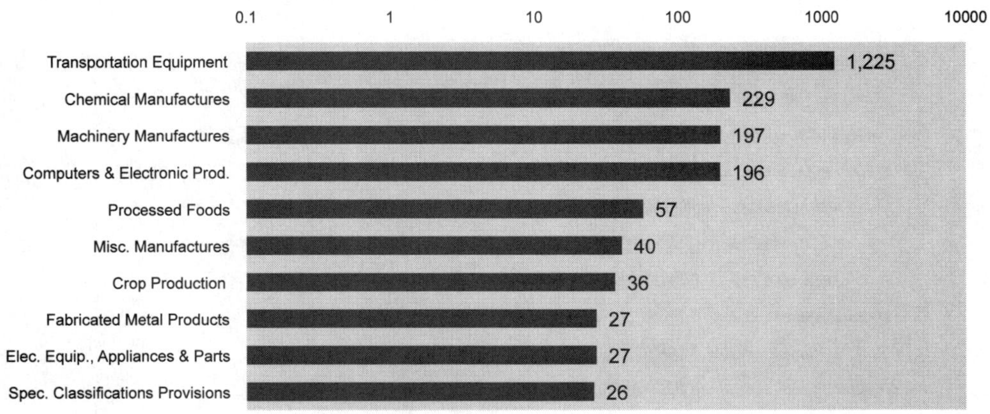

Source: Bureau of Economic Anlaysis, Foreign Trade Division, U.S. Census Bureau
*European investment includes France, Germany, Netherlands, Switzerland, and the United Kingdom
Due to a need to align resources with current funding levels, the Bureau of Economic Analysis has reduced its coverage to major investing countries.

Kentucky and Europe

Employment, Investment, and Trade Linkages

Employment

European* investment in Kentucky supported 39,000 jobs in 2008.

Sources of Employment within Kentucky, 2008	
Country	**Employment**
Japan	35,100
Germany	12,300
United Kingdom	9,900
Switzerland	6,400
Canada	6,100

Investment

Of the $28.2 billion invested in Kentucky in 2007, 41%, or $11.6 billion came from Europe*.

Trade

In 2009, Europe purchased $6 billion worth of goods from Kentucky.
Reflecting the large presence of automobile manufacturers in the state, Kentucky's top export to Europe is transportation equipment.

Top European Export Markets, 2009	
Country	**Exports ($ Millions)**
France	1,845
United Kingdom	1,143
Netherlands	724
Germany	658
Austria	367

Top Ten Exports to Europe ($ Millions)

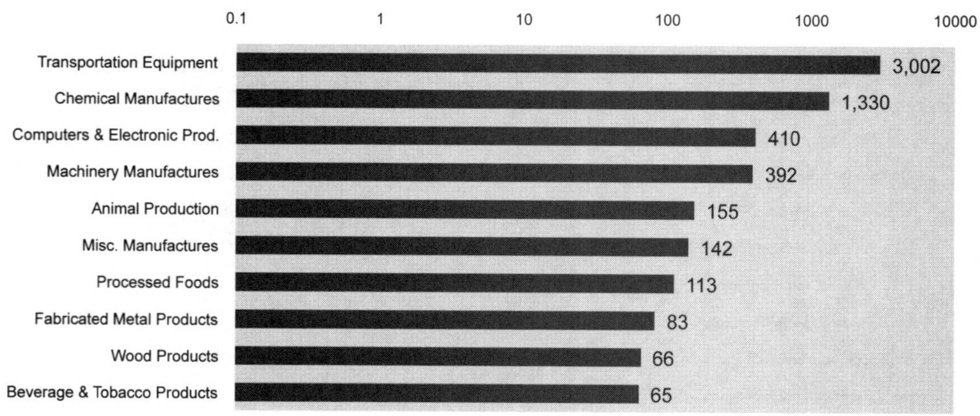

Source: Bureau of Economic Anlaysis, Foreign Trade Division, U.S. Census Bureau

*European investment includes France, Germany, Netherlands, Switzerland, and the United Kingdom

Due to a need to align resources with current funding levels, the Bureau of Economic Analysis has reduced its coverage to major investing countries.

Louisiana and Europe

Employment, Investment, and Trade Linkages

Employment

European* investment in Louisiana supported 26,100 jobs in 2008.

Sources of Employment within Louisiana, 2008	
Country	**Employment**
United Kingdom	8,900
Netherlands	5,400
Canada	5,100
Germany	5,000
France	4,800

Investment

Of the $31.2 billion invested in Louisiana in 2007, 26%, or $8 billion came from Europe*.

Trade

In 2009, Europe purchased $5.1 billion worth of goods from Louisiana.
The state's exports consist of a mix of petroleum and coal products, chemicals and agricultural products.

Top European Export Markets, 2009	
Country	**Exports ($ Millions)**
Netherlands	1,272
Belgium	736
Turkey	582
Germany	559
United Kingdom	308

Top Ten Exports to Europe ($ Millions)

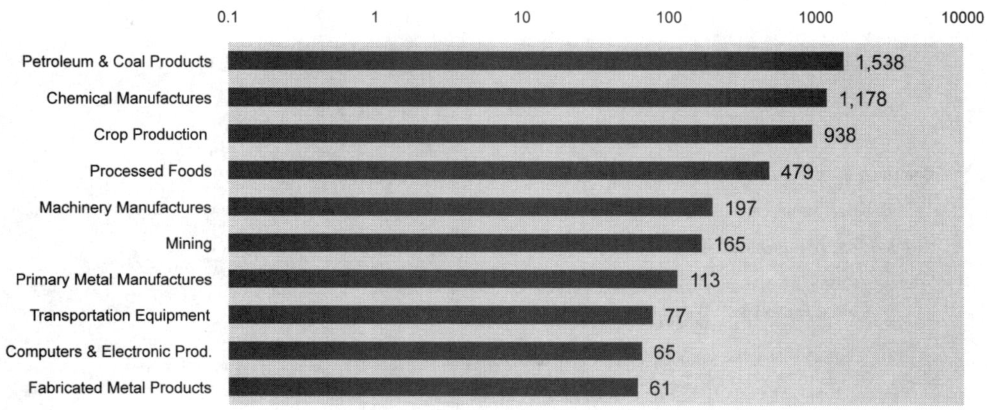

Source: Bureau of Economic Anlaysis, Foreign Trade Division, U.S. Census Bureau

*European investment includes France, Germany, Netherlands, Switzerland, and the United Kingdom

Due to a need to align resources with current funding levels, the Bureau of Economic Analysis has reduced its coverage to major investing countries.

Maine and Europe
Employment, Investment, and Trade Linkages

Employment
European* investment in Maine supported 6,900 jobs in 2008.

Sources of Employment within Maine, 2008	
Country	**Employment**
Canada	6,400
Switzerland	2,300
Germany	1,900
United Kingdom	1,400
France	1,000

Investment
Of the $6.3 billion invested in Maine in 2007, 6%, or $0.4 billion came from Europe*.

Trade
In 2009, Europe purchased $361 million worth of goods from Maine.
Transportation equipment and paper products are the state's top exports to Europe.

Top European Export Markets, 2009	
Country	**Exports ($ Millions)**
France	64
Ukraine	51
Netherlands	49
Belgium	39
Switzerland	33

Top Ten Exports to Europe ($ Millions)

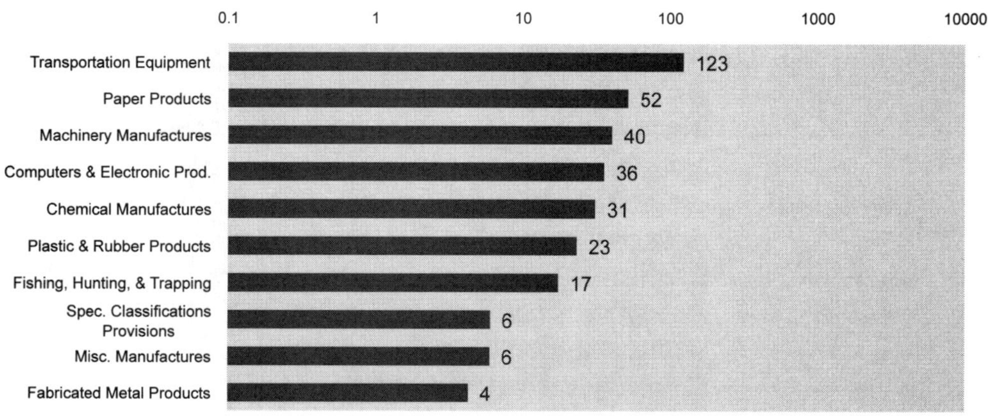

Source: Bureau of Economic Anlaysis, Foreign Trade Division, U.S. Census Bureau
*European investment includes France, Germany, Netherlands, Switzerland, and the United Kingdom
Due to a need to align resources with current funding levels, the Bureau of Economic Analysis has reduced its coverage to major investing countries.

Maryland and Europe

Employment, Investment, and Trade Linkages

Employment

European* investment in Maryland supported 65,000 jobs in 2008.

Sources of Employment within Maryland, 2008	
Country	**Employment**
Netherlands	22,100
United Kingdom	19,800
Canada	9,300
France	8,500
Switzerland	7,800

Investment

Of the $13 billion invested in Maryland in 2007, 60%, or $7.8 billion came from Europe*.

Trade

In 2009, Europe purchased $2.8 billion worth of goods from Maryland.
Top exports are chemicals, transportation equipment, and computers.

Top European Export Markets, 2009	
Country	**Exports ($ Millions)**
Sweden	399
Belgium	379
Netherlands	341
United Kingdom	324
Germany	303

Top Ten Exports to Europe ($ Millions)

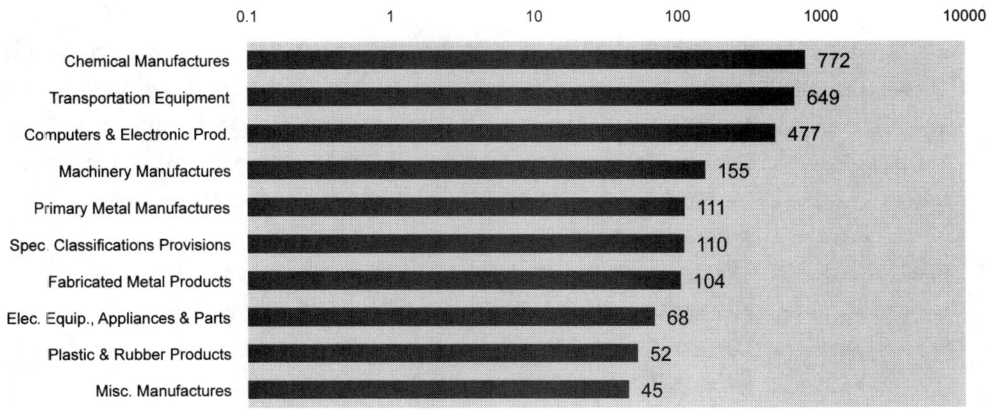

Source: Bureau of Economic Anlaysis, Foreign Trade Division, U.S. Census Bureau

*European investment includes France, Germany, Netherlands, Switzerland, and the United Kingdom

Due to a need to align resources with current funding levels, the Bureau of Economic Analysis has reduced its coverage to major investing countries.

Massachusetts and Europe
Employment, Investment, and Trade Linkages

Employment
European* investment in Massachusetts supported 116,400 jobs in 2008.

Sources of Employment within Massachusetts, 2008	
Country	**Employment**
United Kingdom	40,100
Netherlands	30,700
Canada	22,600
France	17,100
Germany	16,500

Investment
Of the $26.9 billion invested in Massachusetts in 2007, 64%, or $17.1 billion came from Europe*.

Trade
In 2009, Europe purchased $11.1 billion worth of goods from Massachusetts.
Primary metal and chemical manufactures account for 24% and 22% of exports respectively.

Top European Export Markets, 2009	
Country	**Exports ($ Millions)**
United Kingdom	4,049
Netherlands	1,982
Germany	1,750
France	671
Italy	495

Top Ten Exports to Europe ($ Millions)

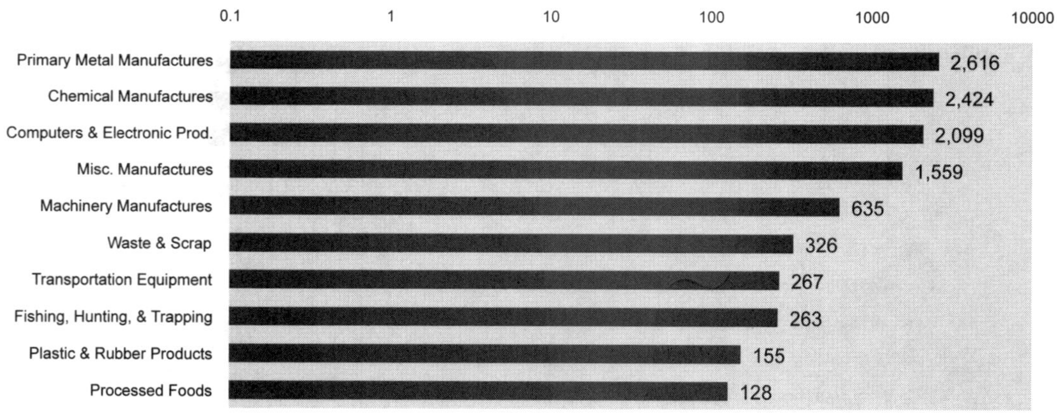

Source: Bureau of Economic Anlaysis, Foreign Trade Division, U.S. Census Bureau
*European investment includes France, Germany, Netherlands, Switzerland, and the United Kingdom
Due to a need to align resources with current funding levels, the Bureau of Economic Analysis has reduced its coverage to major investing countries.

Michigan and Europe

Employment, Investment, and Trade Linkages

Employment

European* investment in Michigan supported 74,700 jobs in 2008.

Sources of Employment within Michigan, 2008	
Country	**Employment**
Japan	32,100
Germany	28,300
United Kingdom	19,300
Canada	16,900
France	12,300

Investment

Of the $24.1 billion invested in Michigan in 2007, 36%, or $8.7 billion came from Europe*.

Trade

In 2009, Europe purchased $4.1 billion worth of goods from Michigan.
Chemical manufactures have surpassed transportation equipment as Michigan's top export to Europe.

Top European Export Markets, 2009	
Country	**Exports ($ Millions)**
Germany	1,258
United Kingdom	542
Belgium	516
France	434
Netherlands	381

Top Ten Exports to Europe ($ Millions)

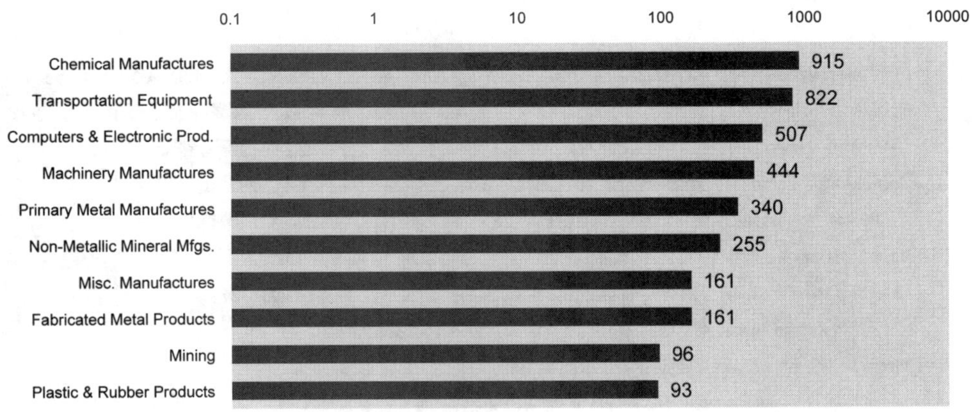

Source: Bureau of Economic Anlaysis, Foreign Trade Division, U.S. Census Bureau

*European investment includes France, Germany, Netherlands, Switzerland, and the United Kingdom

Due to a need to align resources with current funding levels, the Bureau of Economic Analysis has reduced its coverage to major investing countries.

Minnesota and Europe

Employment, Investment, and Trade Linkages

Employment

European* investment in Minnesota supported 41,000 jobs in 2008.

Sources of Employment within Minnesota, 2008	
Country	**Employment**
Canada	18,800
United Kingdom	14,200
Germany	9,000
France	6,800
Netherlands	5,700

Investment

Of the $16.2 billion invested in Minnesota in 2007, 24%, or $3.9 billion came from Europe*.

Trade

In 2009, Europe purchased $4.4 billion worth of goods from Minnesota.
Miscellaneous manufactures and computer and electronic products rank as the top exports to Europe.

Top European Export Markets, 2009	
Country	**Exports ($ Millions)**
Ireland	898
Germany	694
United Kingdom	616
Belgium	566
Netherlands	396

Top Ten Exports to Europe ($ Millions)

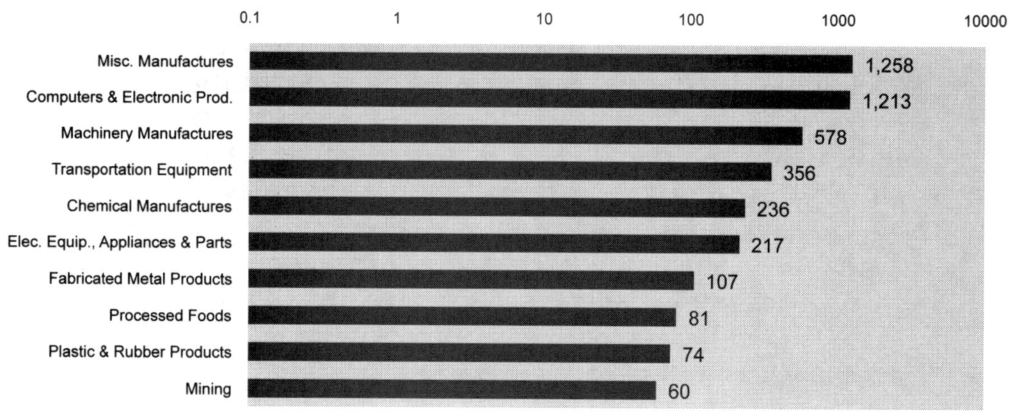

Source: Bureau of Economic Anlaysis, Foreign Trade Division, U.S. Census Bureau
*European investment includes France, Germany, Netherlands, Switzerland, and the United Kingdom
Due to a need to align resources with current funding levels, the Bureau of Economic Analysis has reduced its coverage to major investing countries.

Mississippi and Europe

Employment, Investment, and Trade Linkages

Employment

European* investment in Mississippi supported 10,900 jobs in 2008.

Sources of Employment within Mississippi, 2008	
Country	**Employment**
Japan	5,300
Canada	4,400
Germany	2,900
United Kingdom	2,900
Netherlands	2,400

Investment

Of the $8.3 billion invested in Mississippi in 2007, 20%, or $1.7 billion came from Europe*.

Trade

In 2009, Europe purchased $1.3 billion worth of goods from Mississippi.
Petrolium products and chemicals rank as the top exports to Europe.

Top European Export Markets, 2009	
Country	**Exports ($ Millions)**
Belgium	207
United Kingdom	148
Netherlands	147
Germany	115
Turkey	93

Top Ten Exports to Europe ($ Millions)

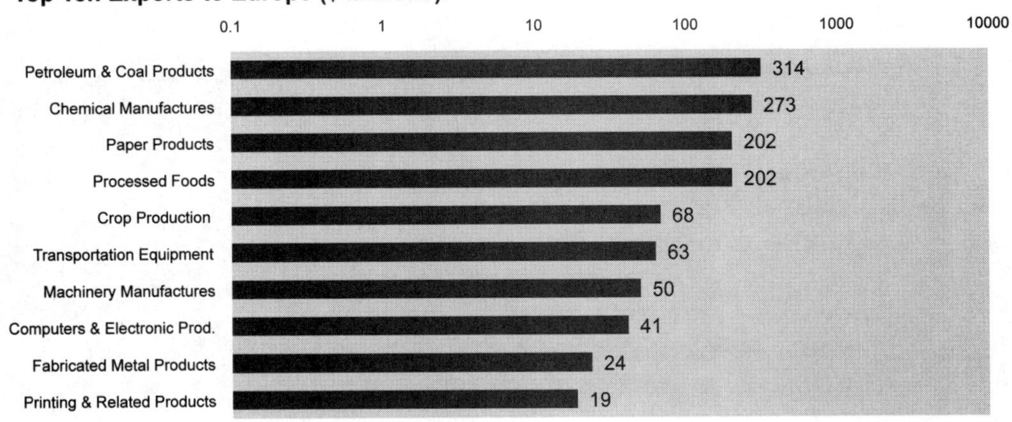

Source: Bureau of Economic Anlaysis, Foreign Trade Division, U.S. Census Bureau

*European investment includes France, Germany, Netherlands, Switzerland, and the United Kingdom

Due to a need to align resources with current funding levels, the Bureau of Economic Analysis has reduced its coverage to major investing countries.

Missouri and Europe

Employment, Investment, and Trade Linkages

Employment

European* investment in Missouri supported 47,000 jobs in 2008.

Sources of Employment within Missouri, 2008	
Country	**Employment**
United Kingdom	17,600
Germany	10,500
Japan	8,400
France	8,000
Switzerland	7,500

Investment

Of the investment in Missouri in 2007, $8.2 billion came from Europe*.

Trade

In 2009, Europe purchased $1.8 billion worth of goods from Missouri.
Top exports include chemicals, machinery and transportation equipment.

Top European Export Markets, 2009	
Country	**Exports ($ Millions)**
Germany	385
United Kingdom	297
Belgium	232
Netherlands	183
France	153

Top Ten Exports to Europe ($ Millions)

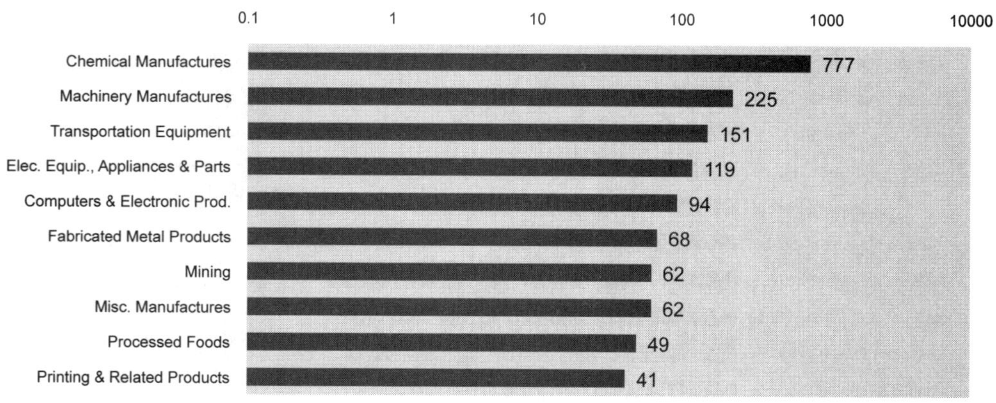

Source: Bureau of Economic Anlaysis, Foreign Trade Division, U.S. Census Bureau

*European investment includes France, Germany, Netherlands, Switzerland, and the United Kingdom

Due to a need to align resources with current funding levels, the Bureau of Economic Analysis has reduced its coverage to major investing countries.

Montana and Europe

Employment, Investment, and Trade Linkages

Employment

European* investment in Montana supported 3,000 jobs in 2008.

Sources of Employment within Montana, 2008	
Country	**Employment**
United Kingdom	1,100
France	1,000
Canada	800
Switzerland	600
Japan	400

Investment

Of the $3.4 billion invested in Montana in 2007, 5%, or $179 million came from Europe*.

Trade

In 2009, Europe purchased $159 million worth of goods from Montana.
Exports are relatively small and skewed towards chemicals, machinery goods and mining.

Top European Export Markets, 2009	
Country	**Exports ($ Millions)**
Belgium	26
Netherlands	25
Germany	25
United Kingdom	23
Denmark	18

Top Ten Exports to Europe ($ Millions)

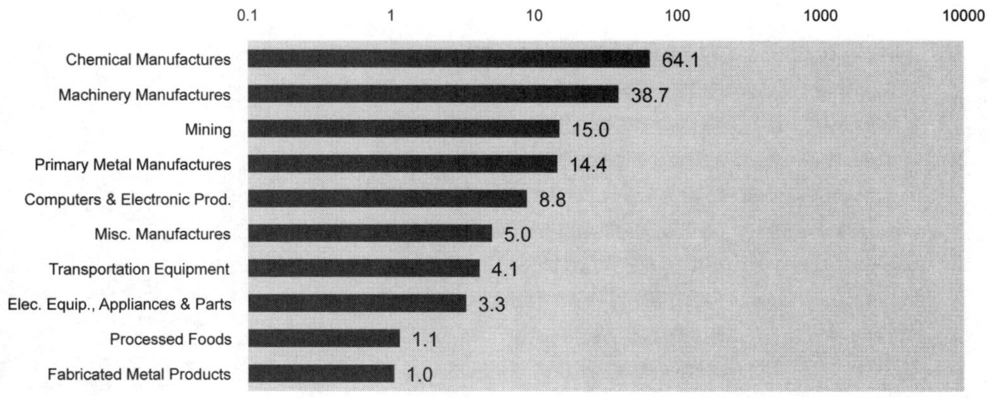

Source: Bureau of Economic Anlaysis, Foreign Trade Division, U.S. Census Bureau
*European investment includes France, Germany, Netherlands, Switzerland, and the United Kingdom
Due to a need to align resources with current funding levels, the Bureau of Economic Analysis has reduced its coverage to major investing countries.

Nebraska and Europe

Employment, Investment, and Trade Linkages

Employment

European* investment in Nebraska supported 9,000 jobs in 2008.

Sources of Employment within Nebraska, 2008	
Country	**Employment**
Japan	3,600
France	3,500
Canada	2,900
United Kingdom	2,200
Switzerland	2,100

Investment

Of the investment in Nebraska in 2007, $0.8 billion came from Europe*.

Trade

In 2009, Europe purchased $637 million worth of goods from Nebraska.
Top exports are machinery and chemical manufactures followed by processed foods.

Top European Export Markets, 2009	
Country	**Exports ($ Millions)**
Netherlands	97
Germany	75
France	73
Belgium	72
Italy	47

Top Ten Exports to Europe ($ Millions)

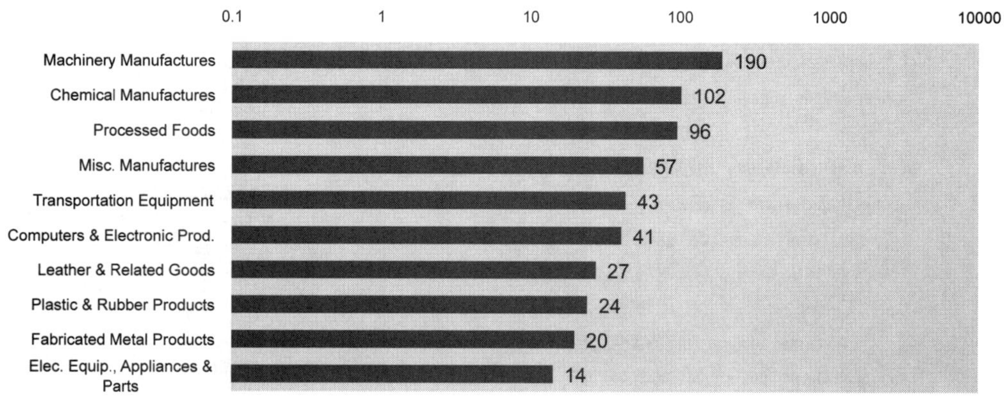

Source: Bureau of Economic Anlaysis, Foreign Trade Division, U.S. Census Bureau
*European investment includes France, Germany, Netherlands, Switzerland, and the United Kingdom
Due to a need to align resources with current funding levels, the Bureau of Economic Analysis has reduced its coverage to major investing countries.

Nevada and Europe

Employment, Investment, and Trade Linkages

Employment

European* investment in Nevada supported 17,900 jobs in 2008.

Sources of Employment within Nevada, 2008	
Country	**Employment**
Canada	8,200
United Kingdom	6,700
France	4,000
Switzerland	3,400
Japan	3,000

Investment

Of the $9.7 billion invested in Nevada in 2007, 24%, or $2.3 billion came from Europe*.

Trade

In 2009, Europe purchased $3.4 billion worth of goods from Nevada.
Primary metal manufactures account for roughly 85% of total exports.

Top European Export Markets, 2009	
Country	**Exports ($ Millions)**
Switzerland	2,899
United Kingdom	84
Germany	76
Netherlands	67
France	59

Top Ten Exports to Europe ($ Millions)

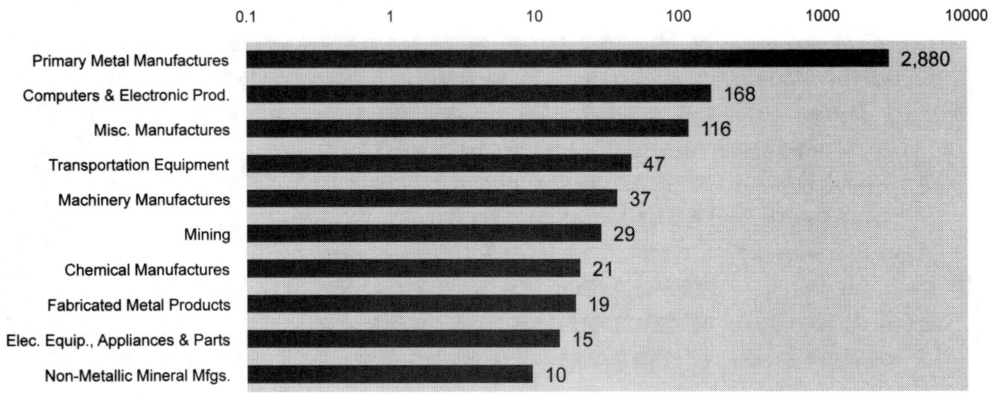

Source: Bureau of Economic Anlaysis, Foreign Trade Division, U.S. Census Bureau
*European investment includes France, Germany, Netherlands, Switzerland, and the United Kingdom
Due to a need to align resources with current funding levels, the Bureau of Economic Analysis has reduced its coverage to major investing countries.

New Hampshire and Europe

Employment, Investment, and Trade Linkages

Employment

European* investment in New Hampshire supported 22,700 jobs in 2008.

Sources of Employment within New Hampshire, 2008	
Country	**Employment**
United Kingdom	10,000
France	4,500
Canada	4,400
Germany	4,100
Japan	3,700

Investment

Of the $5.2 billion invested in New Hampshire in 2007, 48%, or $2.5 billion came from Europe*.

Trade

In 2009, Europe purchased $817 million worth of goods from New Hampshire.
Computers and machinery are the top exports to Europe.

Top European Export Markets, 2009	
Country	**Exports ($ Millions)**
Germany	173
United Kingdom	127
Netherlands	112
France	70
Switzerland	61

Top Ten Exports to Europe ($ Millions)

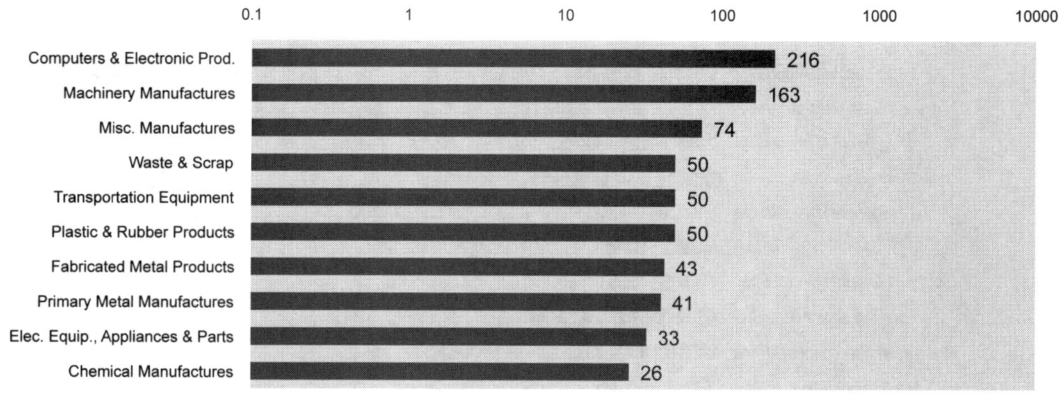

Source: Bureau of Economic Anlaysis, Foreign Trade Division, U.S. Census Bureau
*European investment includes France, Germany, Netherlands, Switzerland, and the United Kingdom
Due to a need to align resources with current funding levels, the Bureau of Economic Analysis has reduced its coverage to major investing countries.

New Jersey and Europe

Employment, Investment, and Trade Linkages

Employment

European* investment in New Jersey supported 145,500 jobs in 2008.

Sources of Employment within New Jersey, 2008	
Country	**Employment**
United Kingdom	36,900
France	34,000
Switzerland	31,800
Germany	26,200
Japan	23,000

Investment

Of the $38.4 billion invested in New Jersey in 2007, 65%, or $25 billion came from Europe*.

Trade

In 2009, Europe purchased $8.8 billion worth of goods from New Jersey.
Top exports consist of chemical manufactures, transportation equipment and waste and scrap.

Top European Export Markets, 2009	
Country	**Exports ($ Millions)**
United Kingdom	1,797
Germany	1,081
Netherlands	851
France	788
Turkey	748

Top Ten Exports to Europe ($ Millions)

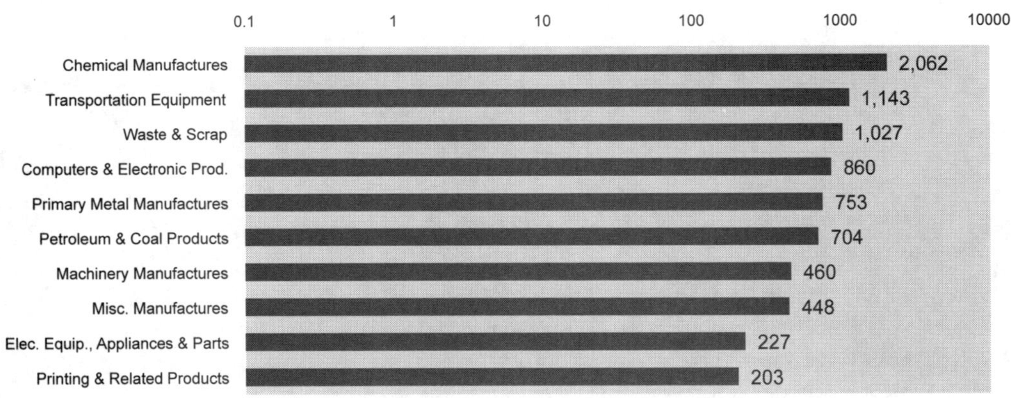

Source: Bureau of Economic Anlaysis, Foreign Trade Division, U.S. Census Bureau
*European investment includes France, Germany, Netherlands, Switzerland, and the United Kingdom
Due to a need to align resources with current funding levels, the Bureau of Economic Analysis has reduced its coverage to major investing countries.

New Mexico and Europe

Employment, Investment, and Trade Linkages

Employment

European* investment in New Mexico supported 8,600 jobs in 2008.

Sources of Employment within New Mexico, 2008	
Country	**Employment**
Canada	4,100
Germany	3,300
United Kingdom	3,000
France	1,700
Japan	1,000

Investment

Of the $4.8 billion invested in New Mexico in 2007, 8%, or $0.4 billion came from Europe*.

Trade

In 2009, Europe purchased $205 million worth of goods from New Mexico.
Exports are relatively small and are skewed toward computers and related goods.

Top European Export Markets, 2009	
Country	**Exports ($ Millions)**
Germany	70
United Kingdom	26
France	21
Italy	19
Ireland	13

Top Ten Exports to Europe ($ Millions)

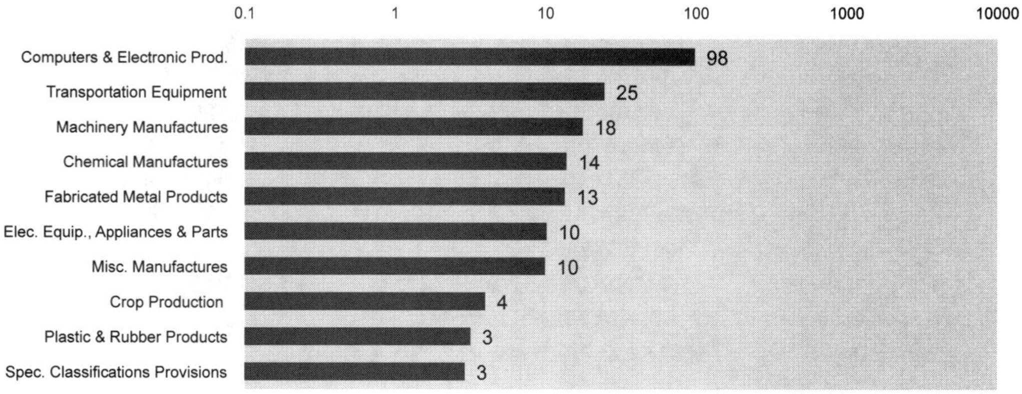

Source: Bureau of Economic Anlaysis, Foreign Trade Division, U.S. Census Bureau
*European investment includes France, Germany, Netherlands, Switzerland, and the United Kingdom
Due to a need to align resources with current funding levels, the Bureau of Economic Analysis has reduced its coverage to major investing countries.

New York and Europe

Employment, Investment, and Trade Linkages

Employment

European* investment in New York supported 255,300 jobs in 2008.

Sources of Employment within New York, 2008	
Country	**Employment**
United Kingdom	98,300
France	52,400
Germany	41,500
Switzerland	38,600
Canada	37,400

Investment

Of the $80.5 billion invested in New York in 2007, 54%, or $43.4 billion came from Europe*.

Trade

In 2009, Europe purchased $19.7 billion worth of goods from New York. Used merchandise, miscellaneous manufactures and chemical manufactures are top export categories to Europe.

Top European Export Markets, 2009	
Country	**Exports ($ Millions)**
United Kingdom	4,532
Switzerland	3,317
Germany	2,377
France	1,769
Belgium	1,751

Top Ten Exports to Europe ($ Millions)

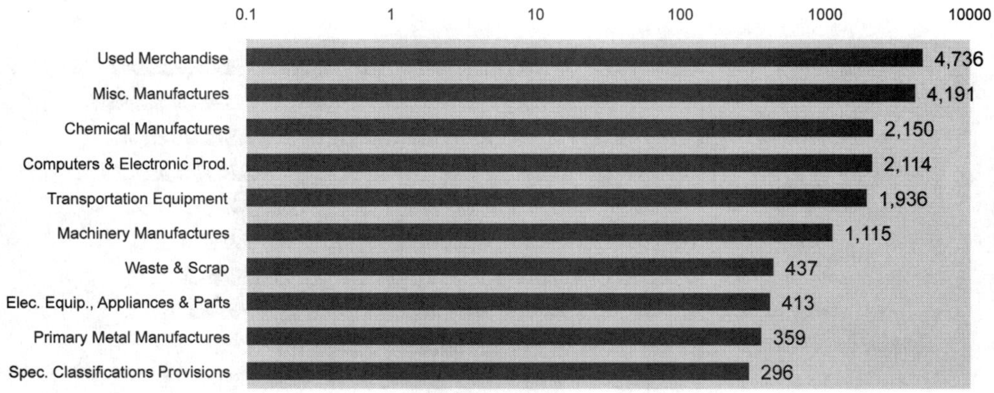

Source: Bureau of Economic Anlaysis, Foreign Trade Division, U.S. Census Bureau

*European investment includes France, Germany, Netherlands, Switzerland, and the United Kingdom

Due to a need to align resources with current funding levels, the Bureau of Economic Analysis has reduced its coverage to major investing countries.

North Carolina and Europe
Employment, Investment, and Trade Linkages

Employment
European* investment in North Carolina supported 95,100 jobs in 2008.

Sources of Employment within North Carolina, 2008	
Country	**Employment**
United Kingdom	30,500
Germany	28,100
Japan	16,800
Switzerland	15,300
France	14,700

Investment
Of the $28.9 billion invested in North Carolina in 2007, 45%, or $13 billion came from Europe*.

Trade
In 2009, Europe purchased $5.8 billion worth of goods from North Carolina.
Chemical manufactures account for more than 37% of total exports to Europe.

Top European Export Markets, 2009	
Country	**Exports ($ Millions)**
Netherlands	1,518
France	928
Germany	801
United Kingdom	713
Belgium	334

Top Ten Exports to Europe ($ Millions)

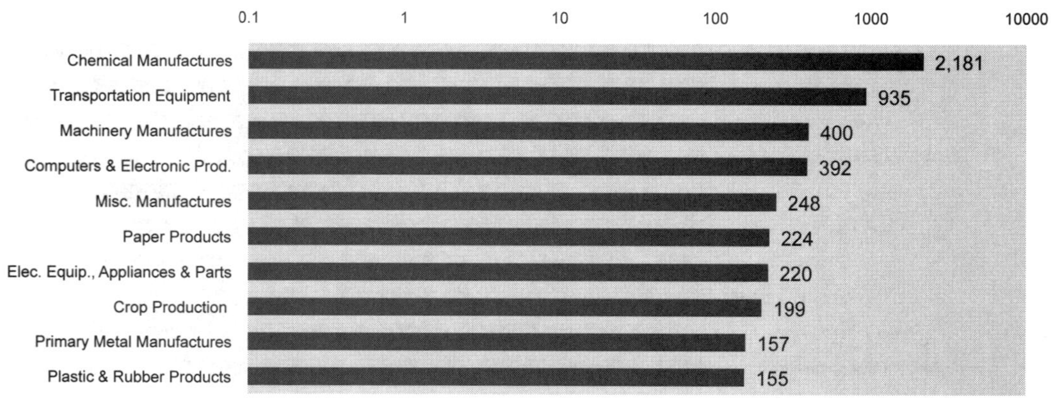

Source: Bureau of Economic Anlaysis, Foreign Trade Division, U.S. Census Bureau
*European investment includes France, Germany, Netherlands, Switzerland, and the United Kingdom
Due to a need to align resources with current funding levels, the Bureau of Economic Analysis has reduced its coverage to major investing countries.

North Dakota and Europe

Employment, Investment, and Trade Linkages

Employment

European* investment in North Dakota supported 1,900 jobs in 2008.

Sources of Employment within North Dakota, 2008	
Country	**Employment**
Netherlands	G
Canada	1,000
France	700
Japan	700
United Kingdom	500

G represents suppressed data that is assigned a range of 1,000 to 2,499 employees

Investment

Of the $1.4 billion invested in North Dakota in 2007, 7%, or $0.1 billion came from Europe*.

Trade

In 2009, Europe purchased $312 million worth of goods from North Dakota.
Nearly 66% of the state's exports consists of machinery manufactures.

Top European Export Markets, 2009	
Country	**Exports ($ Millions)**
United Kingdom	36
Belgium	34
Germany	34
Spain	21
France	20

Top Ten Exports to Europe ($ Millions)

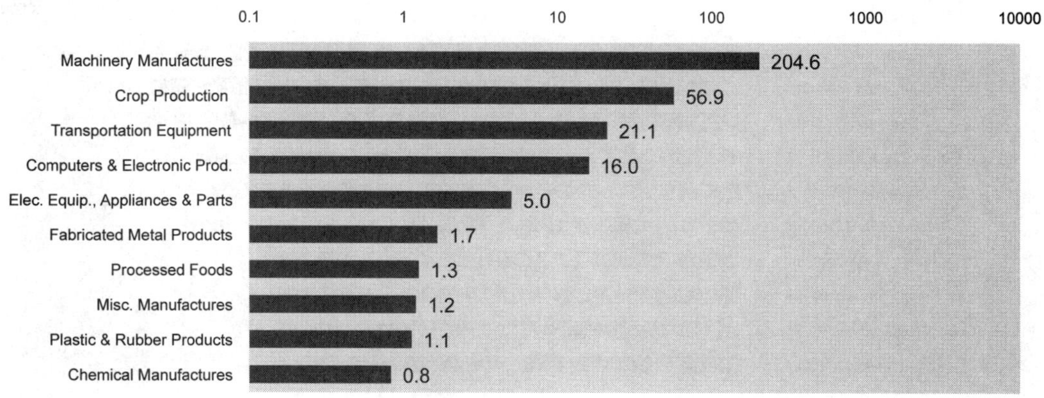

Source: Bureau of Economic Anlaysis, Foreign Trade Division, U.S. Census Bureau
*European investment includes France, Germany, Netherlands, Switzerland, and the United Kingdom
Due to a need to align resources with current funding levels, the Bureau of Economic Analysis has reduced its coverage to major investing countries.

Ohio and Europe

Employment, Investment, and Trade Linkages

Employment

European* investment in Ohio supported 114,000 jobs in 2008.

Sources of Employment within Ohio, 2008	
Country	**Employment**
Japan	53,600
United Kingdom	40,800
Germany	29,600
France	20,700
Switzerland	16,800

Investment

Of the $43.4 billion invested in Ohio in 2007, 40%, or $17.4 billion came from Europe*.

Trade

In 2009, Europe purchased $7.3 billion worth of goods from Ohio.
Transportation equipment and machinery are the state's top exports to Europe.

Top European Export Markets, 2009	
Country	**Exports ($ Millions)**
United Kingdom	1,142
Greece	1,125
Germany	967
France	825
Netherlands	566

Top Ten Exports to Europe ($ Billions)

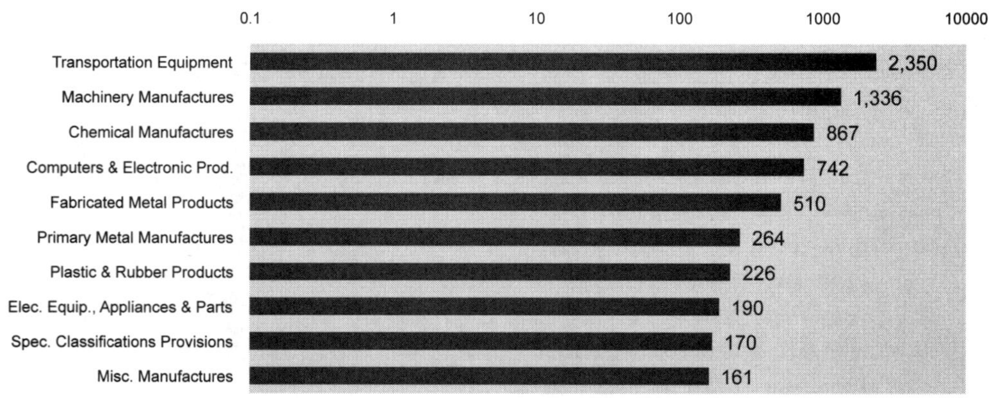

Source: Bureau of Economic Anlaysis, Foreign Trade Division, U.S. Census Bureau
*European investment includes France, Germany, Netherlands, Switzerland, and the United Kingdom
Due to a need to align resources with current funding levels, the Bureau of Economic Analysis has reduced its coverage to major investing countries.

Oklahoma and Europe

Employment, Investment, and Trade Linkages

Employment

European* investment in Oklahoma supported 17,400 jobs in 2008.

Sources of Employment within Oklahoma, 2008	
Country	**Employment**
France	6,400
United Kingdom	6,300
Canada	5,100
Germany	2,200
Switzerland	1,800

Investment

Of the $10.6 billion invested in Oklahoma in 2007, 16%, or $1.7 billion came from Europe*.

Trade

In 2009, Europe purchased $746 million worth of goods from Oklahoma.
Top exports include machinery, transportation equipment and computers.

Top European Export Markets, 2009	
Country	**Exports ($ Millions)**
Germany	116
Belgium	91
United Kingdom	91
Turkey	53
Netherlands	50

Top Ten Exports to Europe ($ Millions)

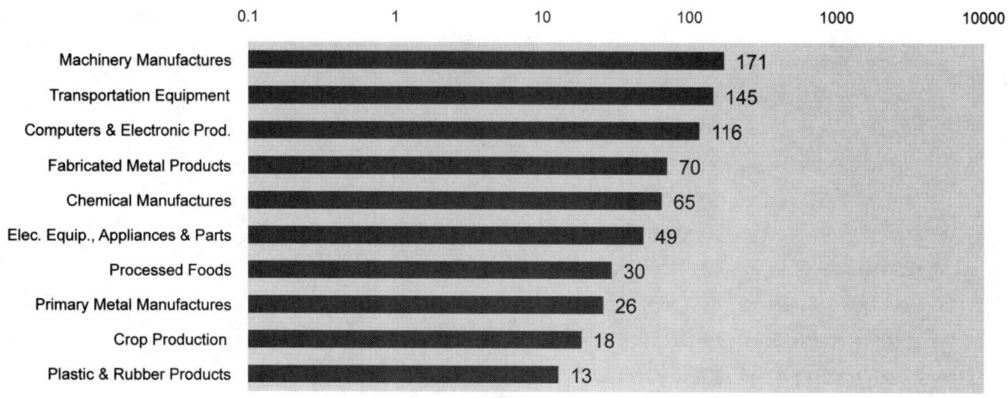

Source: Bureau of Economic Anlaysis, Foreign Trade Division, U.S. Census Bureau
*European investment includes France, Germany, Netherlands, Switzerland, and the United Kingdom
Due to a need to align resources with current funding levels, the Bureau of Economic Analysis has reduced its coverage to major investing countries.

Oregon and Europe

Employment, Investment, and Trade Linkages

Employment

European* investment in Oregon supported 26,000 jobs in 2008.

Sources of Employment within Oregon, 2008	
Country	**Employment**
Germany	10,000
United Kingdom	7,400
Japan	5,400
Canada	3,500
France	3,300

Investment

Of the $10 billion invested in Oregon in 2007, 26%, or $2.6 billion came from Europe*.

Trade

In 2009, Europe purchased $1.8 billion worth of goods from Oregon.
Nearly 38% of Oregon's exports to Europe consist of computers and related products.

Top European Export Markets, 2009	
Country	**Exports ($ Millions)**
Netherlands	385
Germany	362
United Kingdom	194
France	160
Italy	135

Top Ten Exports to Europe ($ Millions)

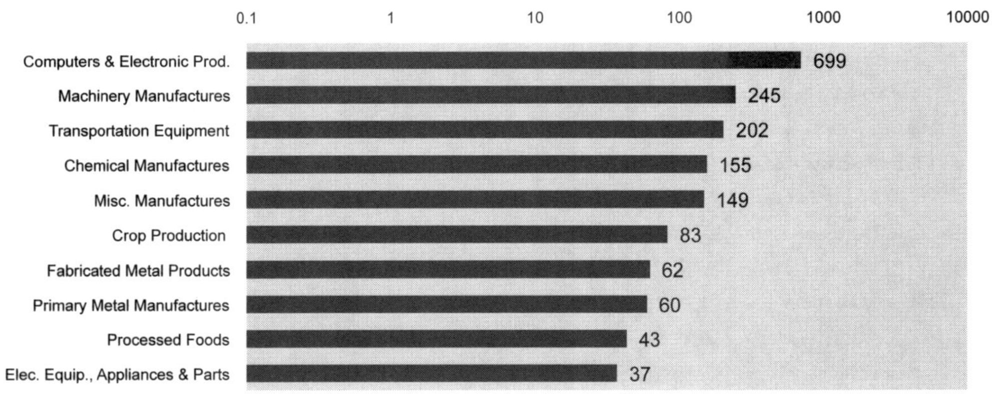

Source: Bureau of Economic Anlaysis, Foreign Trade Division, U.S. Census Bureau
*European investment includes France, Germany, Netherlands, Switzerland, and the United Kingdom
Due to a need to align resources with current funding levels, the Bureau of Economic Analysis has reduced its coverage to major investing countries.

Pennsylvania and Europe
Employment, Investment, and Trade Linkages

Employment
European* investment in Pennsylvania supported 164,400 jobs in 2008.

Sources of Employment within Pennsylvania, 2008	
Country	**Employment**
United Kingdom	52,100
Germany	37,600
Netherlands	35,700
Canada	25,500
France	25,400

Investment
Of the $39.8 billion invested in Pennsylvania in 2007, 54%, or $21.3 billion came from Europe*.

Trade
In 2009, Europe purchased $7.5 billion worth of goods from Pennsylvania.
Exports are relatively diverse, ranging from chemicals & transportation equipment to machinery manufactures & primary metals.

Top European Export Markets, 2009	
Country	**Exports ($ Millions)**
United Kingdom	1,227
Germany	1,063
Belgium	990
Switzerland	836
Netherlands	759

Top Ten Exports to Europe ($ Millions)

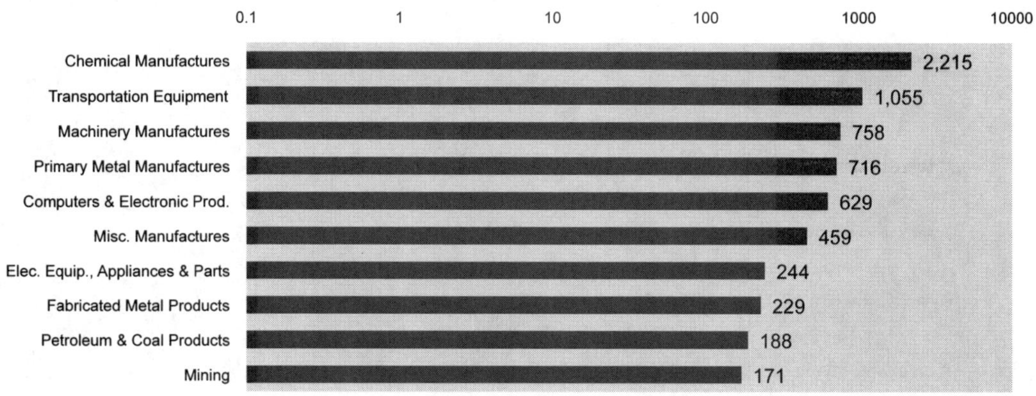

Source: Bureau of Economic Anlaysis, Foreign Trade Division, U.S. Census Bureau
*European investment includes France, Germany, Netherlands, Switzerland, and the United Kingdom
Due to a need to align resources with current funding levels, the Bureau of Economic Analysis has reduced its coverage to major investing countries.

Rhode Island and Europe
Employment, Investment, and Trade Linkages

Employment
European* investment in Rhode Island supported 15,400 jobs in 2008.

Sources of Employment within Rhode Island, 2008	
Country	**Employment**
United Kingdom	7,200
Netherlands	4,200
France	2,100
Japan	1,200
Germany	1,000

Investment
Of the $5.4 billion invested in Rhode Island in 2007, 7%, or $0.4 billion came from Europe*.

Trade
In 2009, Europe purchased $390 million worth of goods from Rhode Island.
Top exports include computers and elctronic products, waste and scrap, miscellaneous manufactures and plastic & rubber products.

Top European Export Markets, 2009	
Country	**Exports ($ Millions)**
United Kingdom	85
Germany	50
Turkey	41
Netherlands	39
France	34

Top Ten Exports to Europe ($ Millions)

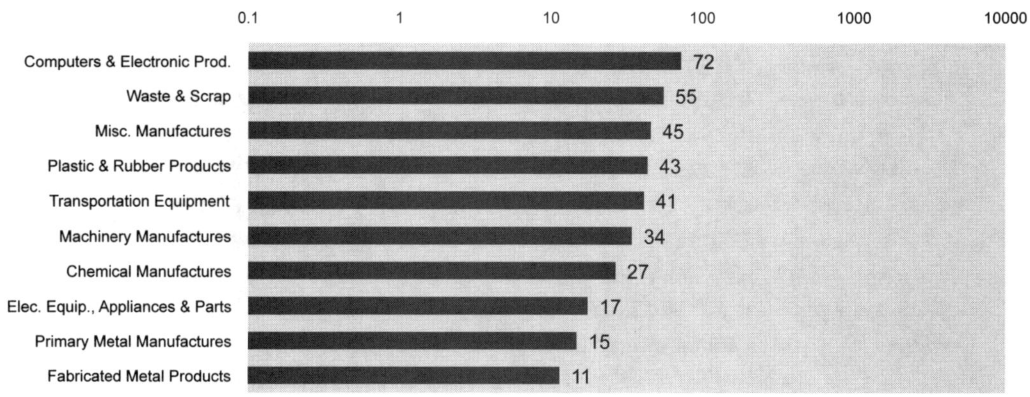

Source: Bureau of Economic Anlaysis, Foreign Trade Division, U.S. Census Bureau
*European investment includes France, Germany, Netherlands, Switzerland, and the United Kingdom
Due to a need to align resources with current funding levels, the Bureau of Economic Analysis has reduced its coverage to major investing countries.

South Carolina and Europe

Employment, Investment, and Trade Linkages

Employment

European* investment in South Carolina supported 59,500 jobs in 2008.

Sources of Employment within South Carolina, 2008	
Country	**Employment**
Germany	20,400
France	17,300
Japan	13,200
United Kingdom	12,700
Switzerland	6,700

Investment

Of the investment in South Carolina in 2007, $14.2 billion came from Europe*.

Trade

In 2009, Europe purchased $6.6 billion worth of goods from South Carolina.
Over 55% of the state's exports consist of transportation equipment.

Top European Export Markets, 2009	
Country	**Exports ($ Millions)**
Germany	3,406
United Kingdom	805
France	493
Belgium	370
Netherlands	267

Top Ten Exports to Europe ($ Millions)

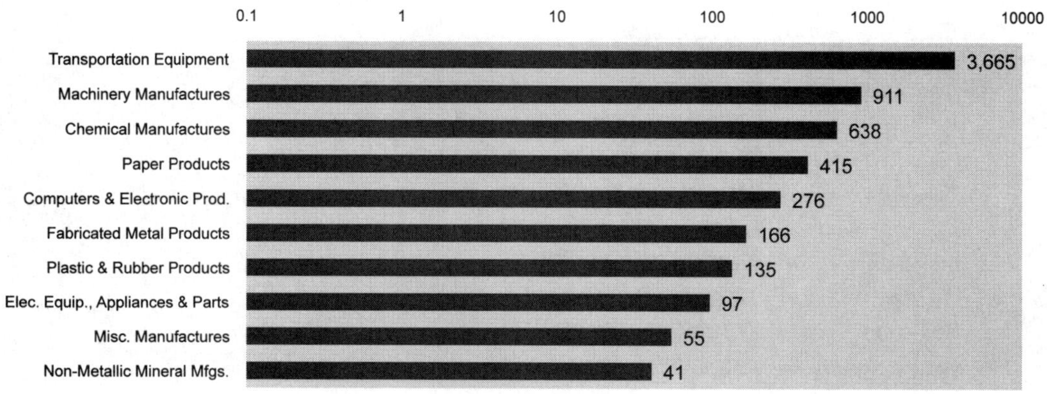

Source: Bureau of Economic Anlaysis, Foreign Trade Division, U.S. Census Bureau

*European investment includes France, Germany, Netherlands, Switzerland, and the United Kingdom

Due to a need to align resources with current funding levels, the Bureau of Economic Analysis has reduced its coverage to major investing countries.

South Dakota and Europe
Employment, Investment, and Trade Linkages

Employment
European* investment in South Dakota supported 3,300 jobs in 2008.

Sources of Employment within South Dakota, 2008	
Country	**Employment**
Canada	2,500
United Kingdom	1,600
France	1,000
Switzerland	300
Japan	300

Investment
Of the $1.3 billion invested in South Dakota in 2007, 8%, or $0.1 billion came from Europe*.

Trade
In 2009, Europe purchased $150 million worth of goods from South Dakota.
Machinery manufactures are the state's top export to Europe.

Top European Export Markets, 2009	
Country	**Exports ($ Millions)**
Germany	36
United Kingdom	33
Netherlands	22
France	12
Italy	9

Top Ten Exports to Europe ($ Millions)

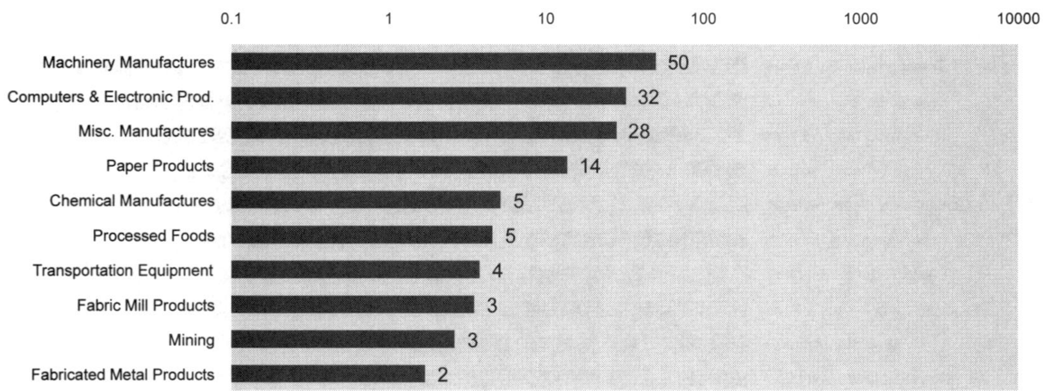

Source: Bureau of Economic Anlaysis, Foreign Trade Division, U.S. Census Bureau
*European investment includes France, Germany, Netherlands, Switzerland, and the United Kingdom
Due to a need to align resources with current funding levels, the Bureau of Economic Analysis has reduced its coverage to major investing countries.

Tennessee and Europe

Employment, Investment, and Trade Linkages

Employment

European* investment in Tennessee supported 57,100 jobs in 2008.

Sources of Employment within Tennessee, 2008	
Country	**Employment**
Japan	38,000
United Kingdom	18,600
Germany	12,900
France	11,800
Netherlands	9,300

Investment

Of the $22.7 billion invested in Tennessee in 2007, 27%, or $6.1 billion came from Europe*.

Trade

In 2009, Europe purchased $4.6 billion worth of goods from Tennessee. Miscellaneous and chemical manufactures as well as computers and electronic products make up the bulk of exports.

Top European Export Markets, 2009	
Country	**Exports ($ Millions)**
United Kingdom	796
Germany	621
Netherlands	582
Belgium	445
Luxembourg	436

Top Ten Exports to Europe ($ Millions)

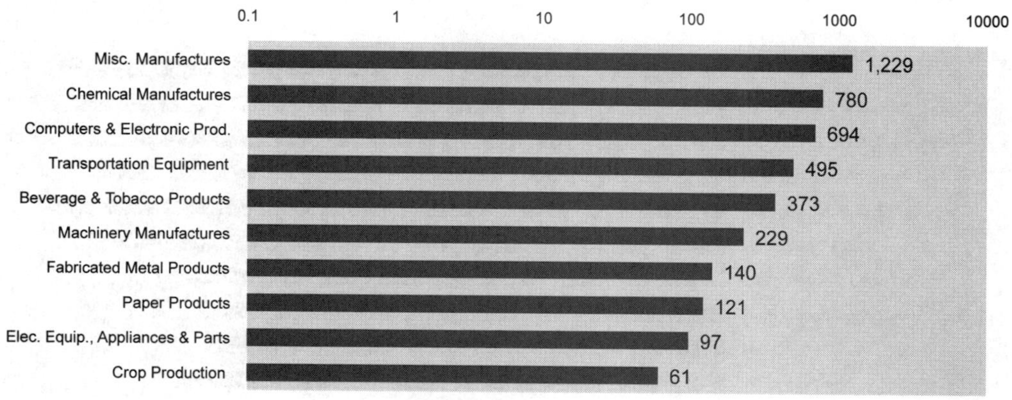

Source: Bureau of Economic Anlaysis, Foreign Trade Division, U.S. Census Bureau

*European investment includes France, Germany, Netherlands, Switzerland, and the United Kingdom

Due to a need to align resources with current funding levels, the Bureau of Economic Analysis has reduced its coverage to major investing countries.

Texas and Europe

Employment, Investment, and Trade Linkages

Employment

European* investment in Texas supported 212,200 jobs in 2008.

Sources of Employment within Texas, 2008	
Country	**Employment**
United Kingdom	69,900
France	43,700
Canada	37,800
Germany	37,400
Netherlands	36,700

Investment

Of the $128.4 billion invested in Texas in 2007, 45%, or $58.2 billion came from Europe*.

Trade

In 2009, Europe purchased $24.2 billion worth of goods from Texas.

Exports are relatively diverse ranging from petroleum, chemicals, computers and machinery manufactuers.

Top European Export Markets, 2009	
Country	**Exports ($ Millions)**
Netherlands	6,064
United Kingdom	3,215
Belgium	2,981
France	2,058
Germany	1,994

Top Ten Exports to Europe ($ Billions)

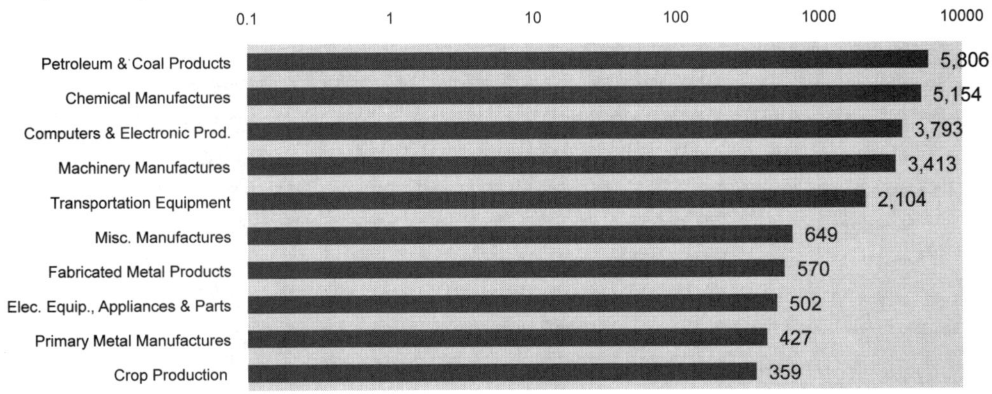

Source: Bureau of Economic Anlaysis, Foreign Trade Division, U.S. Census Bureau

*European investment includes France, Germany, Netherlands, Switzerland, and the United Kingdom

Due to a need to align resources with current funding levels, the Bureau of Economic Analysis has reduced its coverage to major investing countries.

Utah and Europe

Employment, Investment, and Trade Linkages

Employment

European* investment in Utah supported 19,300 jobs in 2008.

Sources of Employment within Utah, 2008	
Country	**Employment**
United Kingdom	6,600
France	4,700
Germany	3,800
Switzerland	2,600
Japan	2,400

Investment

Of the $6.5 billion invested in Utah in 2007, 17%, or $1.1 billion came from Europe*.

Trade

In 2009, Europe purchased $5.3 billion worth of goods from Utah.
Primary metals dominate the state's exports to Europe.

Top European Export Markets, 2009	
Country	**Exports ($ Millions)**
United Kingdom	4,364
Belgium	209
Germany	166
Switzerland	95
Netherlands	93

Top Ten Exports to Europe ($ Millions)

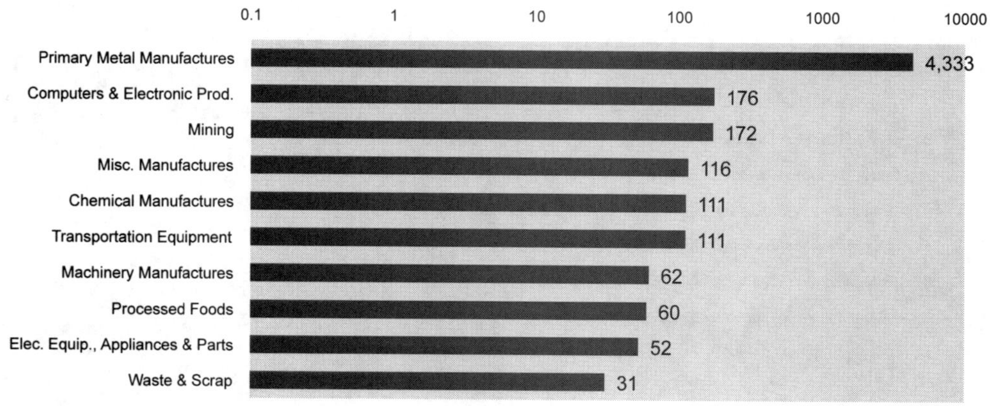

Source: Bureau of Economic Anlaysis, Foreign Trade Division, U.S. Census Bureau

*European investment includes France, Germany, Netherlands, Switzerland, and the United Kingdom

Due to a need to align resources with current funding levels, the Bureau of Economic Analysis has reduced its coverage to major investing countries.

Vermont and Europe

Employment, Investment, and Trade Linkages

Employment

European* investment in Vermont supported 5,000 jobs in 2008.

Sources of Employment within Vermont, 2008	
Country	**Employment**
Canada	1,700
United Kingdom	1,400
Switzerland	1,300
France	900
Japan	900

Investment

Of the $1.7 billion invested in Vermont in 2007, 6%, or $0.1 billion came from Europe*.

Trade

In 2009, Europe purchased $310 million worth of goods from Vermont.
Computers and electronic products are the top export to Europe.

Top European Export Markets, 2009	
Country	**Exports ($ Millions)**
Ireland	74
Germany	48
United Kingdom	44
Belgium	27
France	27

Top Ten Exports to Europe ($ Millions)

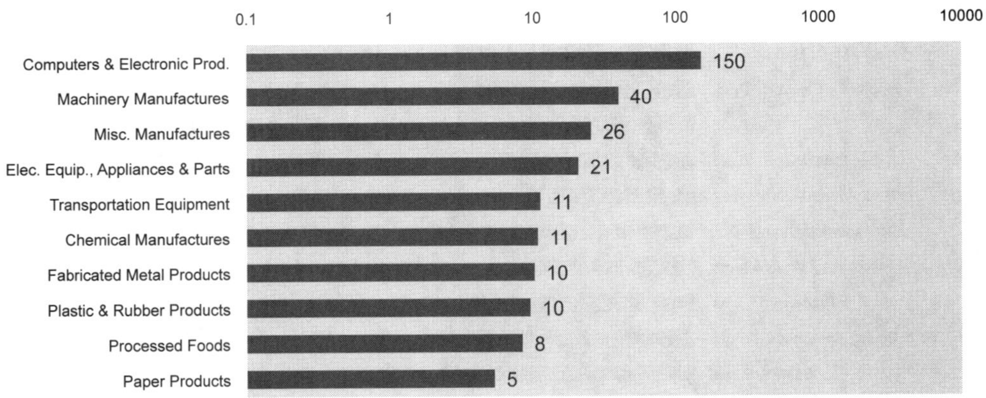

Source: Bureau of Economic Anlaysis, Foreign Trade Division, U.S. Census Bureau
*European investment includes France, Germany, Netherlands, Switzerland, and the United Kingdom
Due to a need to align resources with current funding levels, the Bureau of Economic Analysis has reduced its coverage to major investing countries.

Virginia and Europe

Employment, Investment, and Trade Linkages

Employment

European* investment in Virginia supported 74,000 jobs in 2008.

Sources of Employment within Virginia, 2008	
Country	**Employment**
United Kingdom	28,300
Japan	17,100
Germany	14,000
France	13,200
Netherlands	11,900

Investment

Of the investment in Virginia in 2007, $12.3 billion came from Europe*.

Trade

In 2009, Europe purchased $5.3 billion worth of goods from Virginia.
Top exports include chemicals, transportation equipment and agricultural products.

Top European Export Markets, 2009	
Country	**Exports ($ Millions)**
United Kingdom	1,006
Germany	840
Netherlands	643
Belgium	447
France	424

Top Ten Exports to Europe ($ Millions)

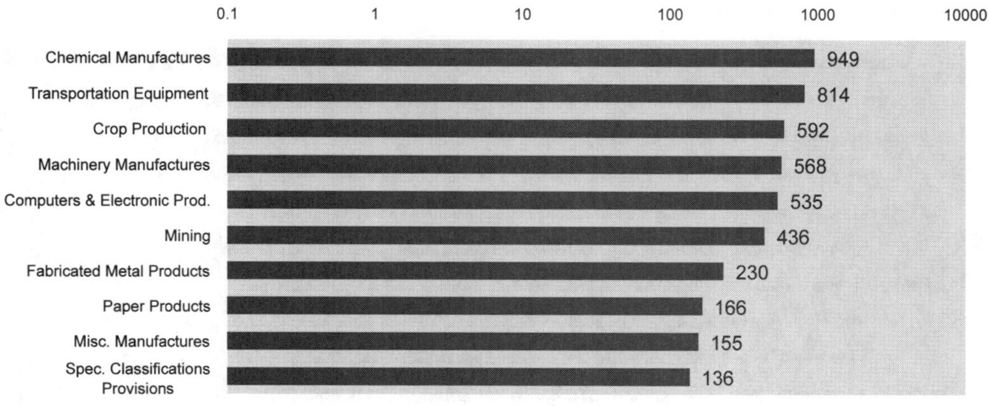

Source: Bureau of Economic Anlaysis, Foreign Trade Division, U.S. Census Bureau
*European investment includes France, Germany, Netherlands, Switzerland, and the United Kingdom
Due to a need to align resources with current funding levels, the Bureau of Economic Analysis has reduced its coverage to major investing countries.

Washington and Europe

Employment, Investment, and Trade Linkages

Employment

European* investment in Washington supported 45,800 jobs in 2008.

Sources of Employment within Washington, 2008	
Country	**Employment**
Germany	14,700
United Kingdom	14,100
Canada	11,800
Japan	11,400
France	7,800

Investment

Of the $21.6 billion invested in Washington in 2007, 43%, or $9.3 billion came from Europe*.

Trade

In 2009, Europe purchased $10 billion worth of goods from Washington.
Transportation equipment dominates Washington's exports to Europe.

Top European Export Markets, 2009	
Country	**Exports ($ Millions)**
Ireland	1,817
France	1,696
Germany	1,437
United Kingdom	1,436
Netherlands	1,050

Top Ten Exports to Europe ($ Billions)

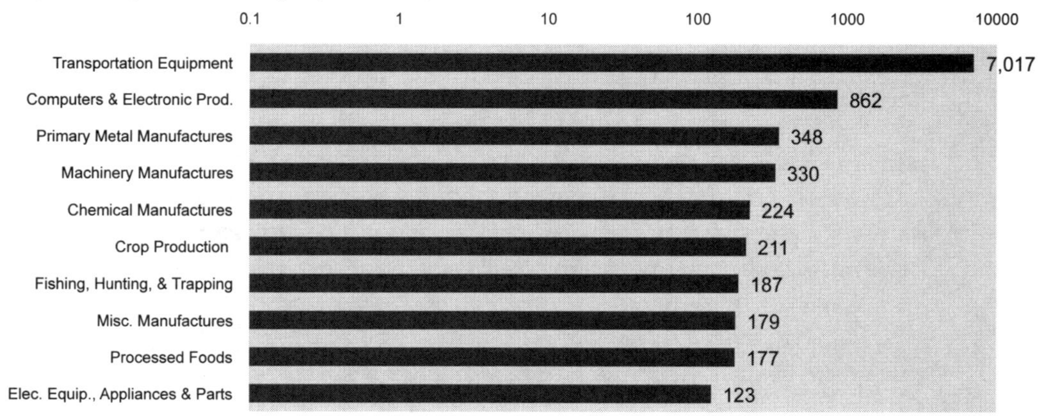

Source: Bureau of Economic Anlaysis, Foreign Trade Division, U.S. Census Bureau
*European investment includes France, Germany, Netherlands, Switzerland, and the United Kingdom
Due to a need to align resources with current funding levels, the Bureau of Economic Analysis has reduced its coverage to major investing countries.

West Virginia and Europe

Employment, Investment, and Trade Linkages

Employment

European* investment in West Virginia supported 11,000 jobs in 2008.

Sources of Employment within West Virginia, 2008	
Country	**Employment**
United Kingdom	4,600
Japan	2,800
Germany	2,300
Canada	1,900
Switzerland	1,800

Investment

Of the $6.3 billion invested in West Virginia in 2007, 21%, or $1.3 billion came from Europe*.

Trade

In 2009, Europe purchased $2 billion worth of goods from West Virginia.
Mining is the state's top export to Europe.

Top European Export Markets, 2009	
Country	**Exports ($ Millions)**
Netherlands	364
Belgium	313
France	288
United Kingdom	227
Italy	166

Top Ten Exports to Europe ($ Millions)

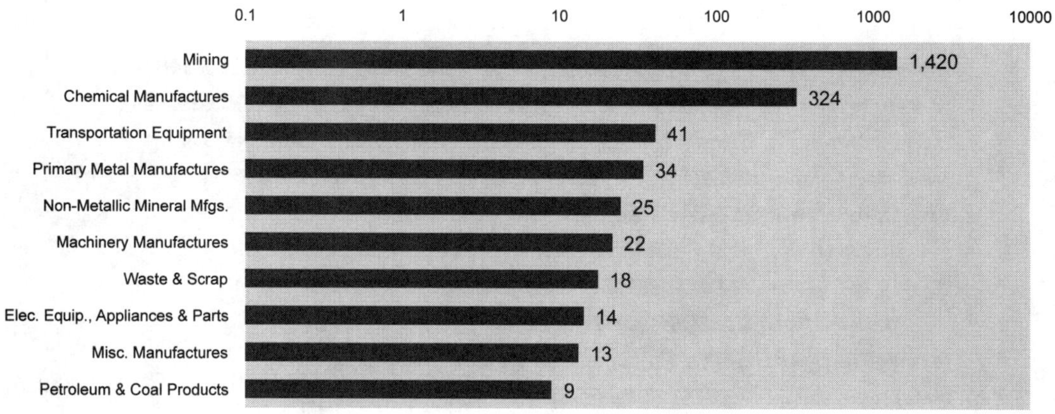

Source: Bureau of Economic Anlaysis, Foreign Trade Division, U.S. Census Bureau
*European investment includes France, Germany, Netherlands, Switzerland, and the United Kingdom
Due to a need to align resources with current funding levels, the Bureau of Economic Analysis has reduced its coverage to major investing countries.

Wisconsin and Europe
Employment, Investment, and Trade Linkages

Employment
European* investment in Wisconsin supported 41,500 jobs in 2008.

Sources of Employment within Wisconsin, 2008	
Country	**Employment**
United Kingdom	14,000
Canada	13,900
Germany	12,000
France	7,100
Switzerland	5,800

Investment
Of the $14.6 billion invested in Wisconsin in 2007, 35%, or $5.1 billion came from Europe*.

Trade
In 2009, Europe purchased $3.7 billion worth of goods from Wisconsin.
Machinery and computers are the state's top exports to Europe.

Top European Export Markets, 2009	
Country	**Exports ($ Millions)**
Germany	641
United Kingdom	531
France	477
Netherlands	313
Italy	295

Top Ten Exports to Europe ($ Millions)

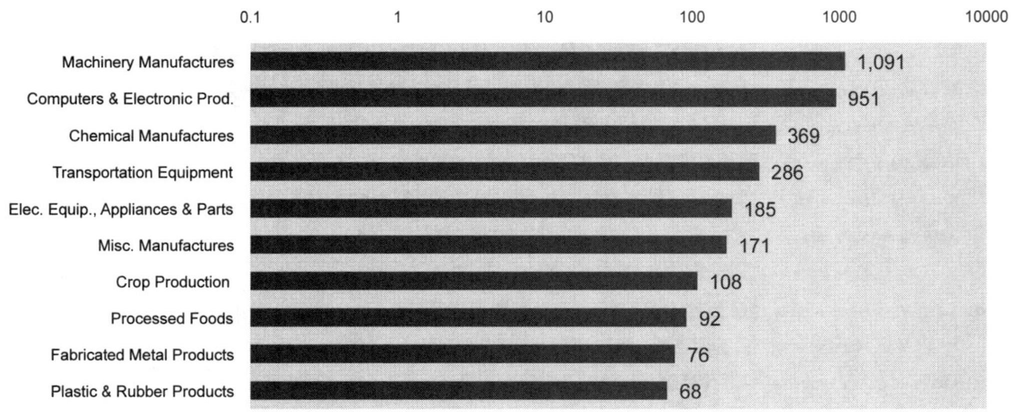

Source: Bureau of Economic Anlaysis, Foreign Trade Division, U.S. Census Bureau
*European investment includes France, Germany, Netherlands, Switzerland, and the United Kingdom
Due to a need to align resources with current funding levels, the Bureau of Economic Analysis has reduced its coverage to major investing countries.

Wyoming and Europe

Employment, Investment, and Trade Linkages

Employment

European* investment in Wyoming supported 4,800 jobs in 2008.

Sources of Employment within Wyoming, 2008	
Country	**Employment**
United Kingdom	3,300
Canada	900
France	800
Switzerland	400
Netherlands	200

Investment

Of the $11.1 billion invested in Wyoming in 2007, 1%, or $0.1 billion came from Europe*.

Trade

In 2009, Europe purchased $125 million worth of goods from Wyoming.
By a wide margin, chemicals are the top export to Europe.

Top European Export Markets, 2009	
Country	**Exports ($ Millions)**
Belgium	31
Netherlands	29
Spain	16
United Kingdom	15
Lithuania	11

Top Ten Exports to Europe ($ Millions)

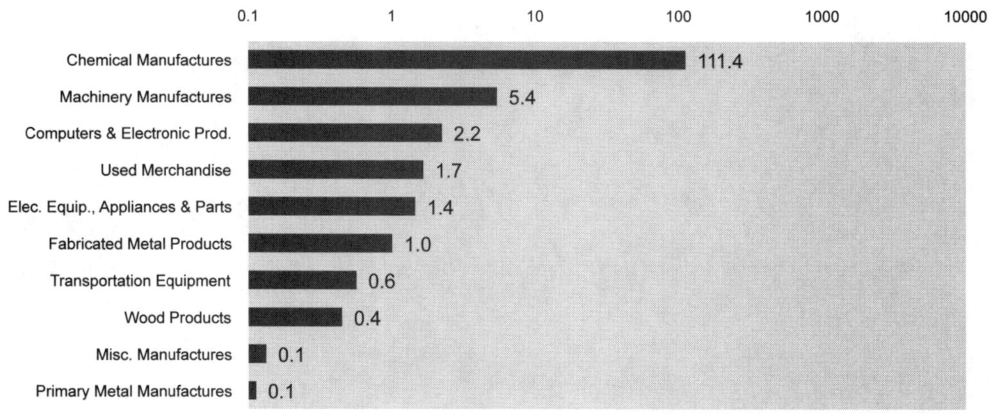

Source: Bureau of Economic Anlaysis, Foreign Trade Division, U.S. Census Bureau
*European investment includes France, Germany, Netherlands, Switzerland, and the United Kingdom
Due to a need to align resources with current funding levels, the Bureau of Economic Analysis has reduced its coverage to major investing countries.

Chapter 4

U.S. Commerce and Europe: A Country-by-Country Comparison

U.S. foreign direct investment (FDI) to the European Union (EU) jumped by nearly 30% during the first nine months of 2010, a solid rebound from the depressed levels of 2009, despite the rolling sovereign debt problems of some European countries and attendant fears over the fate of the euro. The upturn is not surprising given that Europe—notwithstanding some serious structural problems—remains one the largest and wealthiest economic entities in the world. In fact, the EU is the #1 destination of U.S. global FDI, accounting for just over half of such investments worldwide. The U.S. is also the principal source of FDI in the EU, accounting alone for about half of such investments. In 2008, the last year of comparable global data, U.S. FDI stocks in the EU totaled €1.05 trillion, more than that of the next 20 investors combined.[1]

Next to the United States, the European Union is the closest economic entity in the world—in terms of size, scale and open commerce—that resembles anything like a coherent, single pan-continental market, easily accessible to those firms operating from within. Despite all the headline risk swirling around the region, it continues to possess the main attributes that attract foreign investment in the first place—a wealthy consumer market, transparent rule of law, a liberal investment environment, and a large pool of skilled labor. The successful enlargement of the EU to many central and eastern European nations is another factor that makes Europe the most favored destination for U.S. foreign direct investment. Nestled among the nations of the "Old World" are large and dynamic emerging markets such as Poland, the only EU member state that did not experience a decline in output in 2009. In fact, the Polish economy expanded by 1.7% in recession year 2009, versus a -4.1% contraction for the euro area as a whole.

The spike in U.S. FDI to Europe in 2010 was far greater than the increase in global foreign investment; overall FDI inflows rose just 1%, to $1.1 trillion. That is hardly a gangbuster pace, but the aggregate number masks the fact that cross-border M&A deals soared 37% last year, a reflection of rising confidence among global corporations, including those from the United States and Europe. Greenfield operations, in contrast, were a drag on overall global FDI.

Global foreign direct investment flows are highly correlated to real global growth. The stronger the global economy, the more robust global investment flows tend to be to virtually all regions of the world. Hence, over the 2003-07 period, with the world economy expanding by nearly 5% on an annual rate, global and transatlantic FDI flows were quite robust. In 2007, one year before the financial crisis hammered the global economy, U.S. foreign direct investment to Europe hit an all-time high of $240 billion. Thereafter, however, U.S. investment declined along with the slumping global economy; U.S. foreign direct

---

[1] Eurostat.

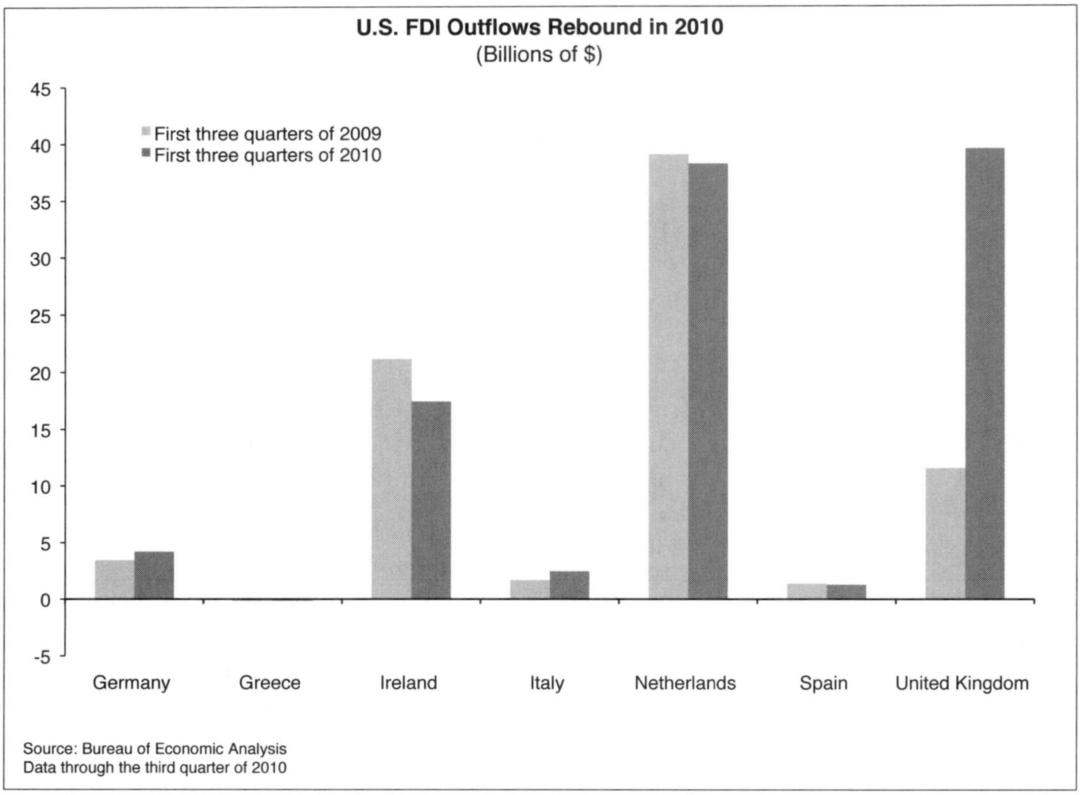

investment to Europe dropped roughly 20% in 2008 and plunged by roughly one-third in 2009. The two-year freefall in investment was one of the worst on record, although as the accompanying chart highlights, 2010 was less destructive. By country, there were signs of strength amidst continued indications of weakness.

To this point, in the first nine months of 2010 versus the same period a year earlier, U.S. FDI flows rose sharply to the United Kingdom (243%), Belgium (172%), Italy (48%), and Germany (22%). Behind the surge in flows to the UK and Belgium: soaring and large M&A deals between U.S. firms and their transatlantic counterparts. Robust flows to Germany reflected the strong nature of Germany's economy, which expanded by 3.6% in 2010, one of the best rates in decades.

In contrast, France's economic growth has been constrained by near 10% unemployment, an unpropitious backdrop that has ingrained caution among U.S. companies considering possible investments in France. U.S. inflows to France rose just 1% during the first nine months of 2010.

The damage was far more extensive in Ireland, with U.S. foreign investment plunging by 17.5%. Ireland's banking crisis and tough austerity measures have dramatically reduced economic activity in a number of sectors, resulting in less investment capital from U.S. multinationals. Over the balance of 2010, Ireland remained in recession, as did Greece, while the rest of Europe gradually experienced a rebound in economic activity. Not surprisingly, U.S. firms continue to disinvest in Greece—U.S. net *dis*investment in Greece of -$157 million in 2009 was followed by -$18 million disinvestment during the first nine months of 2010.

U.S. firms decreased their investment in Spain by nearly 6% in 2010—not bad given all the market worries and concerns about Spain's slumping construction, troubled banks and less than ideal economic prospects. However, should Europe's rolling debt problems ultimately reach Spain, U.S. firms may decide to accelerate the pace of disinvestment. Spain's unemployment rate continues to hover in the 20% range, which does not help matters and is a structural challenge that could undermine foreign confidence in the economy and the country.

Overall, the U.S. investment position in Europe was patchy in 2010, although at high levels and from a very large base. In contrast, U.S. investment inflows into Brazil, India and China surged, but from relatively low levels and a comparatively small base. Higher growth prospects in all three countries stirred greater interest on the part of Corporate America and, in turn, attracted more U.S. investment. Interestingly, as the accompanying chart makes clear, U.S. firms sank more capital into Brazil in the first nine months of 2010 ($7.2 billion) than either China ($6.3 billion) or India ($4.7 billion).

Another key macro variable boosting U.S. investment to Europe in particular and the world in general last year: robust corporate earnings, which in turn gave U.S. companies the cash and confidence to make more long-term investments, both at home and abroad. During 2008 and 2009 U.S. multinationals were largely capital-constrained, a consequence of one of the worse financial crises on record. Less capital in terms of earnings, bank lending and reinvested income curtailed investment outlays, making it financially more difficult to expand abroad. This was a predictable outcome of the financial crisis. In 2010, however, the picture brightened. Robust earnings, low interest rates, a rebound in global growth—all of these factors combined to boost U.S. global FDI, with total foreign investment rising 39% in the first nine months of 2010 versus the same period a year earlier. We estimate that U.S. foreign direct investment totaled $350 billion in 2010, a significant improvement from the prior two years, but a figure still down from a global peak of $394 billion in 2007.

Notwithstanding the plunge in U.S. outward foreign direct investment in 2008/09, the direction of U.S. FDI remains generally towards Europe. That was the case in the 1960s, the 1970s, the 1980s and the 1990s. And to a large degree, things are no different early in the 21st century. Over the 2000-2010 period, for instance, U.S. firms sunk roughly $1.3 trillion into Europe, a figure that equates to just over 60% of total U.S. foreign direct investment for the entire decade. As a footnote, the figures for "Europe" are all encompassing and include non-EU members like Switzerland, Luxembourg, Russia, and Norway. However, due to the patchy nature of U.S. investment flows to Europe in 2010, Europe's share of total U.S. foreign investment was roughly 52%, down from last decade's average.

Over the past decade five of the top ten overseas markets for U.S. investment were in Europe. Of cumulative U.S. foreign investment outflows between 2000 and the third quarter of 2010, the Netherlands ranked first. The United Kingdom was second, followed by Ireland (4th), Switzerland (5th), and Germany (8th). France ranked 13th, Belgium 11th, and

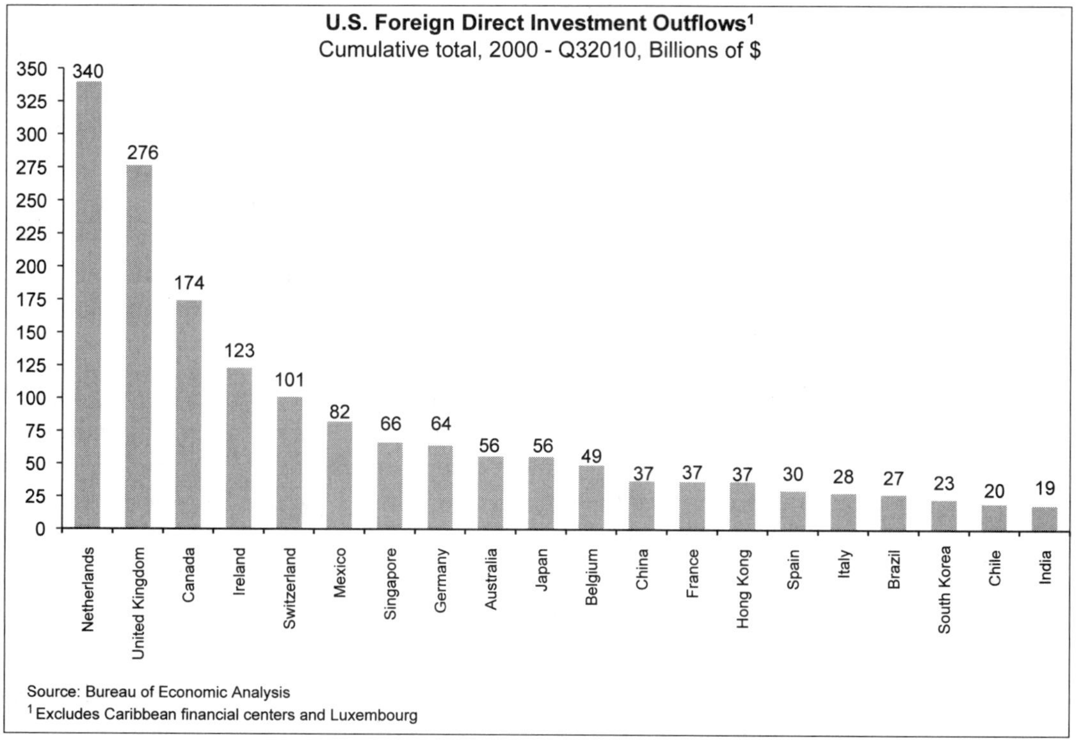

Spain 15th. Also ranking in the top ten were America's Nafta neighbors Canada and Mexico, which ranked third and sixth, respectively. Meanwhile, Singapore ranked 8th, Australia 9th and Japan 10th.

In terms of U.S. mergers and acquisitions in the EU15, the favorite targets of U.S. firms were in the United Kingdom, Norway, Germany, France and the Netherlands.

Interestingly, within Europe, America's top overseas market has shifted from the United Kingdom to the Netherlands. During the 1990s the United Kingdom was Corporate America's overwhelming favorite, accounting for nearly 40% of total U.S. investment in Europe, while the Netherlands attracted around 15% of the European total. In the decade to late 2010, however, the Netherlands accounted for nearly 27% and the UK 22% of total U.S. investment to Europe. The UK has traditionally served as an export platform for U.S. affiliates to greater Europe, but the euro, the Single Market, and EU enlargement have all galvanized more firms to invest directly in the continent. The extension of EU production networks and commercial infrastructure throughout a larger pan-continental Single Market has caused the center of economic gravity in Europe to shift eastward within the EU, with Brussels playing an important role in economic policies and decision-making. As a key export platform and pan-regional distribution hub, the Netherlands has emerged as a critical launching pad for Corporate America to the rest of Europe.

In addition, more countries in the EU have become more attractive to U.S. firms. Greater U.S. investment in new EU member states in central and eastern Europe has helped to re-

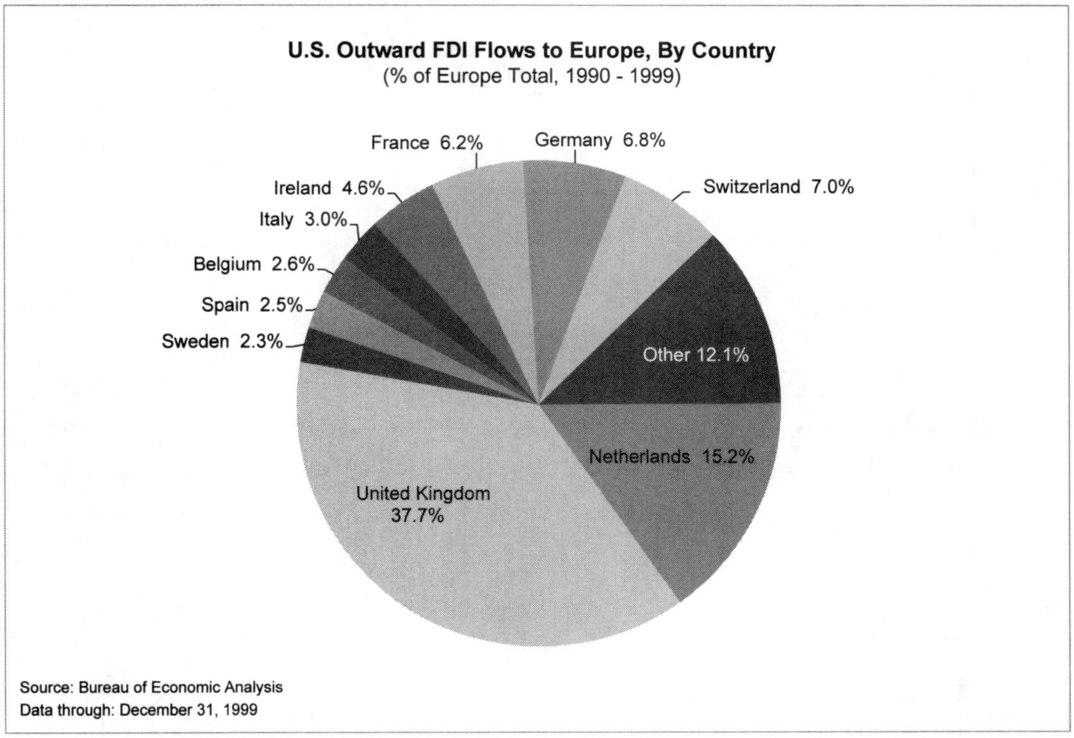
U.S. Outward FDI Flows to Europe, By Country
(% of Europe Total, 1990 - 1999)
France 6.2%
Germany 6.8%
Switzerland 7.0%
Ireland 4.6%
Italy 3.0%
Belgium 2.6%
Spain 2.5%
Sweden 2.3%
Other 12.1%
Netherlands 15.2%
United Kingdom 37.7%
Source: Bureau of Economic Analysis
Data through: December 31, 1999

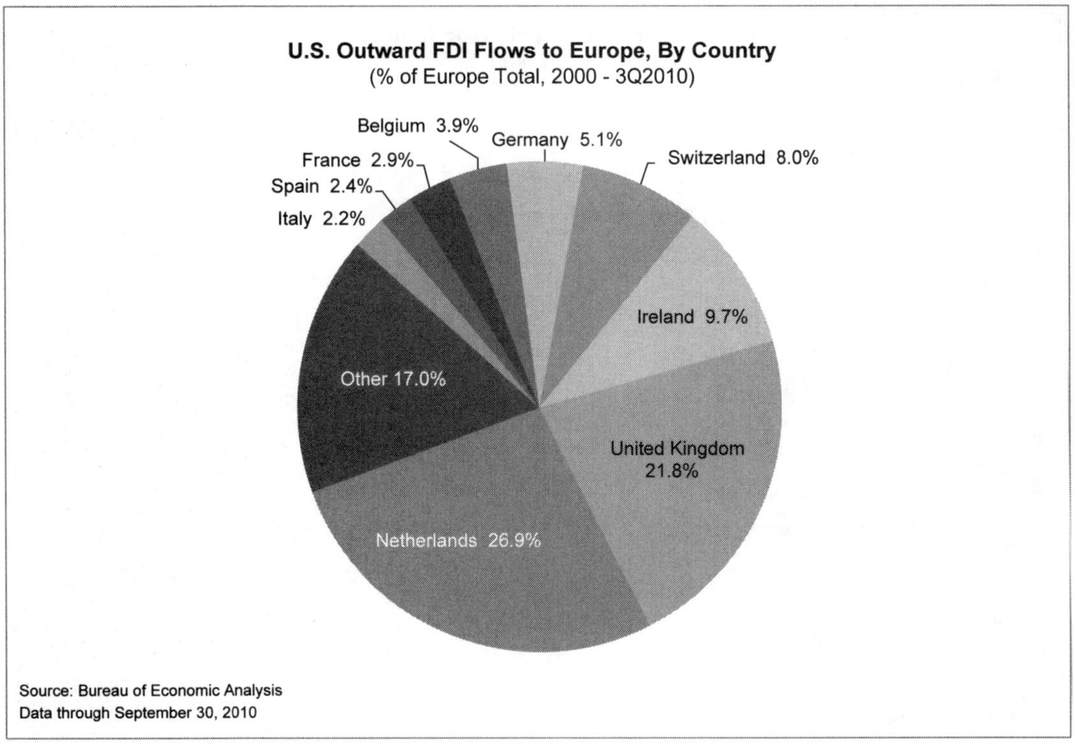
U.S. Outward FDI Flows to Europe, By Country
(% of Europe Total, 2000 - 3Q2010)
Belgium 3.9%
Germany 5.1%
France 2.9%
Switzerland 8.0%
Spain 2.4%
Italy 2.2%
Ireland 9.7%
Other 17.0%
United Kingdom 21.8%
Netherlands 26.9%
Source: Bureau of Economic Analysis
Data through September 30, 2010

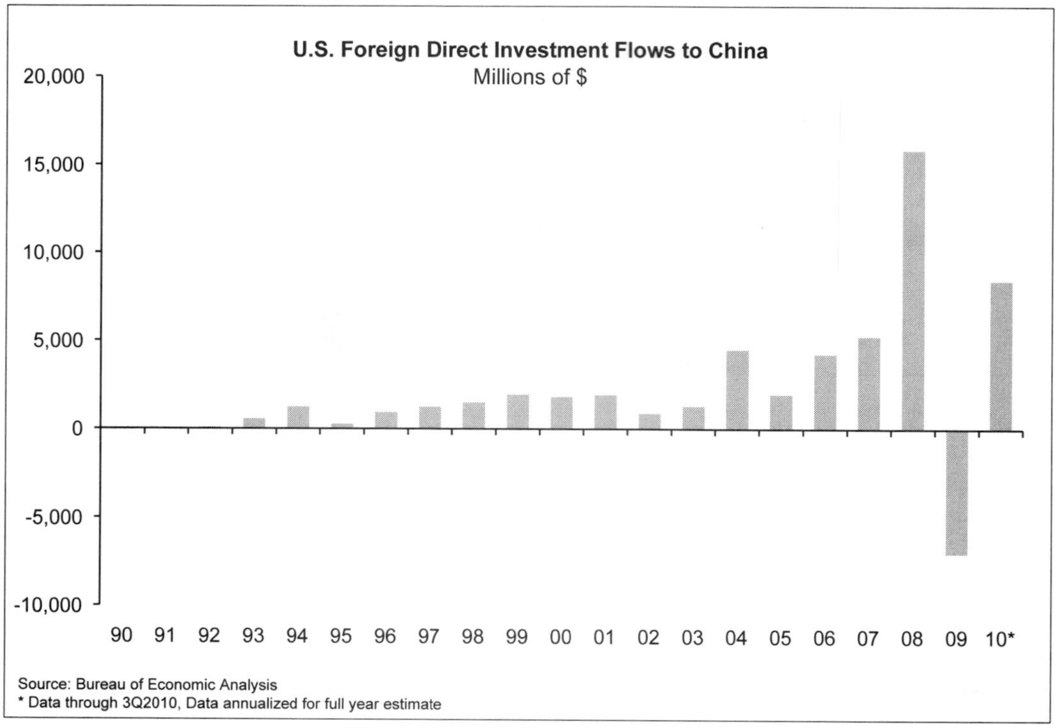
U.S. Foreign Direct Investment Flows to China
Millions of $
20,000
15,000
10,000
5,000
0
-5,000
-10,000
90 91 92 93 94 95 96 97 98 99 00 01 02 03 04 05 06 07 08 09 10*
Source: Bureau of Economic Analysis
* Data through 3Q2010, Data annualized for full year estimate

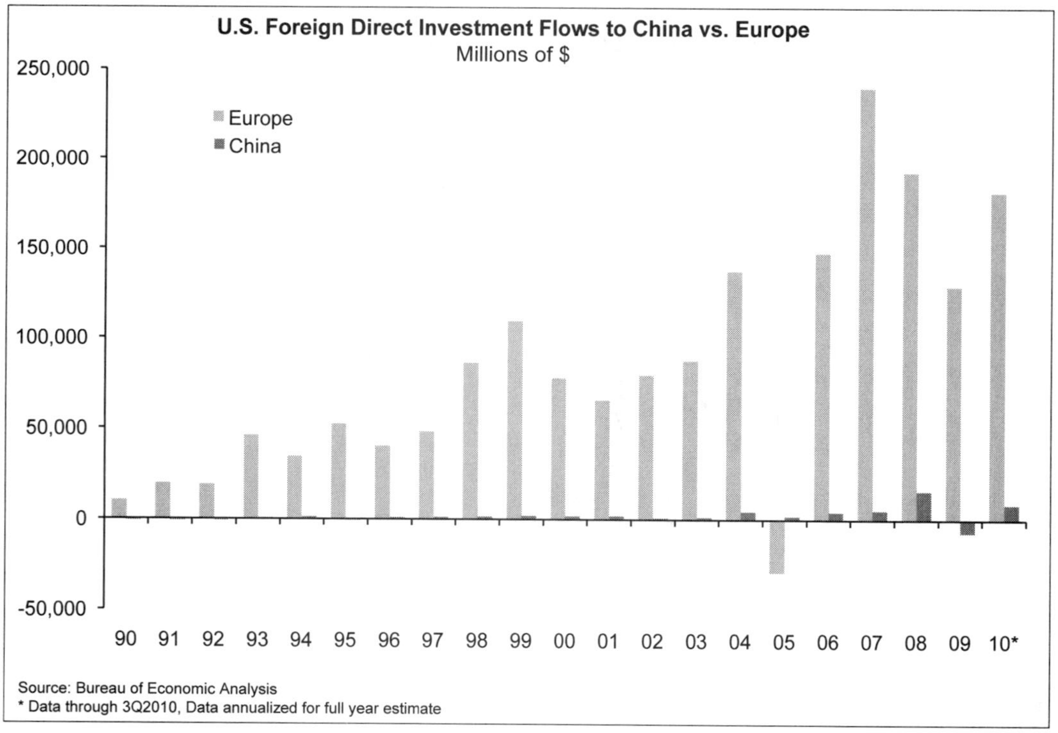
U.S. Foreign Direct Investment Flows to China vs. Europe
Millions of $
Europe
China
250,000
200,000
150,000
100,000
50,000
0
-50,000
90 91 92 93 94 95 96 97 98 99 00 01 02 03 04 05 06 07 08 09 10*
Source: Bureau of Economic Analysis
* Data through 3Q2010, Data annualized for full year estimate

order U.S. flows within Europe. Poland, one of the largest consumer markets in Europe and the one European economy that has weathered the financial and economic storms of the past few years relatively well, has become a key attraction of Corporate America. U.S. firms have sunk $4.3 billion in the country since 2000, more than double U.S. flows to Portugal. Turkey has emerged as another favorite locale of U.S. firms, attracting nearly $7 billion in U.S. investment since 2000, on par with U.S. investment levels in Russia.

Ireland's ties to Corporate America are a special case. Ireland's share of U.S. investment to the EU rose from a share of 4.6% in the 1990s to roughly 10% since the millennium started. U.S. firms have sunk over $120 billion into the Irish economy since 2000, more than double the level over the 1990s. Facilitating this rise in investment has been the country's low-cost, English-speaking labor force, coupled with its low corporate tax rates. The formula made Ireland among the most favored destinations in the world for Corporate America.

Given Ireland's difficulties, however, it hardly looks like past will be prologue. As mentioned above, U.S. foreign direct investment to Ireland plunged 17.5% in the first nine months of 2010; and with Ireland in the grips of a brutal period of fiscal austerity, a prolonged period of weak or no U.S. investment growth would hardly be surprising. On the plus side, Ireland's corporate tax rate remains among the lowest in the European Union and U.S. firms continue to find the trained, English-speaking labor force of Ireland particularly attractive. That said, we would not be surprised to see U.S. firms rethink and reassess their corporate positions in what was once Europe's most dynamic economy.

Beyond the Celtic Tiger-turned-cub, the share of U.S. investment in France and Italy also declined over the past decade compared to the decade before. France has accounted for just 2.9% and Italy only 2.2% of total U.S. investment to the EU since the start of the millennium. Germany's share also fell, dropping to 5.1% of the total. It is important to keep in mind, however, that a good portion of U.S. investment funds that flow first into countries such as the Netherlands, Belgium and Luxembourg finds its way to Europe's economic powerhouse—and some also does to France.

Corporate America's outsized presence in Europe in general runs counter to the prevailing consensus that when it comes to investing overseas, Corporate America is headed for the low-cost nations of Asia and Latin America. This is not quite true, and is a point we continue to emphasis in our annual surveys.

Take China for example. U.S. foreign direct investment to China has increased since 2000, with U.S. firms investing roughly $37 billion into the Middle Kingdom between 2000 and 2010. This represents a significant rise from the prior decade, but some perspective is in order. China ranked 12th overall in terms of aggregate U.S. foreign direct investment in the 2000s, trailing a host of European countries such as Belgium, France, Germany, Switzerland, Ireland, the United Kingdom and the Netherlands. Not only did China trail many European countries, it did so by a wide margin. U.S. investment in Ireland over 2000-2010, for instance, was nearly three times U.S. investment in China. American investment in the Netherlands was nine times greater than in China, and American investment in the UK was more than seven times larger than in China. In fact, since 2000 U.S.

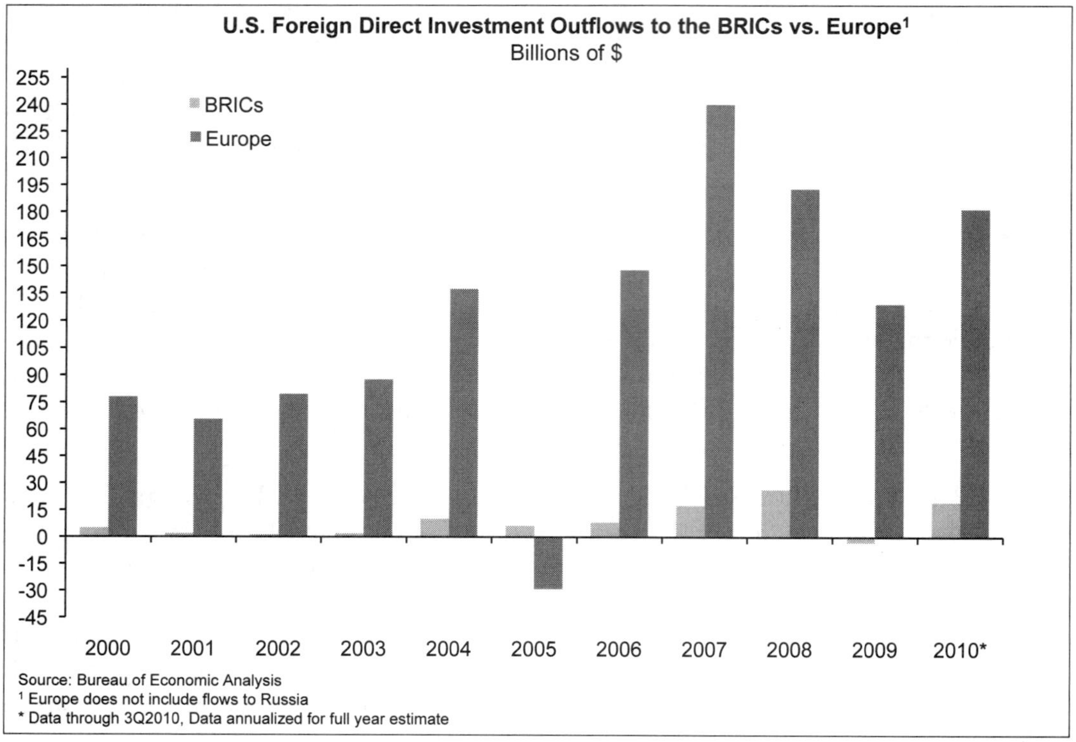
U.S. Foreign Direct Investment Outflows to the BRICs vs. Europe[1]
Billions of $
255
240
225
210
195
180
165
150
135
120
105
90
75
60
45
30
15
0
-15
-30
-45
BRICs
Europe
2000
2001
2002
2003
2004
2005
2006
2007
2008
2009
2010*
Source: Bureau of Economic Analysis
[1] Europe does not include flows to Russia
* Data through 3Q2010, Data annualized for full year estimate

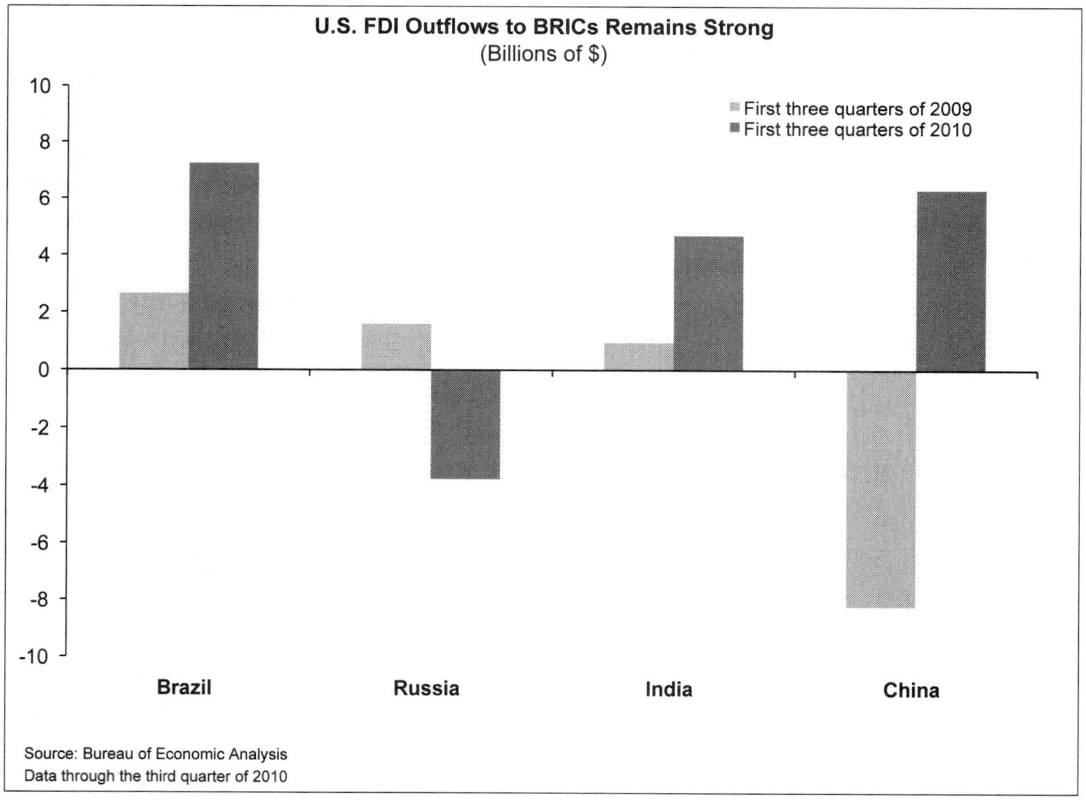
U.S. FDI Outflows to BRICs Remains Strong
(Billions of $)
10
8
6
4
2
0
-2
-4
-6
-8
-10
First three quarters of 2009
First three quarters of 2010
Brazil
Russia
India
China
Source: Bureau of Economic Analysis
Data through the third quarter of 2010

firms have invested more in the Netherlands alone than in South and Central America, the Middle East and Africa combined.

Relative to other BRICs, the story is basically the same. America's cumulative investment in Brazil since 2000 ($27 billion) is less than half of total U.S. investment in Germany. Russia captured more U.S. investment over the past decade ($7 billion), but that was roughly a quarter of the amount of U.S. investment in Italy.

Besides China, no nation has probably attracted as much attention and hope as India. Yet the roughly $19 billion sunk in India by U.S. firms since 2000 was just 60% of total U.S. investment in Norway during that period.

On a combined and cumulative basis, U.S. investment in the BRICs totaled roughly $75 billion over the past decade, up from a total of $48 billion in the 1990s. That represents a 53% rise—an impressive increase and one indicative of the growing interest of Corporate America in key emerging markets. However, the total was less than U.S. investment in tiny Ireland over the same period; moreover, what Corporate America sunk in the BRICs during the past decade was just 8% of total U.S. investment in the European Union. Through the first nine months of 2010 U.S. investment in the BRICs was roughly 11% of total U.S. investment in Europe.

Looked at from the long term, or a historic cost basis, the U.S. investment position in Europe was nearly 14 times larger than the BRICs in 2009. In general U.S. investment in Europe ($2 trillion) was nearly four times larger than Corporate America's investment position in all of Asia at the end of 2009. U.S. investment stakes in Belgium at the end of 2009, $70 billion on a historic cost basis, were on par with the combined U.S. investment position in China and India ($68 billion). Corporate America's investment stakes in Ireland ($166 billion) is much greater than total U.S. investment in South America ($125 billion). U.S. investment in Spain ($51 billion) is greater than U.S. investment in all of Africa ($45 billion).

We continue to highlight these figures since the media hype about the rise of China, the emergence of India, and soaring economic prospects in Brazil tends to ignore the basic fact that at the end of the day, the foreign thrust of Corporate America remains focused on the European Union.

One attraction of the EU to U.S. multinationals is the continent's Single Market in goods and a variety of service activities. In this respect, some U.S. companies view Europe as one large, homogenous market. Others see a Europe with different endowments and attributes and continue to leverage each country accordingly. As the European Union has evolved, so have strategies of U.S. affiliates operating in Europe. While U.S. foreign affiliate sales in Europe remain robust overall, the geographic distribution of those sales has shifted over the past few decades as U.S. firms increasingly slice up their production chains across Europe, producing parts and components where it is most economical and cost-efficient, or where they may be able to generate greater value-added, before final assembly and shipment.

This shift in strategy is evident from the accompanying table. Whereas in 1990 roughly 65% of U.S. affiliate sales were directed to local markets, the percentage dropped sharply to 53% by 2008. Meanwhile, exports to third parties—or other countries within the EU

Special Focus: What China Really Wants From the U.S. and Europe

With some $2.8 trillion in international reserves, China has become a major engine of global finance, a geostrategic advantage not lost on Beijing, but one yet to be fully understood by many in the West. Over the past few years, Chinese capital has underpinned economic growth in various parts of Africa (via foreign direct investment), the U.S. (through massive purchases of U.S. Treasuries), and South America and the Middle East (owing to soaring Chinese demand for commodities). Now, China has turned its financial sights on Europe—a recent development that could stave off a financial meltdown in the eurozone.

Deep in debt and confronting soaring borrowing costs, Europe's debt-plagued countries now need some financial reassurance from the world's largest creditor nation, China. The global financial markets could use the same smooth talk, lest investors continue to dump Portuguese and Irish debt or refuse to buy new debt from countries such as Spain and Belgium. As 2011 dawned, all eyes focused on Portugal, where the yield between Portuguese 10-year bonds and German bunds topped 400 basis points.

Sensing the time was right to ride to Europe's rescue, China publicly came out in support of the euro and was rumored to be considering making sizable purchases of Portuguese and Spanish debt. Writing in the German daily *Süddeutsche Zeitung* in mid-January, Chinese Vice Premier Li Keqiang proclaimed that "China's support of the EU's financial stabilization measures and its help to certain countries in coping with the sovereign debt crisis are all conducive to promoting full economic recovery and steady growth." Translation: coffers stuffed full of dollars, China is ready and willing to ante up some badly needed capital to Europe's near-broke periphery, a move that would not only serve China's own interests by keeping Europe, China's most important export destination, afloat, but also enhance the nation's standing as a responsible stakeholder in the global economy.

Against this backdrop, the global financial crisis of 2008 is the gift that keeps on giving to China. The country's global economic standing and prestige have soared over the past two years, owing to Beijing's adept economic handling of the crisis. By dramatically boosting lending and state spending, China not only posted real GDP growth of nearly 10% at home in 2010, but also provided badly needed support to a global economy stunned by one of the worst financial crises of the past century. Without Chinese demand for copper, oil and other commodities, as well as demand for finished goods like automobiles, cell phones, and computers, 2010 would have been a much tougher year for the world's commodity producers and for a host of Western multinationals that have come to rely on China for earnings growth. This year, absent China's financial presence in debt-wracked Europe, the continent's simmering debt crisis could very well morph into something far more insidious—a protracted recession in the eurozone, for instance, accompanied by rising social and political tensions.

This scenario is not likely to evolve if China's words of support are more than just rhetorical and are backed by actual debt purchases by Beijing. However, China's financial lifeline to Europe comes at a price.

While China still finds the West—the U.S. and Europe—a relatively attractive place to invest its excess savings, China's investing mandarins are keen on diversifying their Western holdings. Starkly put, China wants to buy Western plants, not Western paper. Beijing's preference is for companies rather than coupons.

This tilt in investment bias, however, has not and will not go down very well with the U.S. and Europe, who have been all too happy to see Beijing gorge itself on their sovereign debt while remaining reticent about China's interest in buying U.S. and Europe firms outright. To the latter point, in January 2011 a Chinese firm dropped a $1.3 billion bid for a Dutch cable wire company after the EU's Industry Commissioner expressed hostility toward the planned takeover. The Chinese firm ultimately backed down—although the next time around, China could be less compliant.

Both Europe and the U.S. should expect China to become more aggressive and adamant about sealing deals in the West. Beijing not only wants to diversify its foreign investments, complementing massive holdings of securities with holdings of Western companies, it wants to level the competitive playing field between U.S. and European firms on the one hand and Chinese firms on the other. While China enjoys a trade advantage over the transatlantic partnership, the U.S. and Europe enjoy a massive investment (in-country presence) advantage over China.

To this point, it increasingly irks Beijing that America's foreign direct investment stock in China, some $49 billion, is more than 20 times larger than China's investment presence in the U.S. ($2.3 billion in 2009). The EU's investment position in China, meanwhile, was 10 times larger than China's investment position in the EU in 2009, with EU stock totaling $81 billion versus Chinese stock of $8.1 billion. In other words, when it comes to foreign direct investment, or competing directly in one's own market, American and European firms hold a significant advantage over their Chinese counterparts. The playing field is heavily tilted in favor of the West—a lopsided advantage Beijing would like to correct but cannot if Europe and the U.S. continue to torpedo potential M&A deals.

Large Chinese firms want to go global, which means they want direct access to the markets of the U.S. and Europe, a strategy that entails less trade and more foreign investment. And like Japanese firms in the 1980s, Chinese firms, fearing rising trade barriers in the West, hope to jump or skirt these barriers by investing directly in the West. However, Chinese investors are hardly getting a warm and fuzzy feeling from the U.S. and Europe. Hence, as they are prevented from expanding their corporate presence in the transatlantic economy, it is not surprising that China has become more hostile and less welcoming to U.S. and European investment in China.

In the end, the debt-laden U.S. and Europe will need to face some tough choices. China might only remain a trusted source of portfolio inflows (buying debt) on the condition that its corporations be able to expand their foreign direct investment position in the West. That means being allowed to buy and acquire companies in the U.S. and Europe. If this option is closed, China might just think about leaving the West financially high and dry. And if the option is opened, then Western decision-makers will need to focus much harder on how they can balance their concerns about China's predatory authoritarian capitalism and their security worries about Chinese ambitions with the their need for continued infusions of cold Chinese cash.

U.S. Affiliate Sales in Europe By Destination

% of total

Region	Calendar 1982: Local Market	Calendar 1982: Exports to 3rd Market	Calendar 1982: Exports to U.S.	Calendar 1990: Local Market	Calendar 1990: Exports to 3rd Market	Calendar 1990: Exports to U.S.	Calendar 2008: Local Market	Calendar 2008: Exports to 3rd Market	Calendar 2008: Exports to U.S.
World	**63.7%**	**25.6%**	**10.7%**	**67.0%**	**22.8%**	**10.2%**	**58.6%**	**31.4%**	**10.0%**
Europe	**61.4%**	**35.0%**	**3.6%**	**64.8%**	**31.2%**	**4.0%**	**53.0%**	**40.7%**	**6.3%**
Austria	na	na	na	77.8%	21.1%	1.1%	61.9%	34.1%	4.0%
Belgium	39.7%	57.2%	3.1%	41.5%	55.5%	3.0%	38.3%	57.3%	4.4%
Denmark	n.a.	n.a.	n.a.	75.7%	20.0%	4.3%	50.5%	46.6%	3.0%
Finland	97.6%	na	na	97.4%	2.3%	0.4%	56.4%	40.4%	3.1%
France	74.1%	24.0%	1.9%	72.4%	24.6%	3.0%	66.2%	28.8%	5.0%
Germany	69.8%	28.1%	2.1%	68.4%	29.0%	2.6%	61.3%	34.9%	3.8%
Ireland	n.a.	n.a.	5.3%	29.3%	64.9%	5.8%	24.4%	59.1%	16.5%
Italy	83.0%	16.0%	1.0%	82.3%	16.2%	1.5%	75.6%	21.1%	3.3%
Netherlands	44.1%	53.0%	2.9%	41.8%	55.7%	2.5%	41.1%	53.4%	5.5%
Norway	45.7%	41.7%	12.6%	n.a.	37.7%	n.a.	43.6%	54.1%	2.4%
Poland	n.a.	n.a.	n.a.	n.a.	n.a.	n.a.	60.9%	37.8%	1.3%
Portugal	76.6%	22.8%	0.6%	79.5%	20.1%	0.4%	72.5%	23.0%	4.4%
Spain	72.9%	25.8%	1.3%	74.7%	23.7%	1.7%	68.4%	28.8%	2.8%
Sweden	81.0%	18.1%	0.9%	78.8%	19.1%	2.1%	46.9%	44.4%	8.7%
Switzerland	12.4%	81.3%	6.3%	25.4%	63.5%	11.1%	21.1%	71.1%	7.7%
United Kingdom	68.3%	26.4%	5.3%	74.6%	20.3%	5.1%	68.8%	25.0%	6.2%

Source: Bureau of Economic Analysis

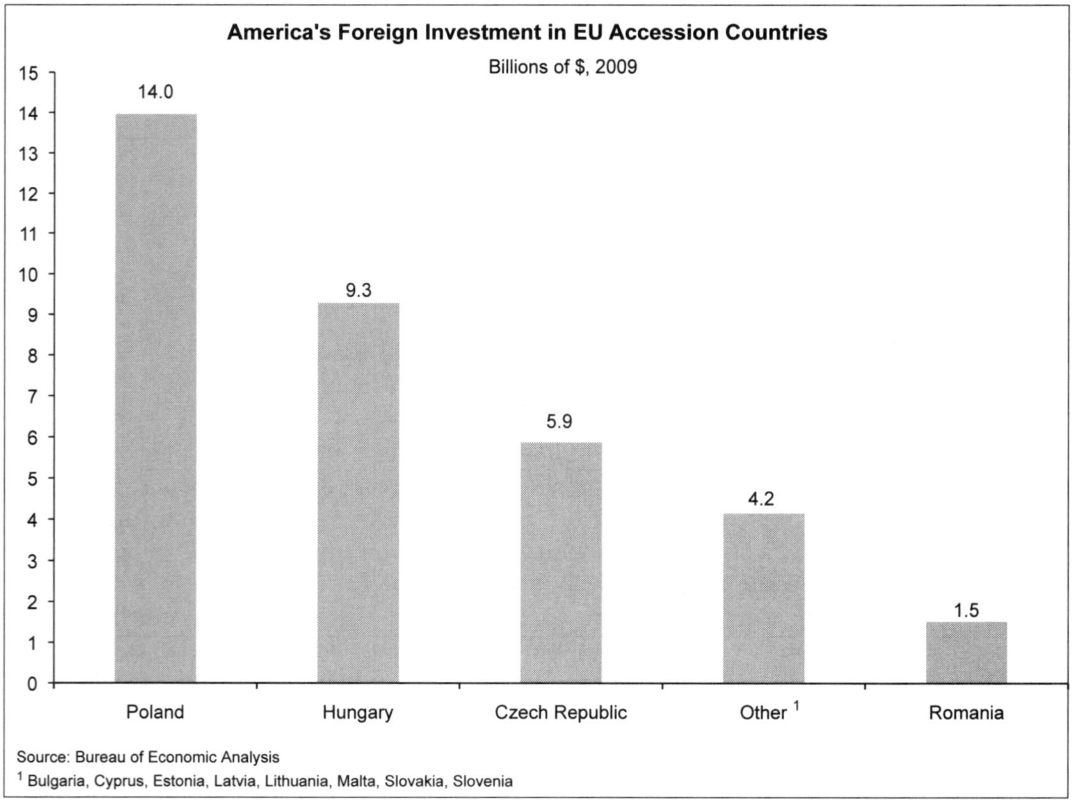

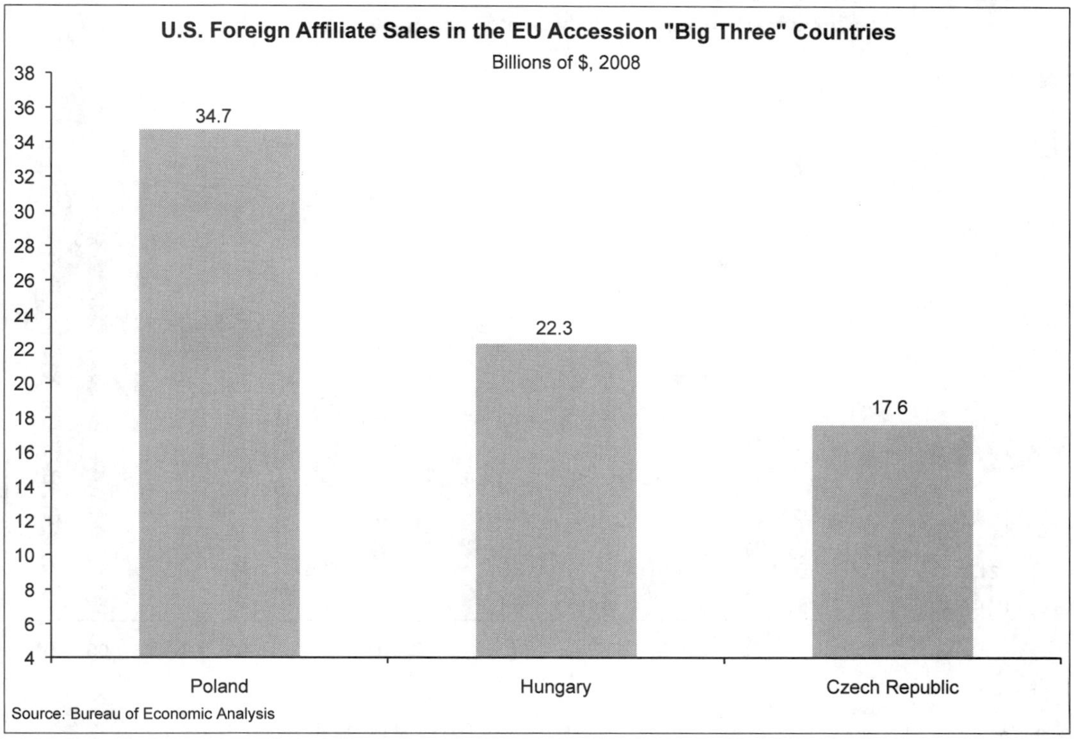

and elsewhere—have gained prominence. In 2008, for instance, nearly 41% of U.S. affiliate sales in Europe were classified as exports to third parties, up from 31% in 1990. The rise reflects the dispersion of U.S. manufacturing activities across Europe, notably between high-wage western Europe and low-cost eastern and central Europe. EU enlargement has allowed U.S. affiliates to slice up their value chains to produce and assemble in various parts of the EU. Belgium, Ireland and the Netherlands have emerged as significant export platforms for U.S. affiliates over the past few decades.

Ireland has been a good example of this phenomenon. U.S. foreign affiliates sales totaled $250 billion in 2008, making Ireland one of the largest markets in the EU in terms of foreign affiliate sales. However, foreign affiliate sales to the local market accounted for just a quarter of the total in 2008; sales to third markets represented nearly 60% of the total; and affiliate sales to the U.S. accounted for roughly 17% of the total.

Belgium, the Netherlands and Switzerland are three more countries where U.S. affiliate sales are greater in third markets and the U.S. than in the local market. The same is true for Hungary, a low-cost center for production and distribution for many U.S. affiliates in the heart of Europe.

The accession of ten countries (Cyprus, Czech Republic, Estonia, Hungary, Lithuania, Latvia, Malta, Poland, Slovenia, and Slovakia) to the EU in 2004, along with the inclusion of Romania and Bulgaria at the start of 2007, has presented U.S. multinationals with a host of new and promising strategic opportunities. EU accession has expanded the size of the

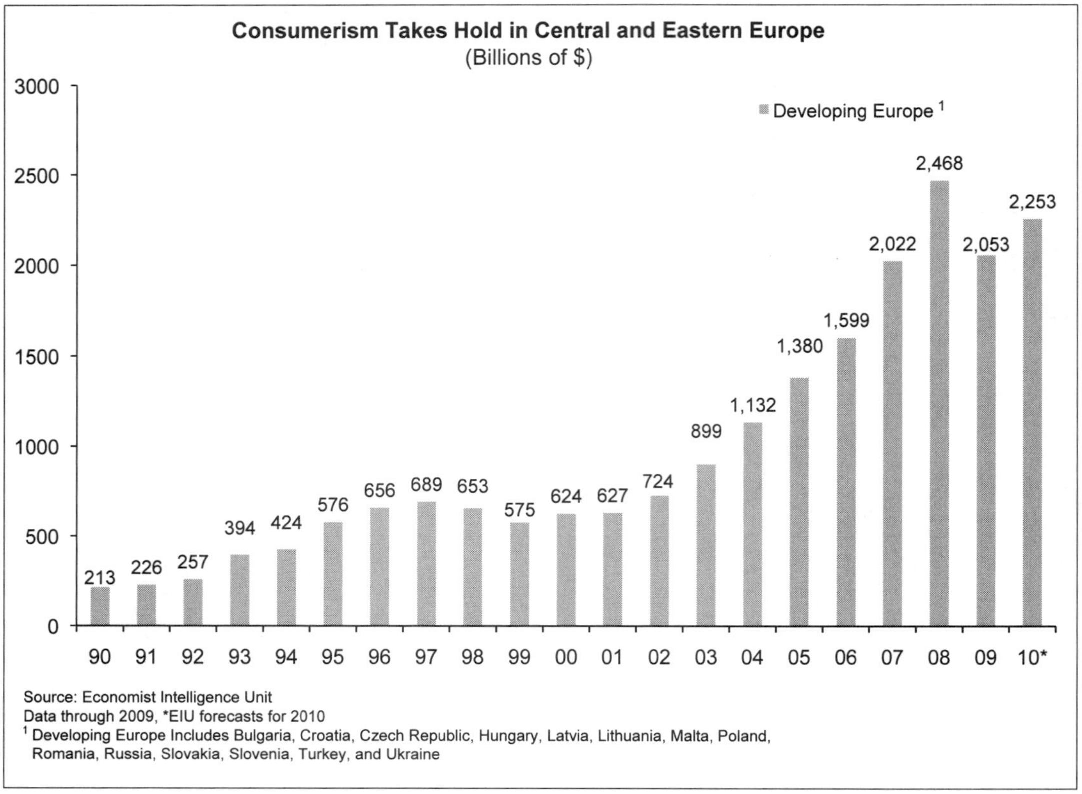

Single European Market and helped to integrate these nations into the mainstream of transatlantic commerce. The last two rounds of enlargement have increased the number of EU member states by over two-thirds, from 15 to 27; boosted the EU's population by nearly 20%; doubled its territory to over 2.5 million square miles; and nearly doubled its official languages. While the 12 new members add only about 5% to the overall output of the EU, before the recession they were registering annual growth rates in excess of the EU annual average. While some are still struggling to recover, overall the eastern member states of the Union present an increasingly attractive picture to U.S. companies. According to IMF estimates, for instance, annual average GDP growth in central and eastern Europe in 2010 was 3.7% versus 1.7% growth from the eurozone.

Trade linkages with the more mature markets of Europe have helped spur growth in central and eastern Europe, but so too have rising consumption levels. Personal consumption and central Europe are rarely used in the same sentence, but over the past decade consumerism has taken hold in Poland, Hungary, the Czech Republic and other neighboring states. The accompanying chart highlights this trend: aggregate personal consumption in developing Europe soared from $213 billion in 1990 to $625 billion in 2000 to roughly $2.2 trillion in 2010. In twenty years, in other words, there has been a ten-fold rise in personal consumption levels in central and eastern Europe, a fact that has not gone unnoticed in the executive suites of Corporate America. Not surprisingly, U.S. multinationals have been very active in the accession states over the past decade, and are already well integrated into central and eastern Europe.

U.S. companies have been particularly focused on the "Big Three" accession states—Poland, Hungary and the Czech Republic. Between 2000 and 2010, these countries, combined, attracted nearly $13.8 billion in U.S. capital, an amount not that far off from India ($18 billion) over the same period. In terms of profits—or affiliate income—U.S. affiliates earned $2.6 billion in the "Big Three" in recession year 2009, four times the level of 2000.

The following pages outline U.S.-sourced jobs, trade, and investment for each of the 27 members of the European Union. Norway and Switzerland are also included.

Special Focus:
The Race to Emerging Markets: The U.S. vs. Europe

As we highlighted in last year's survey, a new race has begun between U.S. firms and their European and Japanese counterparts. Multinationals from all three locations are scrambling to position themselves strategically in the developing world, whose economies, on an aggregate basis, expanded by roughly 7% in 2010, compared with lackluster real growth of roughly 2.8% in the United States and 1.8% in the European Union. The stakes in this race are huge since many large companies domiciled in the slow-growth and saturated developed markets are increasingly dependent on younger, faster-growing developing markets for future earnings growth.

Consumerism is taking hold in developing countries, a global macro trend no serious Western multinational can miss out on. Putting numbers to this dynamic, the World Bank estimates that the middle class in developing countries now numbers roughly 400 million people, a figure roughly one-third larger than the entire U.S. population. More importantly, the middle class in the developing countries is expected to triple in size over the next two decades, increasing to 1.2 billion shoppers and spenders by 2030. By then, developing countries will account for 93% of the global middle class, up from 56% in 2000. This estimate suggests ever rising levels of consumption from developing countries. Yet already today the emerging market consumer outspends the U.S. consumer. In 2010, for instance, the U.S. accounted for roughly 27% of global consumption, whereas emerging markets accounted for 34%. Eight years ago, the percentages were roughly reversed—that is when

Developing Countries' Share of World Total Personal Consumer Expenditures
(Percent of world total)

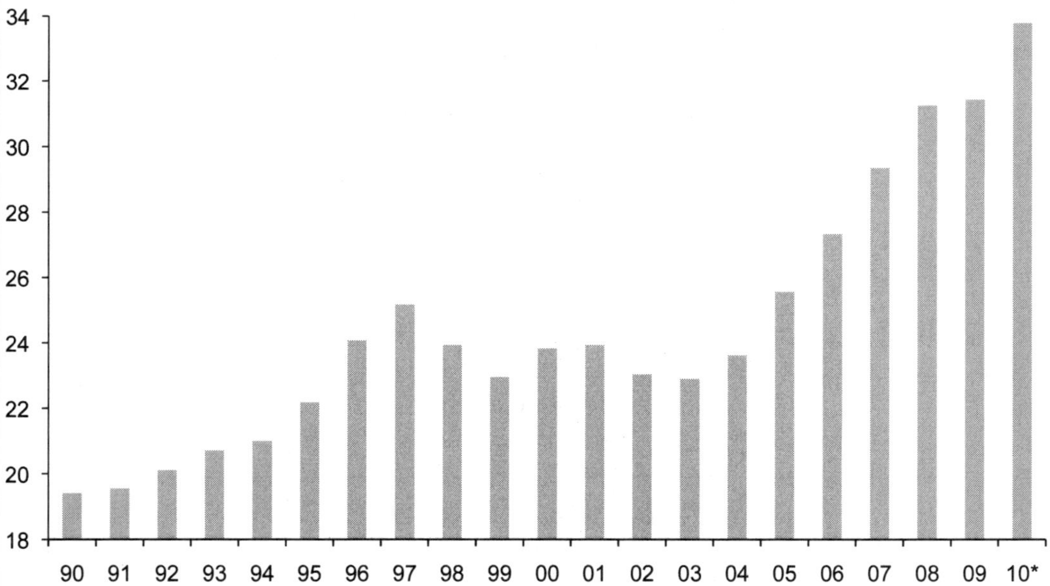

Source: Economist Intelligence Unit
Data through 2009, *EIU forecasts for 2010

the U.S. consumer was the most potent spending machine on earth and when the United States, with a population of less than 5% of the global total, accounted for nearly 20% of global imports in 2000. By 2009, America's share had dropped to 13%.

In other words, times have changed. The spending power of the U.S. consumer has diminished on both a relative and absolute basis. The purchasing power of consumers in developing countries, in contrast, has accelerated. Where in the past factory workers in Asia would trudge off to work on Saturday morning, today they are more likely to head for the local shopping malls for a day of socializing and shopping. Shanghai, Dubai, Mumbai, Ho Chi Minh City, Istanbul, São Paulo—any first-time visitor to these emerging cities is struck by the vigor and vitality of the local consumer, out in force and shopping in an air-conditioned mall that might be mistaken, in some cases, for being located in Short Hills, New Jersey, St. Charles, Missouri or Santa Clara, California. Granted, those trolling the shopping centers on the weekends in the emerging markets are the lucky few relative to the rest of the general population. But the size and scale of these urban buyers, and their pent-up demand for electronic goods, appliances, automobiles, skin-care products, clothing, and other goods, have reached the point whereby emerging market consumers are increasingly setting global trends, leading in global fashion, and driving global sales in a number of industries. In a seminal shift, global consumption is tilting towards the developing countries and away from the United States, Europe and the West.

Thrift and austerity are fast becoming the norm in the West just as conspicuous consumption is rapidly becoming the rage in places like Brazil, India, Turkey and other emerging markets. Emblematic of this trend, China's automobile market is now larger than that of America. While total U.S. vehicle sales imploded in 2009, dropping by over 20% from the prior year, vehicles sales in China exploded, surging roughly 45%. General Motors sold more cars in China last year than in the United States. GM's automobile sales to China soared to over 1.8 million vehicles in 2009, a 67% annual rise that helped offset plunging sales at home and helped stabilize a company that ultimately had to file for bankruptcy. Sales increased by another 28% in 2010. In other words, what is now good for China is good for General Motors, a market leader in China. Many European automakers are enjoying the same robust growth in China. In fact, what is the largest car company in China? Volkswagen.

Given exploding automobile demand in China, soaring cell phone usage in India, and skyrocketing demand for luxury goods in Turkey, we expect more U.S. and Europe investment to shift or tilt towards the developing countries in the coming decade. As the accompanying chart highlights, personal consumption expenditures have soared in the developing countries over the past decade and are likely to continue rising over the medium term. Indeed, between 1990 and 2010, personal consumption expenditures in emerging markets rose fivefold, from $2.4 trillion in 1990 to roughly $12.4 trillion in 2010. In the process, the developing countries' share of global consumption has soared, from 19.4% in 1990 to roughly 34% today.

All of the above should not be read as a sign that the U.S. and Europe are giving up on each other, however; rather, the coming shift reflects the simple yet glaring fact that many U.S. and European multinationals are behind the curve when it comes to having an in-country

Developed Countries are Underweight in Emerging Markets

Foreign direct investment (FDI) position abroad, percent of total to developing markets, annually

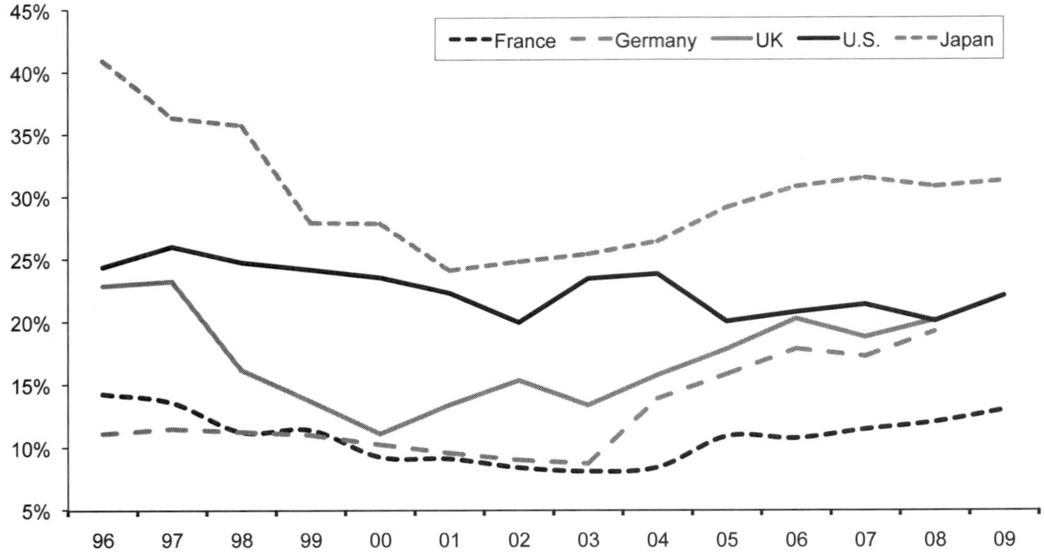

Source: Bureau of Economic Analysis, Banque de France, Bundesbank, JETRO, U.K. Office for National Statistics
Data for Japan, U.S., and France through 2009, all others through 2008
Note: Developing nations total does not include FDI to offshore financial centers or in the case of the U.S. the other Western Hemisphere where funds are frequently re-deployed to other destinations.

presence in many key emerging markets. Rather than having too much investment in such markets, as is commonly assumed, there is too little.

To this point, the bulk of America's global infrastructure—foreign capital stock, overseas workforce, R&D expenditures, foreign affiliates—is sunk in Europe, Canada and Japan. Of the $2.3 trillion U.S. firms have invested overseas since 2000, roughly 70% was directed at the developed markets. U.S. investment in Ireland last decade was roughly 35% greater than combined U.S. investment in the fabled BRIC countries.

Other key metrics tell a similar tale. According to figures from the Bureau of Economic Analysis, more than 80% of the R&D conducted by U.S. foreign affiliates takes place in developed markets. This is despite all the chatter about the millions of science and engineering graduates being pumped out by Chinese and Indian universities each year.

Even on the employment front, the bias remains towards wealthy, high-wage countries. In 2008, the last year of available data, U.S. affiliates employed just over 10 million foreign workers worldwide, with the bulk of this workforce toiling in the developed countries. Many in America blame China for declining U.S. manufacturing employment—yet the combined number of workers employed by U.S. affiliates in Germany, France and the United Kingdom is more than double those employed in China. While America's global manufacturing workforce is slowly shifting towards the developing world, over half of this cohort is still located in Europe, Australia, Canada and Japan.

And where it matters the most—corporate earnings—it is the developed countries that still yield the greatest windfall to U.S. companies. Since 2000 rich countries have accounted for roughly 70% of U.S. foreign affiliate income, a proxy for global earnings.

All of the above suggests that the global infrastructure of Corporate America and Corporate Europe is presently configured for a bygone era in which the developed countries drove the global economy. Since the late 1950s, the principal focus of U.S. multinationals has been on the developed countries, a strategy that has served them well given the wealthy consumer markets and availability of skilled labor in these locations.

Many European companies face the same dilemma. The U.S. is not the only country that is underweight in its investment in the developing markets; France, Germany, Japan and the United Kingdom are as well. While EU FDI to developing countries has accelerated, it has done so from a very low base. The EU's FDI links to China, for instance, are weak, largely because of Chinese barriers and concerns over intellectual property. According to latest comparable global data from Eurostat, EU FDI in China in 2008 was 26 times less than in North America; over 15 times less than in Wider Europe; almost 6 times less than in Rising Asia; almost 5 times less than in the Caribbean and in Latin America; almost 3 times less than in Africa; and half of EU FDI in Russia.

Nonetheless, European companies provide more FDI than North American or Japanese companies in each of the BRIC countries. EU FDI outflows to the BRICs are directed primarily to Russia and Brazil, rather than to China or India.[2]

EU goods exporters have also withstood the challenge of rising economies better than Japan or the United States. Research by Angela Cheptea, Lionel Fontagne and Soledad Zignago offers evidence that over the past 15 years the EU has essentially maintained its 19% market share of world exports, despite the rise of China, which tripled its performance and on the eve of the recession accounted for 16.1% of world market shares. In contrast, Japan and the U.S. each lost around 6% in market shares, so that the U.S. accounted for 12.5% and Japan 8.6% of world market shares in 2007. And while North America is the #1 regional market for EU goods (23% of EU total) and the U.S. is the #1 country market (19%) for EU goods, its share has declined 9% over the past decade. Between 1999 and 2008 total EU export shares to the old member states, the advanced OECD countries and Asia declined, while total EU export shares increased to the new member states, the BRICs and to the rest of the world outside the advanced countries and Asia. The EU is the most important trading partner for the BRICs—especially for Russia, Brazil and India. Of the major developed economies, the EU is the top supplier of goods to the developing nations—by a significant margin—and has enjoyed far greater growth rates than either Japan or the United States.[3]

---

[2] The accompanying figure highlights that on a country basis Japan has the highest percentage of its foreign investment assets in developing markets (31% of the total in 2009), followed by the United States, the United Kingdom, Germany and France.

[3] Angela Cheptea, Lionel Fontagne, Soledad Zignago, "European Export Performance," Document de Travail, No. 2010 – 12, Centre d'Etudes Prospectives et d' Informations Internationales (CEPII); Hamilton and Quinlan, *Globalization and Europe*, op. cit.

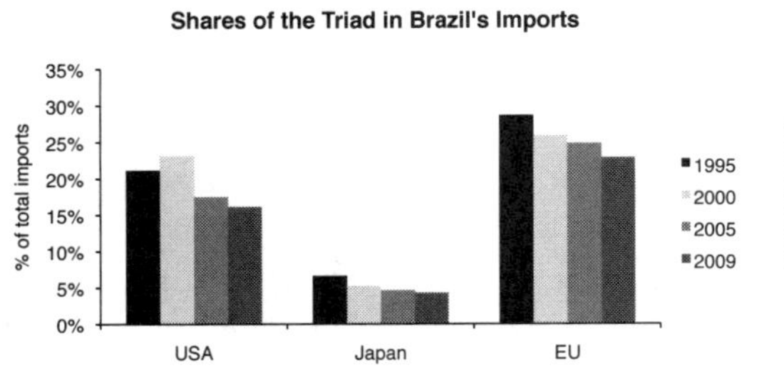

Sources: IMF; WTO; European Competitiveness Report 2009.

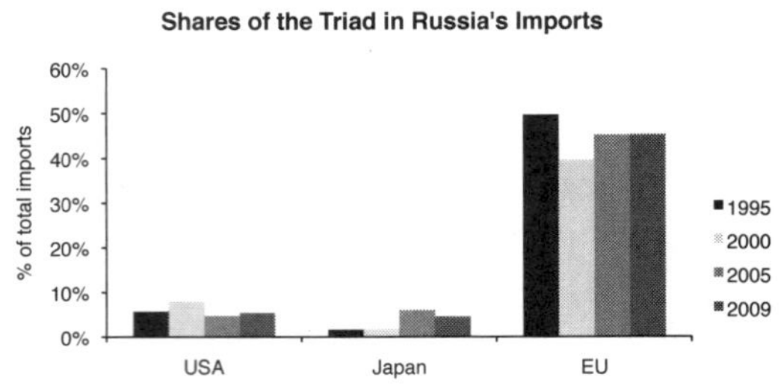

Sources: IMF; WTO; European Competitiveness Report 2009.

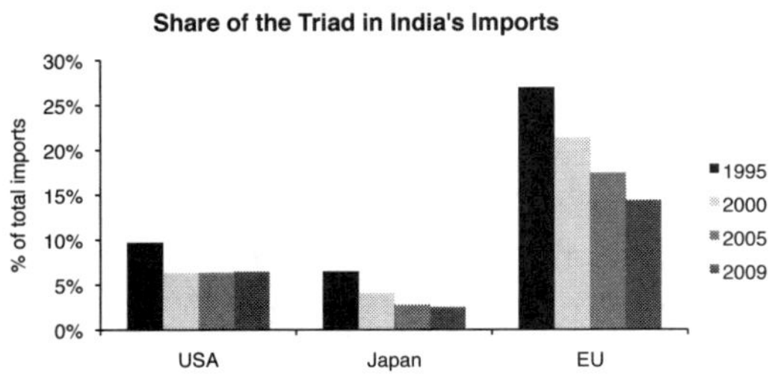

Sources: IMF; WTO; European Competitiveness Report 2009.

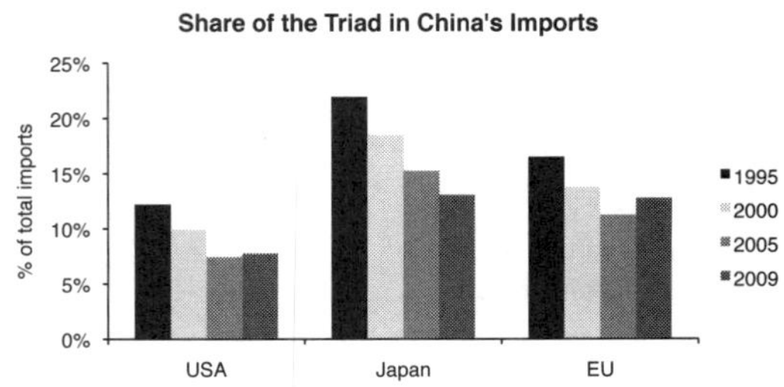

Sources: IMF; WTO; European Competitiveness Report 2009.

Despite this shift, EU exports to key developing countries remain relatively low. In essence, many EU companies are "overweight" in their export presence in developed countries and "underweight" in their exports to high growth developing markets. For instance, even though EU goods exports to China have been growing at a 30% annual average growth rate over the past decade—faster than any other goods export destination—China is only the sixth largest regional destination for EU goods exports. The EU exports more to Switzerland than to China. Moreover, the EU has trade deficits in goods with all BRICs except India.

In the years ahead, however, emerging markets will drive global growth and come to possess the key endowments—expanding consumer markets, a skilled labor force, critical resources—desired by both U.S. and European multinationals.

That said, the irony is that at precisely the moment when U.S. and European multinationals need to build out their presence in the developing nations, the latter have become pickier and somewhat less welcoming of foreign investment. U.S. oil companies, for instance, increasingly confront resource nationalism in a number of petro-states. Both U.S. and European firms have found it slow going in markets such as China and India. In general, a whiff of investment protectionism permeates many key developing countries at a time when Western companies are seeking to increase their local presence.

The bottom line: if developing countries—with their burgeoning middle classes and massive infrastructure needs—represent the future of global economic activity, then many U.S. and European companies are not ready for the future. The race is on to correct this strategic gap. That said, however, we repeat again that should investment flows of the U.S. and Europe begin to shift more towards the developing nations, as we suspect, this should not be viewed as catastrophic for the transatlantic economy. The shift reflects the reality that global economic activity is dispersing to multiple engines of economic dynamism and growth.

U.S. and European companies are challenged to boost their export shares and their corporate presence in fast-growing new markets, rather than overly relying on marginal increases in slower-growing "legacy" markets; without at the same time relinquishing core developed world markets, which in many sectors still provide the foundation for their competitive position.

We think of the shift as a next—and perhaps healthier—phase of globalization. Whereas globalization between 1980 and 2005 was largely about the further integration of the U.S. and Europe, globalization in future will be more about the further integration of the developing countries into the global economy. The transatlantic economy will remain first among equals, but the spread of globalization to the other parts of the world, facilitated in part by rising U.S. and Europe investment levels, will become more prominent. This, in our opinion, represents a positive development for the transatlantic economy.

Austria & the United States
Investment and Trade Figures

Investment

Not surprisingly, America's direct investment position in Austria exceeds Austria's investment stakes in the U.S. American affiliates employed roughly three times as many workers in Austria than Austrian firms employed in the U.S.

Austria - U.S. Global Linkages, 2008

($ billions)

	U.S. in Austria	Austria in U.S.
Foreign Direct Investment* (2009)	18.2	2.9
Total Assets of Affiliates	41.8	13.8
Foreign Affiliate Sales	23.6	5.8
Value Added of Affiliates	6.5	1.3
Affiliate Employees	44,000	14,400

*Based on a historic-cost basis, data for 2009; all data for majority-owned nonbank affiliates

Trade

On a global basis, the U.S. received $5.5 billion, or 4.0% of the total goods Austria exported to the world in 2009, but the share going to the U.S. rises to 14.1% of the global total after excluding intra-EU trade, this is down from a high of 22.6% in 2004. Imports of U.S. goods constituted $2.3 billion, or 1.6% of the total amount Austria imported from the world the same year and 7.2% when intra-EU imports were removed from the global total, down from a share of nearly 20.6% at the start of the past decade.

Top Ten U.S. Imports from Austria, 2009 (in $ millions)

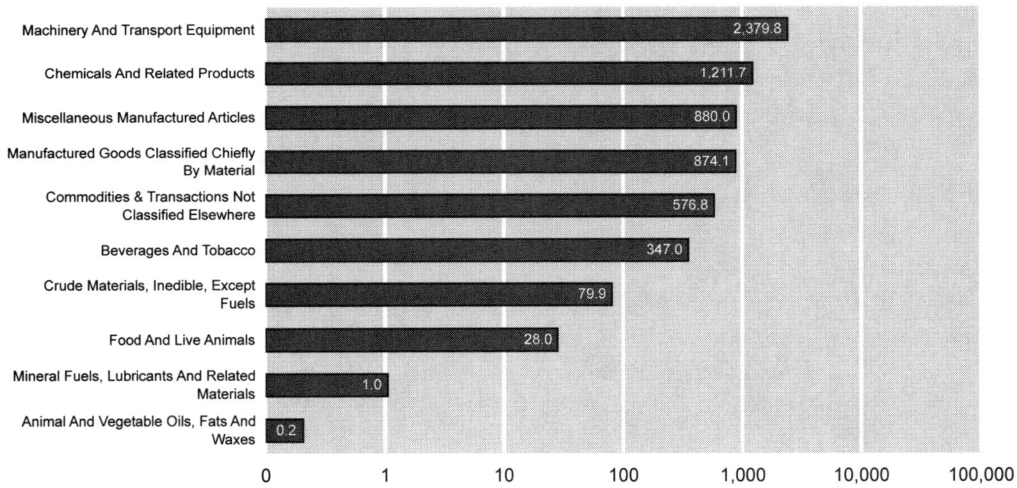

Source: Bureau of Economic Analysis, International Monetary Fund; Office of Trade and Industry Information

Belgium & the United States
Investment and Trade Figures

Investment

America's direct investment position in Belgium is nearly twice as large as Belgium's investment stakes in the U.S. U.S. direct investments in Belgium are increasingly made in the services sector and the manufacturing sector though the latter is larger in terms of jobs supported. Belgian affiliates employed 39% more workers in the U.S. than U.S. affiliates in Belgium. Value added by U.S. affiliates in Belgium totaled $22.5 billion in 2008, 30% more than that of Belgian affiliates in the United States.

Belgium - U.S. Global Linkages, 2008
($ billions)

	U.S. in Belgium	Belgium in U.S.
Foreign Direct Investment* (2009)	69.8	38.5
Total Assets of Affiliates	319.7	241.7
Foreign Affiliate Sales	138.9	66.7
Value Added of Affiliates	22.5	17.3
Affiliate Employees	129,000	179,300

*Based on a historic-cost basis, data for 2009; all data for majority-owned nonbank affiliates

Trade

The U.S. accounted for 5.4%, or $19.9 billion, of total exports from Belgium in 2009. The share of total exports rises to 22.2% when intra-EU trade is excluded, down from a high of 31.8% in 2002. Chemicals and manufactured goods lead the way as the top export categories. Regarding imports, the U.S. supplied 5.7% of total imports by Belgium in 2009, although the share rises to 19.9% after accounting for intra-EU trade.

Top Ten U.S. Imports from Belgium, 2009 (in $ millions)

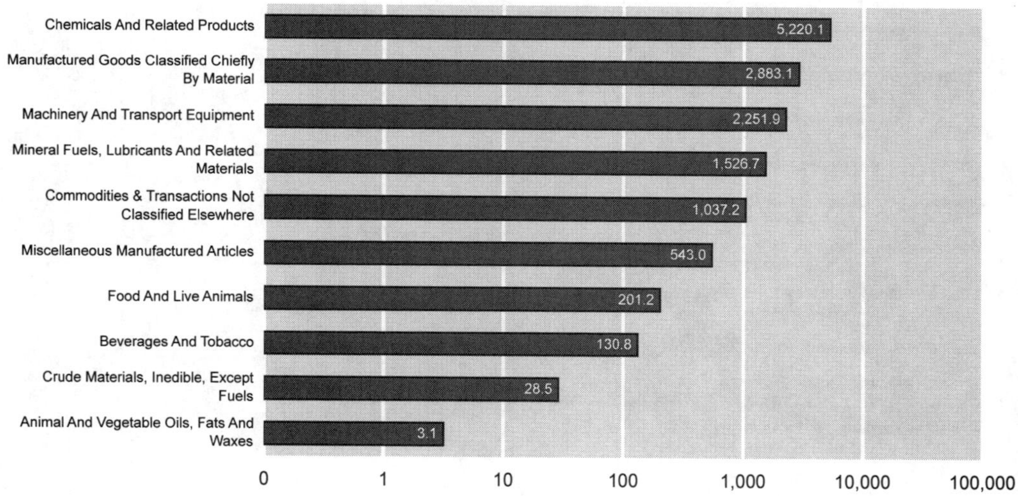

Source: Bureau of Economic Analysis, International Monetary Fund; Office of Trade and Industry Information

Bulgaria & the United States
Investment and Trade Figures

Investment

America's investment base in Bulgaria is rather small, although U.S. investment doubled from $300 million in 2008 to $600 million in 2009. U.S. affiliates employed 3,500 workers in 2008, placing Bulgaria 7th among the EU12 in terms of employment.

Bulgaria - U.S. Global Linkages, 2008
($ billions)

	U.S. in Bulgaria	Bulgaria in U.S.
Foreign Direct Investment* (2009)	0.6	-
Total Assets of Affiliates	1.8	-
Foreign Affiliate Sales	0.4	-
Value Added of Affiliates	0.1	-
Affiliate Employees	3,500	-

*Based on a historic-cost basis, data for 2009; all data for majority-owned nonbank affiliates

Trade

The U.S. accounted for just 1.6% of Bulgaria's total exports in 2009; the percentage rises to just 4.4% when intra-EU trade is excluded from the total, down from a high of 14.4% in 2001. Imports from the U.S. are rather small, totaling just $200 million in 2009, only 2.1% of Bulgaria's extra-EU imports.

Top Ten U.S. Imports from Bulgaria, 2009 (in $ millions)

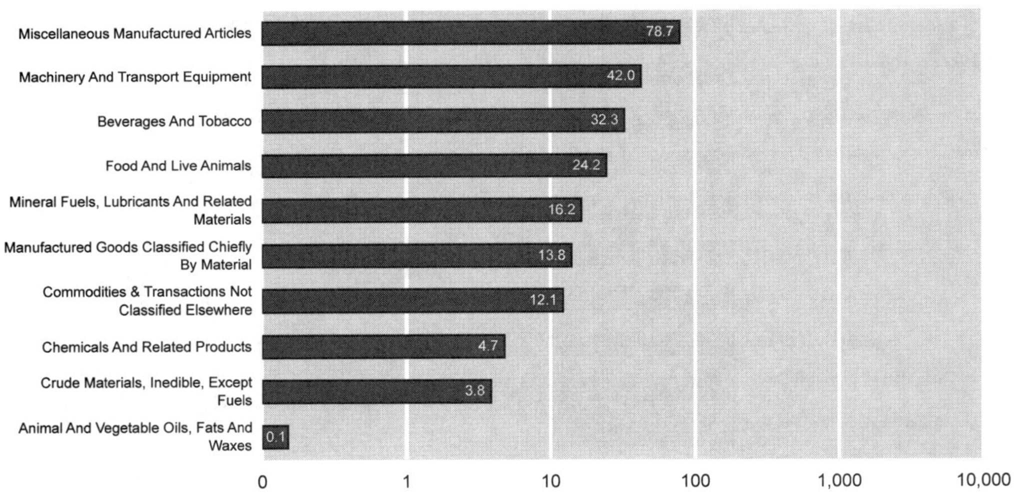

Source: Bureau of Economic Analysis, International Monetary Fund; Office of Trade and Industry Information

Cyprus & the United States
Investment and Trade Figures

Investment

Given the the country's small market the nation has not attracted much with regards to U.S. foreign direct investment relatively but it is currently over six times larger at $1.6 billion compared to investment levels seen in the middle of the decade.

Cyprus - U.S. Global Linkages, 2008
($ billions)

	U.S. in Cyprus	Cyprus in U.S.
Foreign Direct Investment* (2009)	1.6	-
Total Assets of Affiliates	4.4	0.019
Foreign Affiliate Sales	1.5	0.004
Value Added of Affiliates	0.4	-0.003
Affiliate Employees	1,500	-

*Based on a historic-cost basis, data for 2009; all data for majority-owned nonbank affiliates

Trade

Cyprus is an increasingly insignificant supplier of goods to the United States; the U.S. accounted for 1.4% of total exports in 2009. Imports from the U.S. were equally small in 2009, totaling $120 million, 1.5% of Cyprus' total imports from the world.

Top Ten U.S. Imports from Cyprus, 2009 (in $ millions)

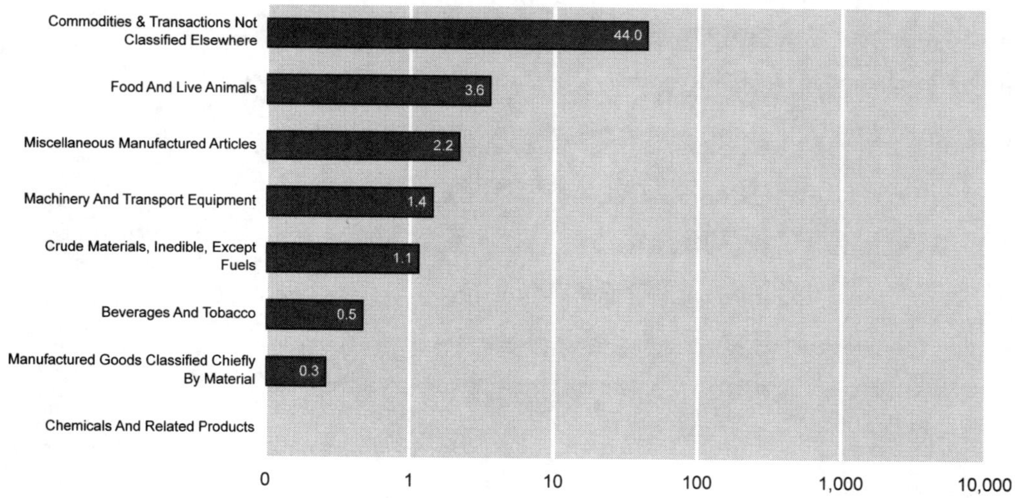

Source: Bureau of Economic Analysis, International Monetary Fund; Office of Trade and Industry Information

Czech Republic & the United States
Investment and Trade Figures

Investment

America's investment base in the Czech Republic is small but expanding, more than doubling since 2005. U.S. foreign direct investment totaled $5.9 billion on a historic cost basis in 2009. Value added by U.S.-owned affiliates totaled $4.8 billion. Affiliate employment in the Czech Republic (70,000 workers) is among the highest in Eastern Europe. Foreign investment from the Czech Republic in the U.S. is still relatively very small.

Czech Republic - U.S. Global Linkages, 2008
($ billions)

	U.S. in Czech Republic	Czech Republic in U.S.
Foreign Direct Investment* (2009)	5.9	0.028
Total Assets of Affiliates	17.4	0.006
Foreign Affiliate Sales	17.6	0.005
Value Added of Affiliates	4.8	0.001
Affiliate Employees	70,000	-

*Based on a historic-cost basis, data for 2009; all data for majority-owned nonbank affiliates

Trade

U.S. imports from the Czech Republic totaled $1.8 billion in 2009, more than double the amount imported at the start of this decade, but down from $2.6 billion in 2008. Imports consist of transportation equipment and electronic machinery. U.S. imports make-up only 10.4% of the country's extra-EU trade, down from 22.5% in 2001, as the Czech Republic diversifies its export base. Czech imports from the U.S. were relatively small, totaling $1.2 billion in 2009.

Top Ten U.S. Imports from Czech Republic, 2009 (in $ millions)

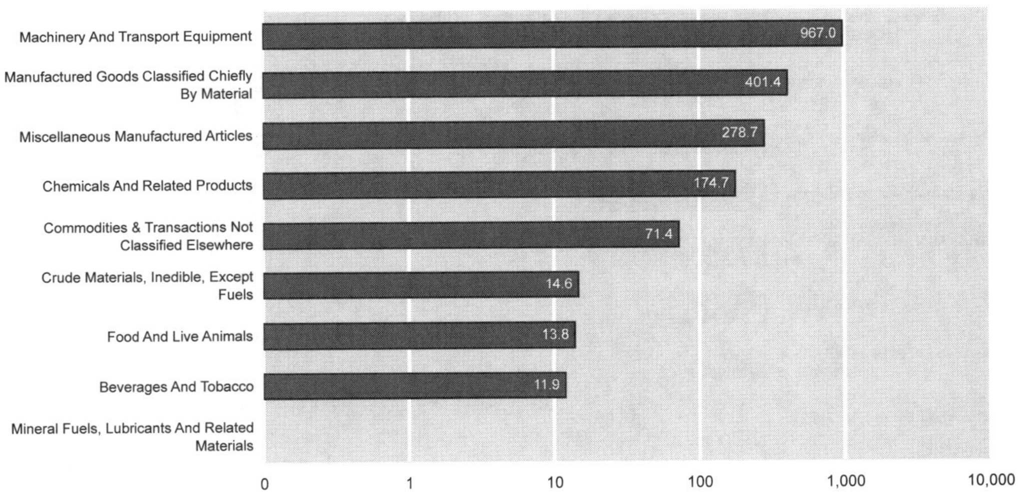

Source: Bureau of Economic Analysis, International Monetary Fund; Office of Trade and Industry Information

Denmark & the United States
Investment and Trade Figures

Investment

Bilateral investment between the U.S. and Denmark favored Denmark in 2009 with the U.S. investing nearly double that which Denmark invested in the United States. Affiliate sales in the U.S. market hit $16.2 billion in 2008 while U.S. affiliate sales in Denmark were $23.4 billion. The affiliate employment balance favors Denmark, with U.S. affiliates in Denmark employing 45% more than Danish affiliates in the U.S.

Denmark - U.S. Global Linkages, 2008
($ billions)

	U.S. in Denmark	Denmark in U.S.
Foreign Direct Investment* (2009)	9.3	5.2
Total Assets of Affiliates	42.6	41.0
Foreign Affiliate Sales	23.4	16.2
Value Added of Affiliates	12.2	4.0
Affiliate Employees	38,900	26,800

*Based on a historic-cost basis, data for 2009; all data for majority-owned nonbank affiliates

Trade

Exports from Denmark to the U.S. totaled $5.7 billion in 2009, or 6.0% of the global total. Excluding intra-EU trade, the share of exports to the U.S. rises to 18.1%. Danish imports from the U.S. totaled $2.7 billion the same year, 3.2% of the global total and 10.7% excluding intra-EU trade. Machinery and transportation equipment, chemicals, and misc. manufactured articles dominate U.S. imports from the country.

Top Ten U.S. Imports from Denmark, 2009 (in $ millions)

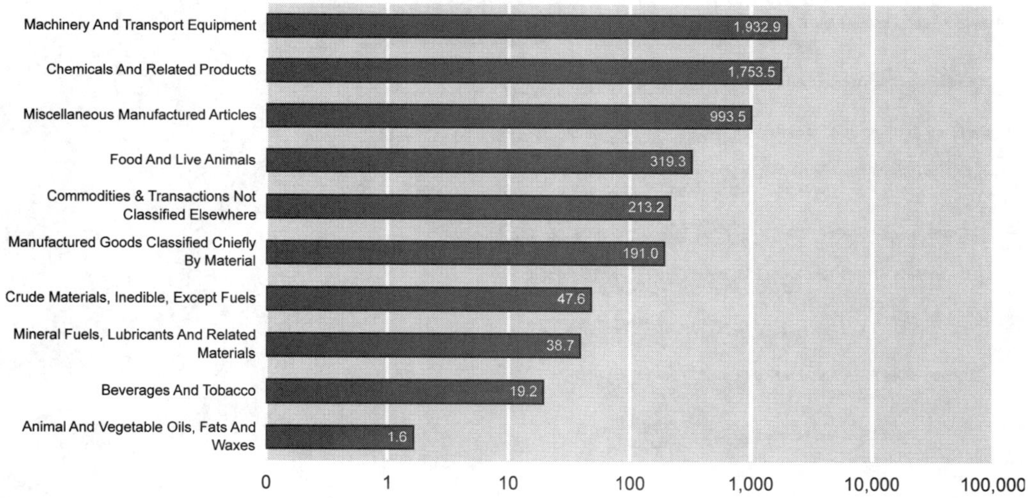

Source: Bureau of Economic Analysis, International Monetary Fund; Office of Trade and Industry Information

Estonia & the United States
Investment and Trade Figures

Investment

America's direct investment base in Estonia is one of the smallest out of all the EU12 countries. U.S. affiliates employed 2,400 people in 2008, placing Estonia 8th among the EU12 in terms of employment. U.S. investment in the country is expected to increase as the Baltic states emerge as a key gateway to Russia and beyond.

Estonia - U.S. Global Linkages, 2008
($ billions)

	U.S. in Estonia	Estonia in U.S.
Foreign Direct Investment* (2009)	0.04	-
Total Assets of Affiliates	0.35	-
Foreign Affiliate Sales	0.43	-
Value Added of Affiliates	0.12	-
Affiliate Employees	2,400	-

*Based on a historic-cost basis, data for 2009; all data for majority-owned nonbank affiliates

Trade

U.S. imports from Estonia totaled $390 million in 2009, over five times greater than imports at the start of the decade, but reflecting a significant drop from 2008. Mineral fuels, lubricants and related materials made up over half of U.S. imports from Estonia in 2008 at $207 million, but have fallen significantly to $47 million in 2009. Estonia imports very little from the U.S., only 1.3% of total imports and 6.5% excluding intra-EU imports come from the United States.

Top Ten U.S. Imports from Estonia, 2009 (in $ millions)

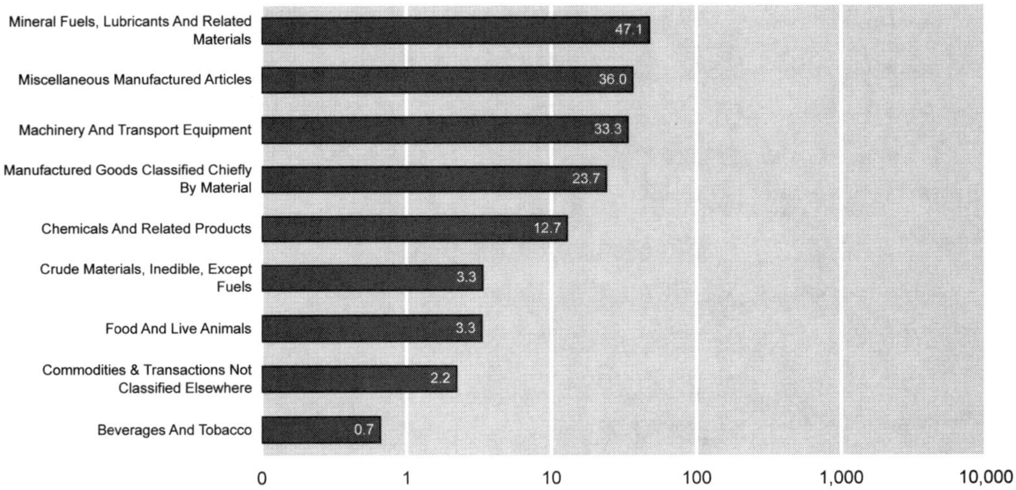

Source: Bureau of Economic Analysis, International Monetary Fund; Office of Trade and Industry Information

Finland & the United States
Investment and Trade Figures

Investment

The direct investment balance favors the United States, with Finnish investment in the U.S. totaling $7.6 billion in 2009 versus just $2.1 billion of U.S. investment in Finland. The affiliate employment balance slightly favors the U.S. by 7,700 jobs.

Finland - U.S. Global Linkages, 2008
($ billions)

	U.S. in Finland	Finland in U.S.
Foreign Direct Investment* (2009)	2.1	7.6
Total Assets of Affiliates	19.7	55.4
Foreign Affiliate Sales	14.5	20.5
Value Added of Affiliates	3.8	4.4
Affiliate Employees	23,800	31,500

*Based on a historic-cost basis, data for 2009; all data for majority-owned nonbank affiliates

Trade

The U.S. received $5 billion, or 7.9% of the total goods exported to the world in 2009, but the share going to the U.S. rises to 17.8% of the global total after excluding intra-EU trade. Imports of U.S. goods constituted $1.3 billion, or 2.1% of the total amount imported from the world the same year and 6.1% when intra-EU imports are removed from the global total, down from a high of nearly 22% in 1998.

Top Ten U.S. Imports from Finland, 2009 (in $ millions)

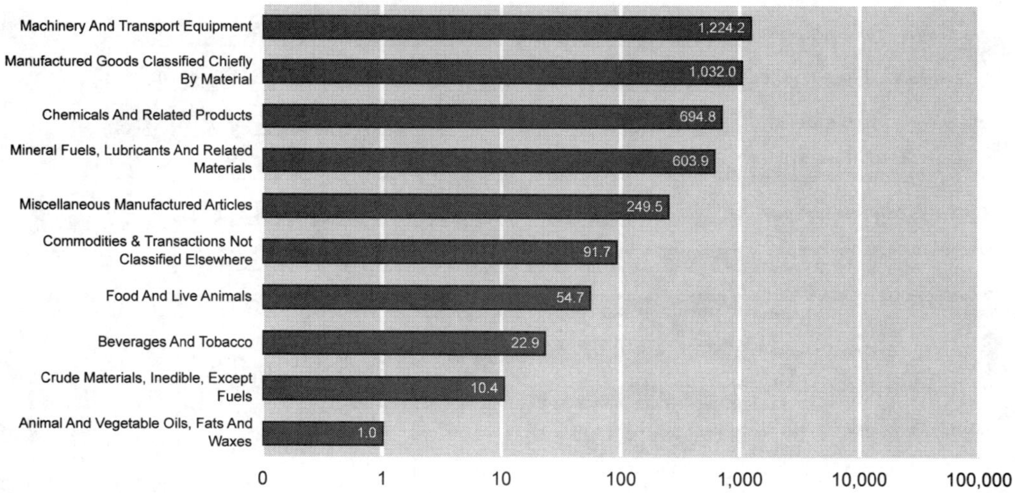

Source: Bureau of Economic Analysis, International Monetary Fund; Office of Trade and Industry Information

France & the United States
Investment and Trade Figures

Investment

The direct investment balance favors the U.S., with U.S. investment in France ($85.8 billion) just 45%of total French investment in the U.S. in 2009 ($189.3 billion). The U.S. is a significant market for French firms, with U.S. affiliates of French firms recording $278.5 billion in sales during 2008. The employment balance now favors France. U.S. and French affiliates combined employed over 1 million workers in 2008.

France - U.S. Global Linkages, 2008
($ billions)

	U.S. in France	France in U.S.
Foreign Direct Investment* (2009)	85.8	189.3
Total Assets of Affiliates	334.2	1,263.2
Foreign Affiliate Sales	231.9	278.5
Value Added of Affiliates	56.7	57.5
Affiliate Employees	604,400	550,200

*Based on a historic-cost basis, data for 2009; all data for majority-owned nonbank affiliates

Trade

The U.S. accounted for 5.7% of total exports from France in 2009, but a share of 14.7% of total exports when intra-EU trade is excluded. Products exported to the U.S. ran the gamut, from heavy machinery and transportation equipment to chemicals and agricultural products. Regarding imports, the U.S. supplied 4.7% of total imports by France in 2009, although the share rises to 15.2% after accounting for intra-EU trade, down from 25.2% in 1999.

Top Ten U.S. Imports from France, 2009 (in $ millions)

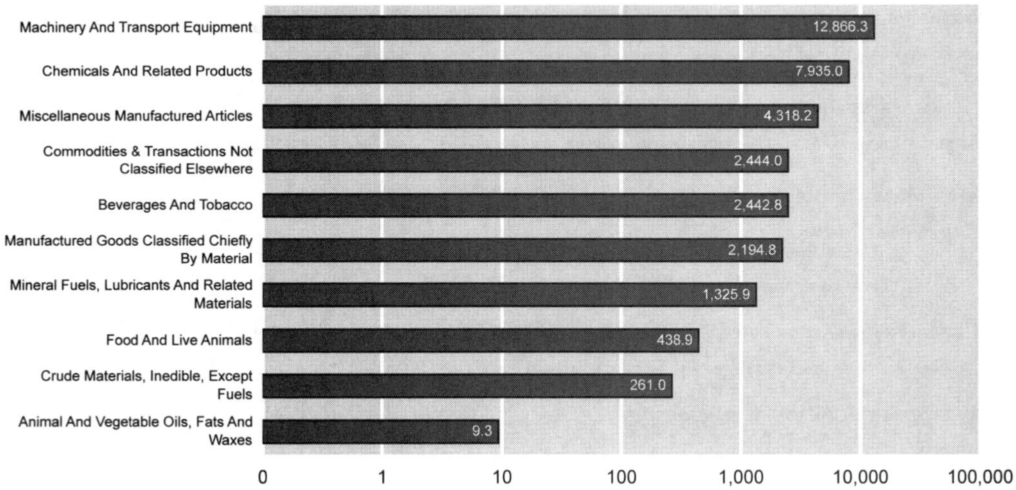

Source: Bureau of Economic Analysis, International Monetary Fund; Office of Trade and Industry Information

Germany & the United States

Investment and Trade Figures

Investment

The investment balance favors the U.S., with U.S. investment in Germany totaling $116.8 billion in 2009 versus $218.2 billion of German investment in the U.S. America's total asset base in Germany was only about one-third that of Germany's asset base in the U.S in 2008, although the value added by American affiliates operating in Germany ($94.1 billion in 2008) exceeded that of German affiliates in the United States. The employment balance favored Germany in 2008. U.S. and German affiliates combined employed over 1.2 million workers.

Germany - U.S. Global Linkages, 2008
($ billions)

	U.S. in Germany	Germany in U.S.
Foreign Direct Investment* (2009)	116.8	218.2
Total Assets of Affiliates	546.5	1,583.0
Foreign Affiliate Sales	347.4	394.1
Value Added of Affiliates	94.1	82.4
Affiliate Employees	621,300	614,200

*Based on a historic-cost basis, data for 2009; all data for majority-owned nonbank affiliates

Trade

Germany is the largest European exporter to the U.S., with exports to the U.S. totaling $74.7 billion in 2009, a drastic decline from $104 billion in 2008. The U.S. accounted for just over 6.7% of total German exports, but 17.8% when intra-EU trade flows are excluded. Imports from the U.S. into Germany totaled $39.6 billion—that equates to 4.3% of total German imports or 12.1% excluding intra-EU trade. Nearly three-fourths of U.S. imports from Germany consist of chemicals and machinery and transportation equipment.

Top Ten U.S. Imports from Germany, 2009 (in $ millions)

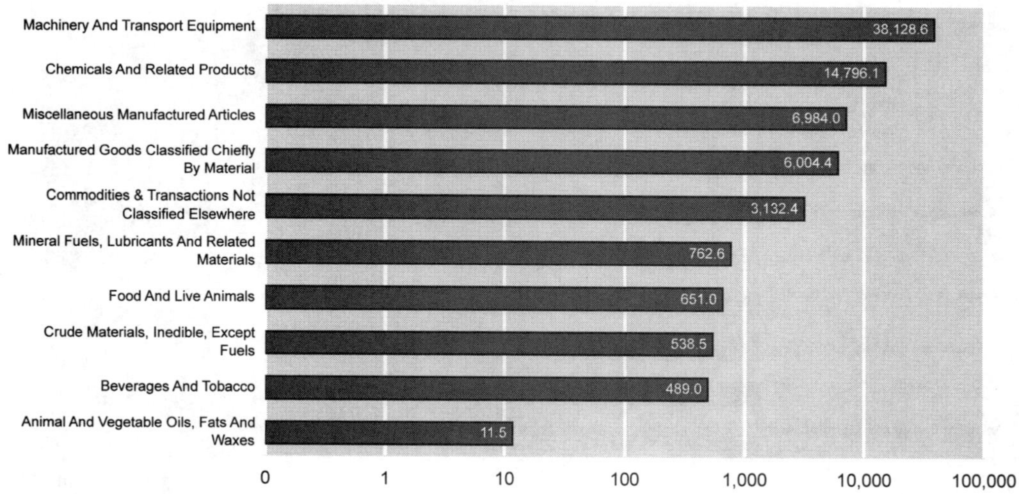

Source: Bureau of Economic Analysis, International Monetary Fund; Office of Trade and Industry Information

Greece & the United States
Investment and Trade Figures

Investment

The investment balance clearly favors Greece with America's investment position totaling $2 billion in 2009. No data is available regarding the investment position of Greece in the U.S. U.S. affiliate sales of just $8.7 billion in 2008 ranked among the lowest in the EU.

Greece - U.S. Global Linkages, 2008
($ billions)

	U.S. in Greece	Greece in U.S.
Foreign Direct Investment* (2009)	2.0	-
Total Assets of Affiliates	9.9	3.0
Foreign Affiliate Sales	8.7	2.1
Value Added of Affiliates	3.9	-0.34
Affiliate Employees	17,000	3,800

*Based on a historic-cost basis, data for 2009; all data for majority-owned nonbank affiliates

Trade

Greek exports to the U.S. totaled nearly $1 billion in 2009, down from a peak OF $1.28 billion in 2008. Imports from the U.S. amounted to $1.8 billion. The U.S. accounted for 4.9% of total exports but were 13.2% excluding intra-EU exports. Greek imports from the U.S. were 3.0% of total imports from the world in 2009 and 8.6% excluding intra-EU imports.

Top Ten U.S. Imports from Greece, 2009 (in $ millions)

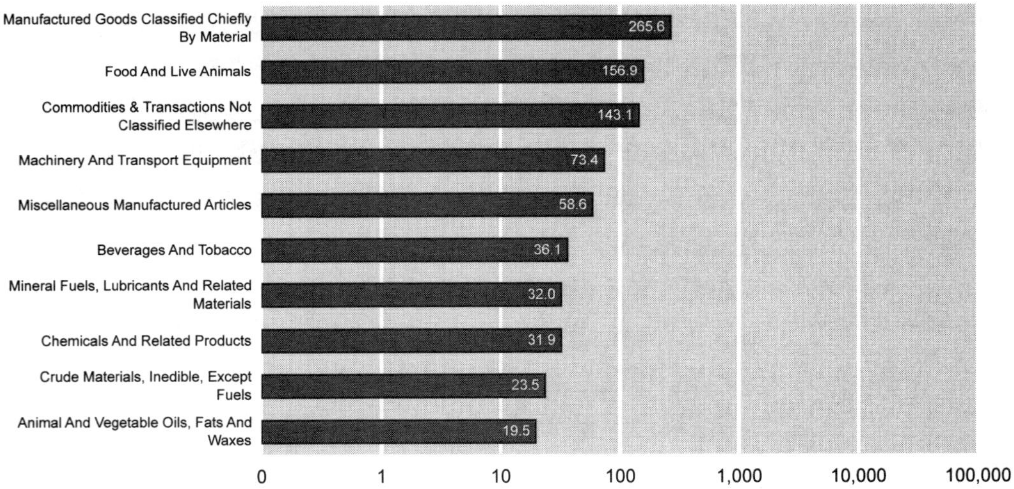

Source: Bureau of Economic Analysis, International Monetary Fund; Office of Trade and Industry Information

Hungary & the United States
Investment and Trade Figures

Investment

America's investment base in Hungary is among the largest in central Europe, with U.S. foreign direct investment totaling $9.3 billion on a historic cost basis in 2009, almost double that of 2008. Value added by U.S.-owned affiliates totaled $5.1 billion. Affiliate employment in Hungary (61,300 workers) ranked third among EU12 countries. Hungarian affiliate investment in the U.S. is suppressed for 2009 to avoid disclosure of data of individual companies.

Hungary - U.S. Global Linkages, 2008
($ billions)

	U.S. in Hungary	Hungary in U.S.
Foreign Direct Investment* (2009)	9.3	-
Total Assets of Affiliates	37.1	-
Foreign Affiliate Sales	22.3	-
Value Added of Affiliates	5.1	0.02
Affiliate Employees	61,300	400

*Based on a historic-cost basis, data for 2009; all data for majority-owned nonbank affiliates

Trade

U.S. imports from Hungary totaled $1.9 billion in 2009, up from $620 million in 1997. The bulk of imports consists of parts and components, including those used in nuclear reactors. Hungarian exports to the World and the U.S have fallen from 2008 to 2009, 23.2% and 24.8% respectively. Hungary bought $1.2 billion worth of U.S. goods in 2009, 5% of the country's extra-EU imports.

Top Ten U.S. Imports from Hungary, 2009 (in $ millions)

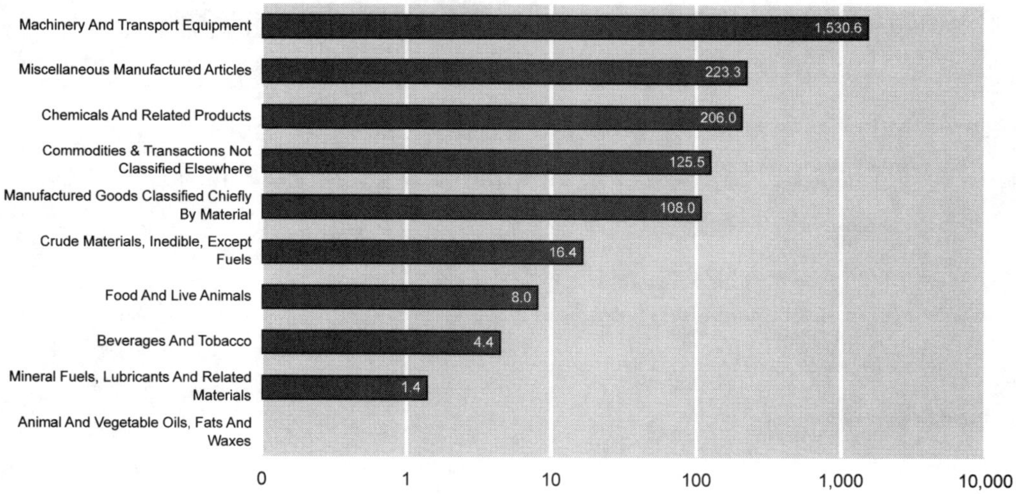

Source: Bureau of Economic Analysis, International Monetary Fund; Office of Trade and Industry Information

Ireland & the United States
Investment and Trade Figures

Investment

The investment balance favors Ireland, with U.S. investment in Ireland totaling some $165.9 billion in 2009 versus $32.6 billion of Ireland's investment in the U.S. Value added by U.S. affiliates totaled $55.6 billion in 2008. The affiliate employment balance favors Ireland by roughly 23,000 jobs.

Ireland - U.S. Global Linkages, 2008
($ billions)

	U.S. in Ireland	Ireland in U.S.
Foreign Direct Investment* (2009)	165.9	32.6
Total Assets of Affiliates	650.5	88.4
Foreign Affiliate Sales	249.7	27.8
Value Added of Affiliates	55.6	6.7
Affiliate Employees	89,000	66,200

*Based on a historic-cost basis, data for 2009; all data for majority-owned nonbank affiliates

Trade

The U.S. is a key export destination for Ireland, with exports to the U.S. totaling $24.3 billion in 2009. The U.S. accounted for 21.0% of total exports from Ireland; when intra-EU exports are excluded from the total, the share of exports to the U.S. jumps to 54.1%. Over seventy percent of U.S. imports from Ireland consist of chemicals and related products. The U.S. is also a key supplier to Ireland, with the U.S. accounting for 16.8% of total imports into Ireland in 2009 and 46.4% after excluding intra-EU trade.

Top Ten U.S. Imports from Ireland, 2009 (in $ millions)

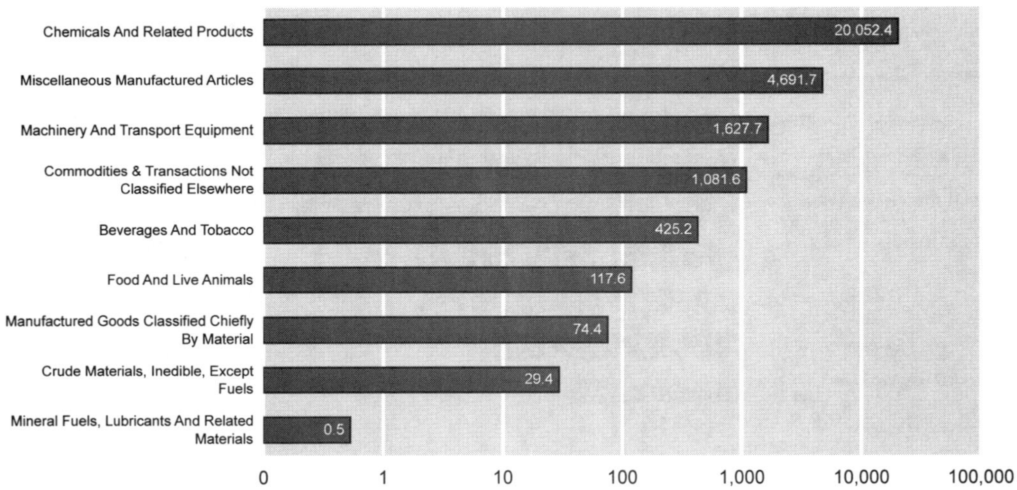

Source: Bureau of Economic Analysis, International Monetary Fund; Office of Trade and Industry Information

Italy & the United States
Investment and Trade Figures

Investment

The investment balance favors Italy—U.S. investment in Italy totaled $31.5 billion in 2009, versus the $9.7 billion invested by Italian firms in the U.S. U.S. investment was mostly concentrated in manufacturing, wholesale trade, information, and finance. Value added by U.S. affiliates in Italy was over three times as much as that produced by Italian affiliates in the U.S. With U.S. foreign affiliates employing some 232,900 workers in 2008, the employment balance clearly favors Italy.

Italy - U.S. Global Linkages, 2008
($ billions)

	U.S. in Italy	Italy in U.S.
Foreign Direct Investment* (2009)	31.5	9.7
Total Assets of Affiliates	139.9	174.8
Foreign Affiliate Sales	129.3	38.6
Value Added of Affiliates	33.0	9.0
Affiliate Employees	232,900	86,500

*Based on a historic-cost basis, data for 2009; all data for majority-owned nonbank affiliates

Trade

The U.S. accounted for 5.9% of total exports from Italy in 2009, but a share of 13.8% of total exports after excluding intra-EU trade, down from 26.6% at the start of the decade. Machinery, transportation goods, and manufactured goods were the top exports to the U.S. Regarding imports, the U.S. supplied 3.2% of total imports by Italy in 2009, although the share rises to 7.5% after accounting for intra-EU imports.

Top Ten U.S. Imports from Italy, 2009 (in $ millions)

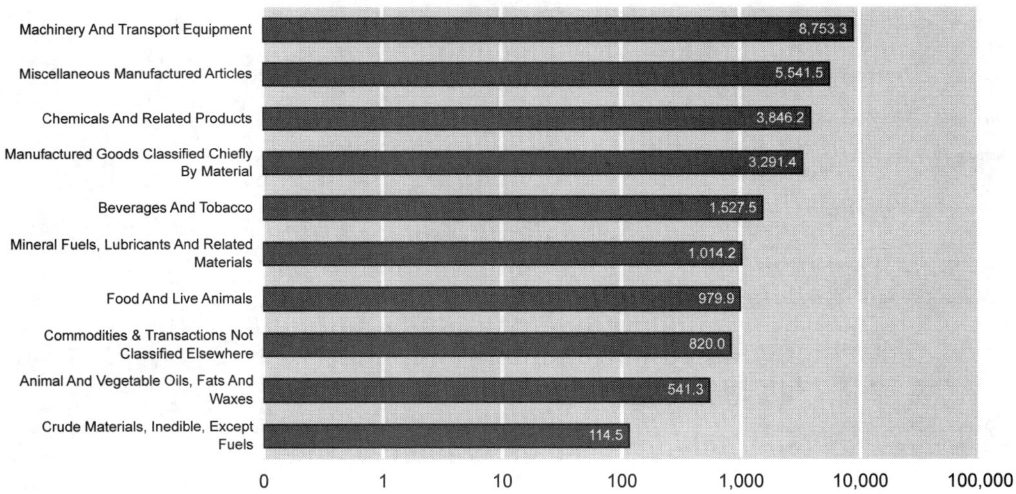

Source: Bureau of Economic Analysis, International Monetary Fund; Office of Trade and Industry Information

Latvia & the United States
Investment and Trade Figures

Investment

Latvia has attracted the least amount of foreign direct investment from the United States. Investment linkages are slightly negative but are expected to gradually expand over the next decade. U.S. affiliates supported only 1,000 jobs, the lowest among EU12 countries, but more than double the jobs supported in Latvia in 2000.

Latvia - U.S. Global Linkages, 2008
($ billions)

	U.S. in Latvia	Latvia in U.S.
Foreign Direct Investment* (2009)	-0.006	-0.001
Total Assets of Affiliates	0.54	-
Foreign Affiliate Sales	0.29	-
Value Added of Affiliates	0.01	-
Affiliate Employees	1,000	-

*Based on a historic-cost basis, data for 2009; all data for majority-owned nonbank affiliates

Trade

U.S. imports from Latvia have increased steadily over the past decade, with imports consisting mainly of mineral fuels, beverages and tobacco and machinery and transport equipment. The U.S. imported $120 million worth of goods from Latvia in 2009. The U.S. is a small supplier to Latvia, with Latvian imports of U.S. goods totaling just $80 million in 2009, 3.4% of Latvia's extra-EU imports.

Top Ten U.S. Imports from Latvia, 2009 (in $ millions)

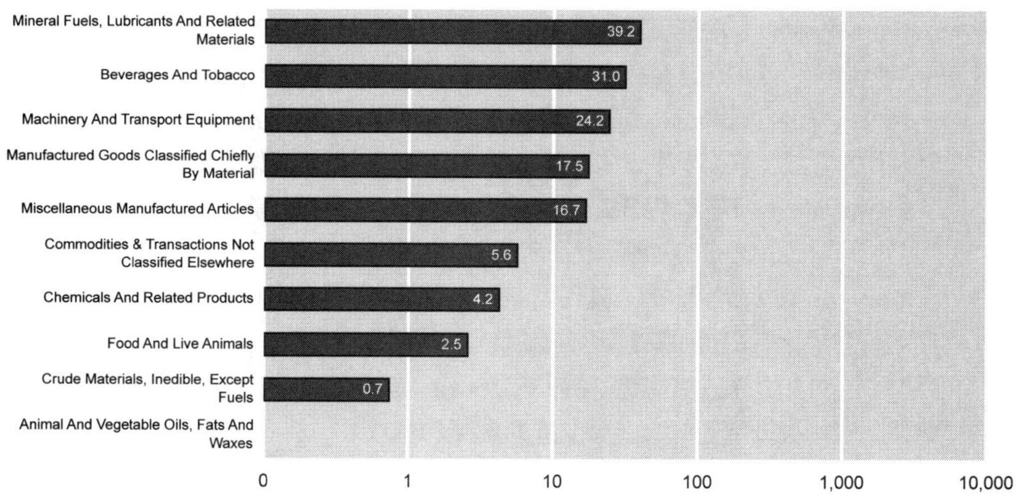

Source: Bureau of Economic Analysis, International Monetary Fund; Office of Trade and Industry Information

Lithuania & the United States
Investment and Trade Figures

Investment

Lithuania has yet to attract significant levels of U.S. foreign direct investment, however, as the Baltic states develop and become more integrated into the greater European market, U.S. investment flows are expected to increase.

Lithuania - U.S. Global Linkages, 2008
($ billions)

	U.S. in Lithuania	Lithuania in U.S.
Foreign Direct Investment* (2009)	0.1	-0.009
Total Assets of Affiliates	0.3	-
Foreign Affiliate Sales	0.3	-
Value Added of Affiliates	0.1	-
Affiliate Employees	1,600	-

*Based on a historic-cost basis, data for 2009; all data for majority-owned nonbank affiliates

Trade

U.S. imports from Lithuania rose from just $6 million in 1997 to a record $760 million in 2008. Rising shipments of mineral fuel led the import surge. But U.S. imports from Lithuania slumped in 2009 to $490 million. Lithuanian imports from the U.S. fell from $540 million in 2008 to $200 million in 2009, or 2.7% of the country's extra-EU imports.

Top Ten U.S. Imports from Lithuania, 2009 (in $ millions)

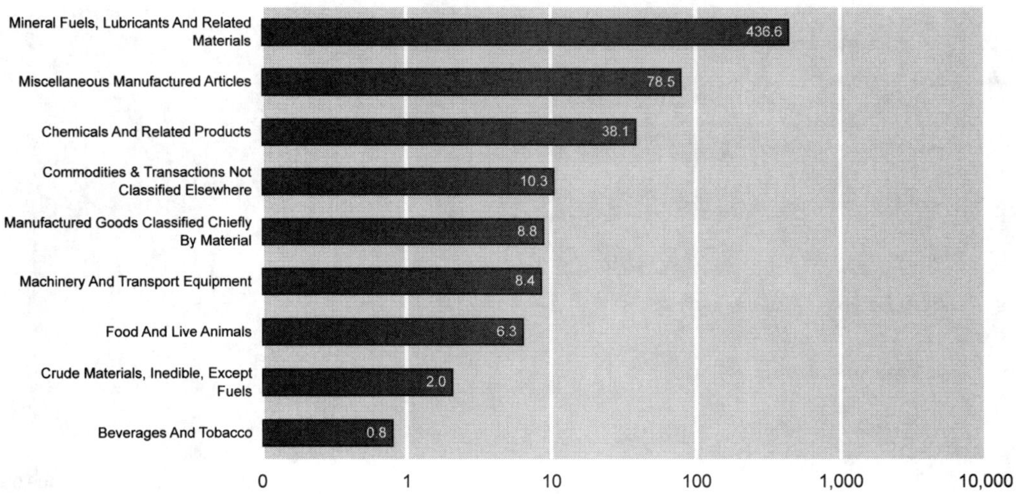

Source: Bureau of Economic Analysis, International Monetary Fund; Office of Trade and Industry Information

Luxembourg & the United States
Investment and Trade Figures

Investment

Investment between the U.S. and Luxembourg is skewed in favor of Luxembourg. The bulk of bilateral investment flows remain in financial services and related industries. U.S. affiliate sales in Luxembourg were almost triple that of affiliates in the U.S. The employee balance favors the U.S. with almost three times the amount of affiliate employees.

Luxembourg - U.S. Global Linkages, 2008
($ billions)

	U.S. in Luxembourg	Luxembourg in U.S.
Foreign Direct Investment* (2009)	174.1	127.8
Total Assets of Affiliates	907.9	14.3
Foreign Affiliate Sales	18.2	7.0
Value Added of Affiliates	0.7	2.6
Affiliate Employees	13,600	35,500

*Based on a historic-cost basis, data for 2009; all data for majority-owned nonbank affiliates

Trade

Trade volumes are rather small—with exports to the U.S. totaling just $440 million in 2009, while imports from the U.S. are $530 million. The U.S. accounted for only 2.1% of total exports but over 13% excluding intra-EU exports. Imports from the U.S. accounted for 2.2% of the total in 2009 and 7.7% excluding intra-EU imports.

Top Ten U.S. Imports from Luxembourg, 2009 (in $ millions)

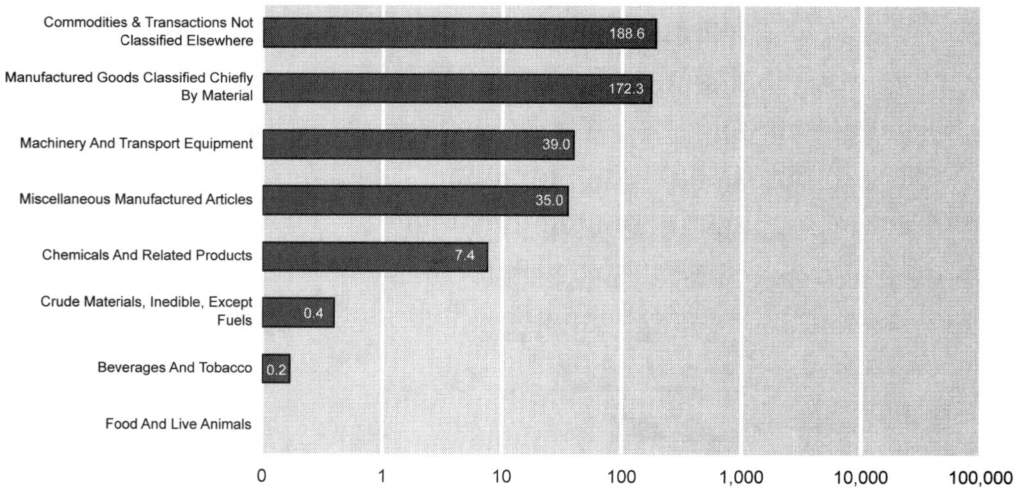

Source: Bureau of Economic Analysis, International Monetary Fund; Office of Trade and Industry Information

Malta & the United States
Investment and Trade Figures

Investment

Given its small size, Malta has not attracted much U.S. foreign direct investment. The country received close to $700 million in U.S. investment in 2009, up from roughly $500 million in 2008

Malta - U.S. Global Linkages, 2008
($ billions)

	U.S. in Malta	Malta in U.S.
Foreign Direct Investment* (2009)	0.7	0.003
Total Assets of Affiliates	2.4	-
Foreign Affiliate Sales	0.3	-
Value Added of Affiliates	0.1	-
Affiliate Employees	1,300	-

*Based on a historic-cost basis, data for 2009; all data for majority-owned nonbank affiliates

Trade

Trade between the two countries remains rather small. U.S. imports from Malta totaled $210 million in 2009 and were primarily concentrated in machinery, chemicals, and other manufactured items. Malta's imports from the U.S. totalled $110 million in 2009, 2.6% of total imports and 9.6% excluding intra-EU imports.

Top Ten U.S. Imports from Malta, 2009 (in $ millions)

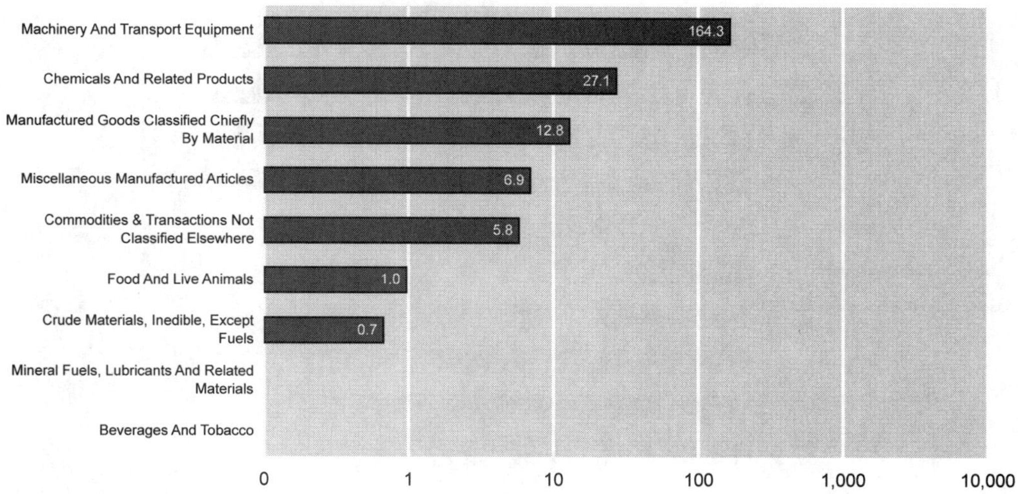

Source: Bureau of Economic Analysis, International Monetary Fund; Office of Trade and Industry Information

Netherlands & the United States

Investment and Trade Figures

Investment

Investment between the U.S. and the Netherlands is slightly skewed toward the latter, with America's investment stake in the Netherlands totaling $471.6 billion in 2009, versus $238 billion of Dutch investment in the U.S. The U.S. is a prime foreign destination for Dutch firms, which recorded $331.6 billion in affiliate sales in the U.S. during 2008. The employment balance favors the U.S. by more than 140,000 jobs, a smaller margin than previous years, though still a substantial gap.

Netherlands - U.S. Global Linkages, 2008
($ billions)

	U.S. in Netherlands	Netherlands in U.S.
Foreign Direct Investment* (2009)	471.6	238.0
Total Assets of Affiliates	1,197.5	883.4
Foreign Affiliate Sales	232.8	331.6
Value Added of Affiliates	33.3	56.2
Affiliate Employees	228,800	371,500

*Based on a historic-cost basis, data for 2009; all data for majority-owned nonbank affiliates

Trade

The U.S. has accounted for 3.9% of total exports from the Netherlands, but a share of 17.4% of total exports when intra-EU trade is excluded, down from 23.4% in 2000. Top exports were diversified across several capital-intensive industries. Regarding imports, the U.S. supplied 7.8% of total imports by the Netherlands in 2009, although the share rises to 15.2% after accounting for intra-EU trade.

Top Ten U.S. Imports from Netherlands, 2009 (in $ millions)

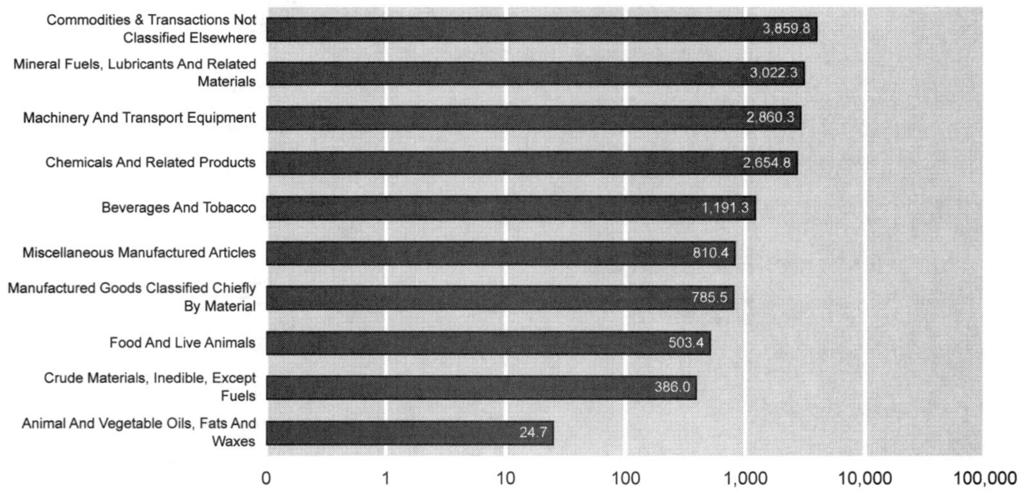

Source: Bureau of Economic Analysis, International Monetary Fund; Office of Trade and Industry Information

Norway & the United States
Investment and Trade Figures

Investment

The investment balance favors Norway, with U.S. direct investment totaling $27 billion in 2009 versus $7.3 billion of Norwegian direct investment in the U.S. The employment balance favors Norway, with U.S. foreign affiliates employing 33,700 Norwegian workers in 2008.

Norway - U.S. Global Linkages, 2008 ($ billions)	U.S. in Norway	Norway in U.S.
Foreign Direct Investment* (2009)	27.0	7.3
Total Assets of Affiliates	71.4	27.4
Foreign Affiliate Sales	60.1	15.7
Value Added of Affiliates	32.5	0.9
Affiliate Employees	33,700	8,000

*Based on a historic-cost basis, data for 2009; all data for majority-owned nonbank affiliates

Trade

Norwegian exports to the U.S. totaled $5.8 billion in 2009, and were skewed toward mineral fuels (i.e. petroleum products). The U.S. accounted for just 4.8% of total Norwegian exports, but nearly 25% after accounting for intra-EU trade. Imports from the U.S. into Norway totaled $4.2 billion—that equates to 6.2% of total Norwegian imports or 18.3% excluding Norway's trade with the EU.

Top Ten U.S. Imports from Norway, 2009 (in $ millions)

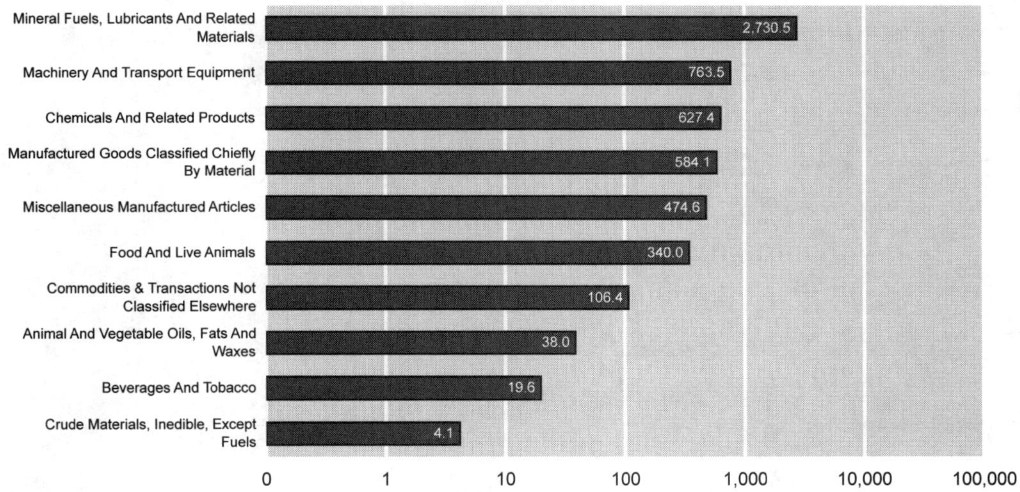

Source: Bureau of Economic Analysis, International Monetary Fund; Office of Trade and Industry Information

Poland & the United States
Investment and Trade Figures

Investment

As one of the largest markets in Central Europe, Poland has attracted significant sums of market-seeking U.S. foreign direct investment. At $30.5 billion, the U.S. asset base in Poland is larger than America's asset base in small developed nations like Finland or Greece. The U.S. affiliate work force of 132,900 workers is the largest among EU12 countries. Polish affiliates in the U.S. have yet to make significant investments in the country.

Poland - U.S. Global Linkages, 2008
($ billions)

	U.S. in Poland	Poland in U.S.
Foreign Direct Investment* (2009)	14.0	-
Total Assets of Affiliates	30.5	-
Foreign Affiliate Sales	34.7	-
Value Added of Affiliates	8.4	0.007
Affiliate Employees	132,900	100

*Based on a historic-cost basis, data for 2009; all data for majority-owned nonbank affiliates

Trade

U.S. imports from Poland have increased sharply over the past few years, clearing $2 billion in 2006 from just $680 million in 1997 and reaching $2.5 billion in 2009. Imports run the gamut - from heavy machinery, to chemicals, to agricultural products. U.S. exports to Poland totaled $2.1 billion in 2009, a share of 1.4% and rising to 5.1% excluding intra-EU trade.

Top Ten U.S. Imports from Poland, 2009 (in $ millions)

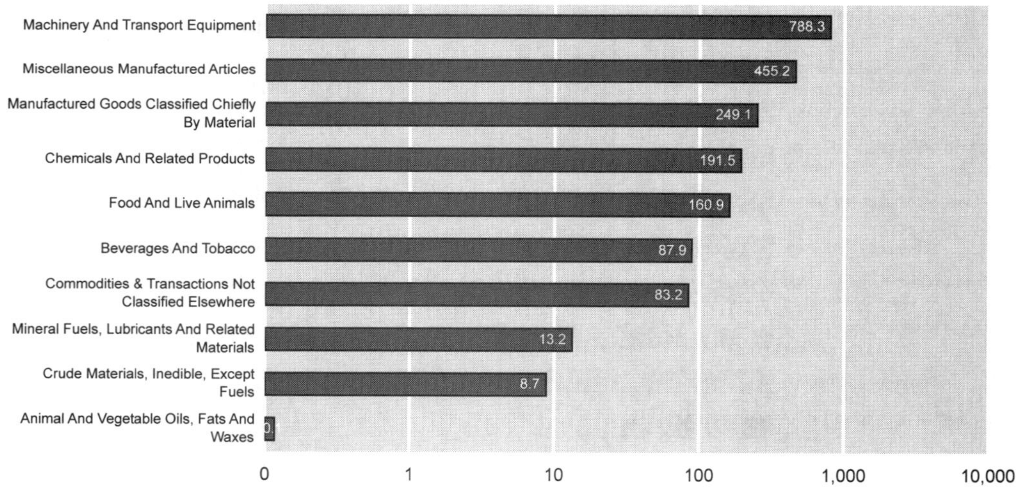

Source: Bureau of Economic Analysis, International Monetary Fund; Office of Trade and Industry Information

Portugal & the United States

Investment and Trade Figures

Investment

U.S. direct investment in Portugal totaled $2.5 billion in 2009, largely concentrated in wholesale trade, while U.S. affiliates employed 57,200 Portuguese workers.

Portugal - U.S. Global Linkages, 2008
($ billions)

	U.S. in Portugal	Portugal in U.S.
Foreign Direct Investment* (2009)	2.5	0.11
Total Assets of Affiliates	40.6	12.04
Foreign Affiliate Sales	11.9	0.48
Value Added of Affiliates	4.7	0.13
Affiliate Employees	57,200	500

*Based on a historic-cost basis, data for 2009; all data for majority-owned nonbank affiliates

Trade

Portuguese exports to the U.S. fell to $1.4 billion in 2009, while imports from the U.S. fell to $1.2 billion. The U.S. accounted for 3.3% of total exports but a 12.2% share of Portugal's exports excluding intra-EU trade. Portuguese imports from the U.S. were 2% of total imports from the world in 2009 and 7.3% excluding intra-EU imports, down from an average of 13% in the 1990s.

Top Ten U.S. Imports from Portugal, 2009 (in $ millions)

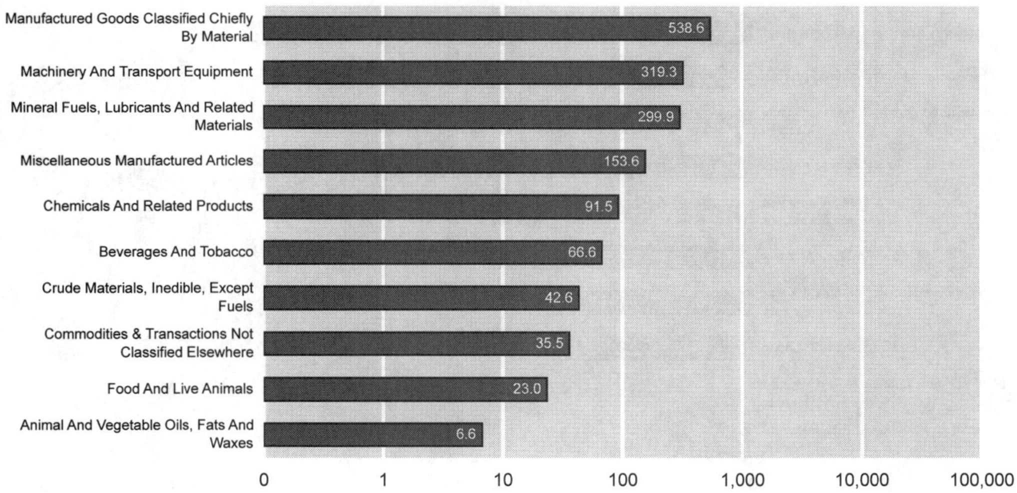

Source: Bureau of Economic Analysis, International Monetary Fund; Office of Trade and Industry Information

Romania & the United States
Investment and Trade Figures

Investment

America's asset base in Romania is rather small, with assets totaling $5.5 billion in 2009. However, with Romania's inclusion into the EU, more U.S. firms are expected to increase their presence in Romania—albeit modestly—over the medium-term. U.S. affiliates employed 38,800 employees in 2008, placing Romania 4th among the EU12 countries in terms of jobs supported.

Romania - U.S. Global Linkages, 2008 ($ billions)	U.S. in Romania	Romania in U.S.
Foreign Direct Investment* (2009)	1.5	-0.004
Total Assets of Affiliates	5.5	-
Foreign Affiliate Sales	6.5	-
Value Added of Affiliates	2.1	-
Affiliate Employees	38,800	0

*Based on a historic-cost basis, data for 2009; all data for majority-owned nonbank affiliates

Trade

U.S. imports from Romania totaled $480 million in 2009, a gradual rise from the levels of the late 1990s but off from a high of $1.1 billion in 2005. Imports included a variety of manufactured goods. The U.S. is a rather small supplier to Romania, with the U.S. accounting for just 1.3% of the nation's total imports and 4.8% excluding intra-EU trade.

Top Ten U.S. Imports from Romania, 2009 (in $ millions)

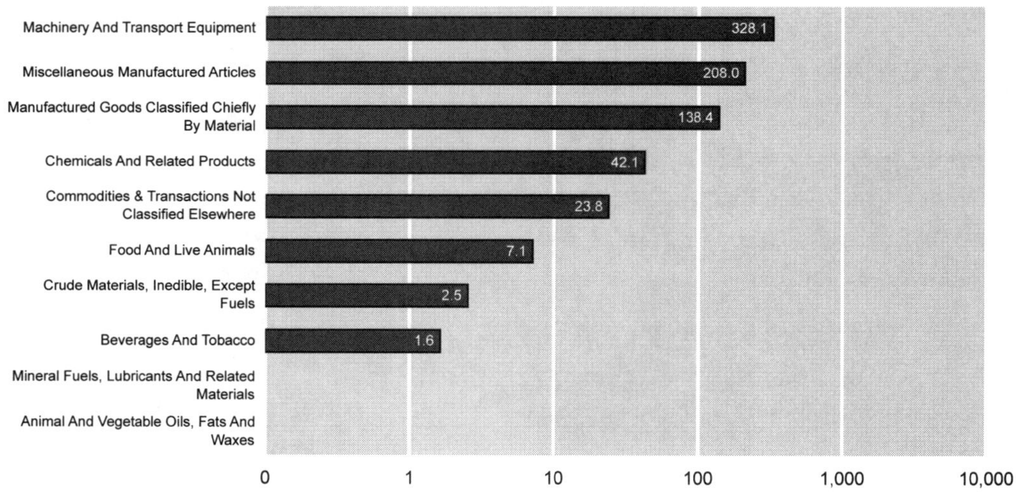

Source: Bureau of Economic Analysis, International Monetary Fund; Office of Trade and Industry Information

Slovakia & the United States
Investment and Trade Figures

Investment

America's asset base in Slovakia is small but expanding — total assets of U.S. affiliates in 2008 amounted to $7.6 billion, while foreign affiliate sales reached $8.6 billion. Centered in the heart of eastern Europe, the nation is well positioned to capture U.S. investment in distribution, transportation, wholesale trade and other service-like activities. U.S. affiliates employed 37,600 workers in 2008, the 5th largest U.S. affiliate work force among the EU12 countries.

Slovakia - U.S. Global Linkages, 2008
($ billions)

	U.S. in Slovakia	Slovakia in U.S.
Foreign Direct Investment* (2009)	0.8	-
Total Assets of Affiliates	7.6	-
Foreign Affiliate Sales	8.6	-
Value Added of Affiliates	2.1	-
Affiliate Employees	37,600	-

*Based on a historic-cost basis, data for 2009; all data for majority-owned nonbank affiliates

Trade

U.S. imports from Slovakia have surged, rising to over $1.4 billion in 2007 from levels under $200 million in the late 1990s. However, U.S. imports fell significantly in 2009 to $600 million. Accounting for the past surge has been rising motor vehicle imports from foreign affiliates producing in the country. Other imports include nuclear reactors, footwear and rubber. Imports from the U.S. have risen gradually as well, hitting $460 million in 2008, and falling slightly to $320 million in 2009, 2.3% of total imports excluding intra-EU trade.

Top Ten U.S. Imports from Slovakia, 2009 (in $ millions)

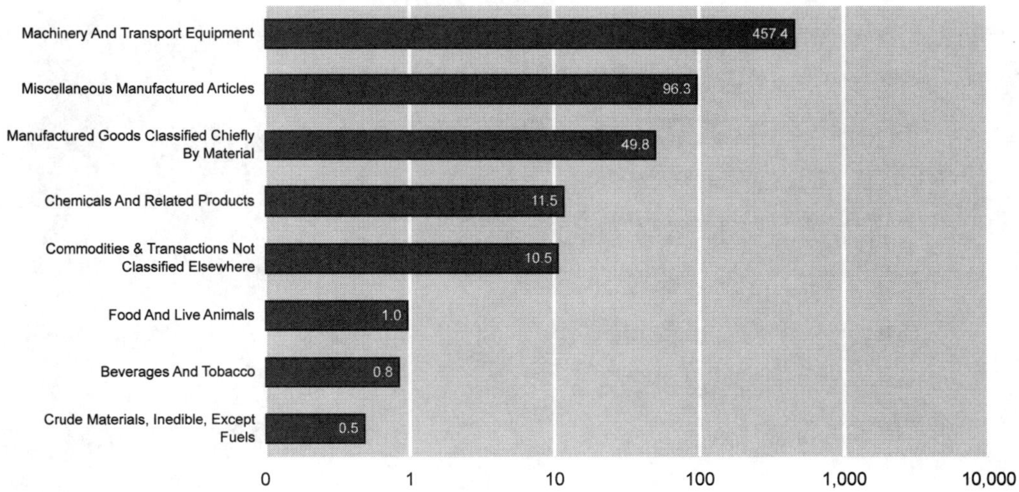

Source: Bureau of Economic Analysis, International Monetary Fund; Office of Trade and Industry Information

Slovenia & the United States
Investment and Trade Figures

Investment

Slovenia has experienced a gradual rise in U.S. foreign investment over the past few years. Total assets of affiliates amounted to $1.1 billion in 2008. U.S. affiliates employed 4,600 workers in 2008, placing Slovenia in the middle of the EU12 countries in terms of employment. The country is expected to emerge as a bridge to the Balkan states over the next decade.

Slovenia - U.S. Global Linkages, 2008 ($ billions)	U.S. in Slovenia	Slovenia in U.S.
Foreign Direct Investment* (2009)	0.3	0.001
Total Assets of Affiliates	1.1	-
Foreign Affiliate Sales	1.3	-
Value Added of Affiliates	0.3	-
Affiliate Employees	4,600	-

*Based on a historic-cost basis, data for 2009; all data for majority-owned nonbank affiliates

Trade

U.S. imports from Slovenia have grown steadily since the late 1990s, however, falling slightly to $300 million in 2009. Imports included machinery, chemicals, furniture and glassware. Slovenia imported only 1.7% of the country's total imports from the U.S. or 5.9% excluding intra-EU trade in 2009.

Top Ten U.S. Imports from Slovenia, 2009 (in $ millions)

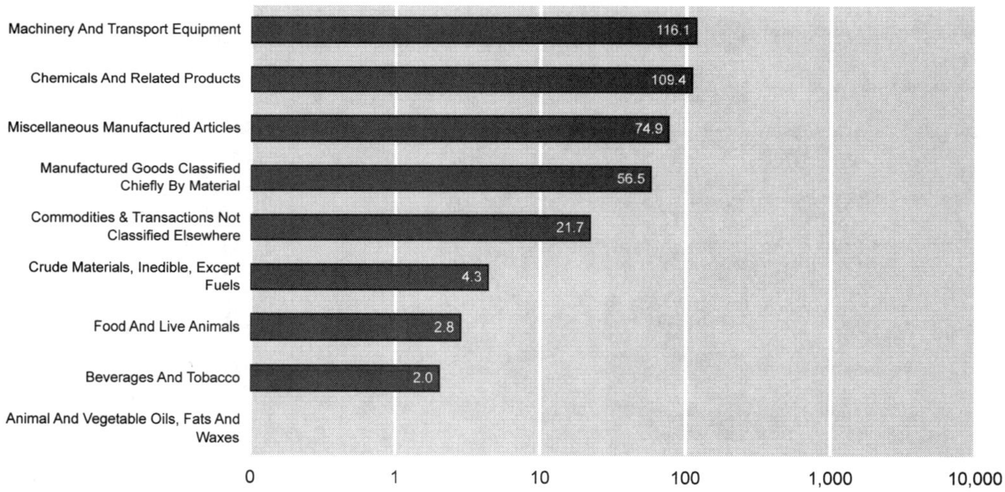

Source: Bureau of Economic Analysis, International Monetary Fund; Office of Trade and Industry Information

Spain & the United States
Investment and Trade Figures

Investment

The investment balance favored Spain in 2009, with U.S. direct investment in Spain totaling $50.6 billion. The U.S., originally not a strategic priority to Spanish firms, received over three times more direct investment in 2009 from Spain than it did in 2006. The majority of 2009 investments were made in depository institutions. The employment balance is skewed in favor of Spain.

Spain - U.S. Global Linkages, 2008
($ billions)

	U.S. in Spain	Spain in U.S.
Foreign Direct Investment* (2009)	50.6	43.9
Total Assets of Affiliates	147.5	265.3
Foreign Affiliate Sales	96.2	31.6
Value Added of Affiliates	17.4	6.2
Affiliate Employees	188,100	66,800

*Based on a historic-cost basis, data for 2009; all data for majority-owned nonbank affiliates

Trade

The U.S. received $8 billion worth of goods, or 3.7% of total exports from Spain in 2009, but a share of 11.6% of total exports when intra-EU trade is excluded. Regarding imports, the U.S. supplied only 3.3% of total imports by Spain in 2009, although the share rises to 8.5% after accounting for intra-EU trade.

Top Ten U.S. Imports from Spain, 2009 (in $ millions)

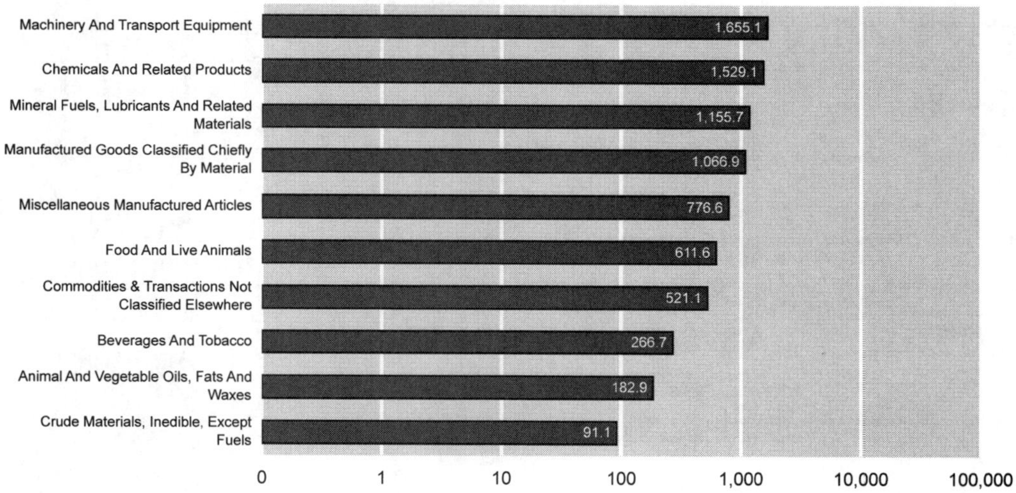

Source: Bureau of Economic Analysis, International Monetary Fund; Office of Trade and Industry Information

Sweden & the United States
Investment and Trade Figures

Investment

The investment balance slightly favors the U.S., with Swedish direct investment in the U.S. totaling $38.9 billion, while U.S. firms invested $27.4 billion in Sweden in 2009. The employment balance is heavily in favor of the United States.

Sweden - U.S. Global Linkages, 2008
($ billions)

	U.S. in Sweden	Sweden in U.S.
Foreign Direct Investment* (2009)	27.4	38.9
Total Assets of Affiliates	122.4	70.7
Foreign Affiliate Sales	53.2	51.7
Value Added of Affiliates	7.7	13.4
Affiliate Employees	88,900	181,500

*Based on a historic-cost basis, data for 2009; all data for majority-owned nonbank affiliates

Trade

U.S. exports from Sweden totalled $8.4 billion in 2009, accounting for 6.4% of Sweden's global total and 15.2% of the total excluding intra-EU trade. Sweden imports $4.5 billion from the U.S., accounting for 3.7% of Sweden's total imports in 2009, although the share rises to 11.7% excluding intra-EU imports.

Top Ten U.S. Imports from Sweden, 2009 (in $ millions)

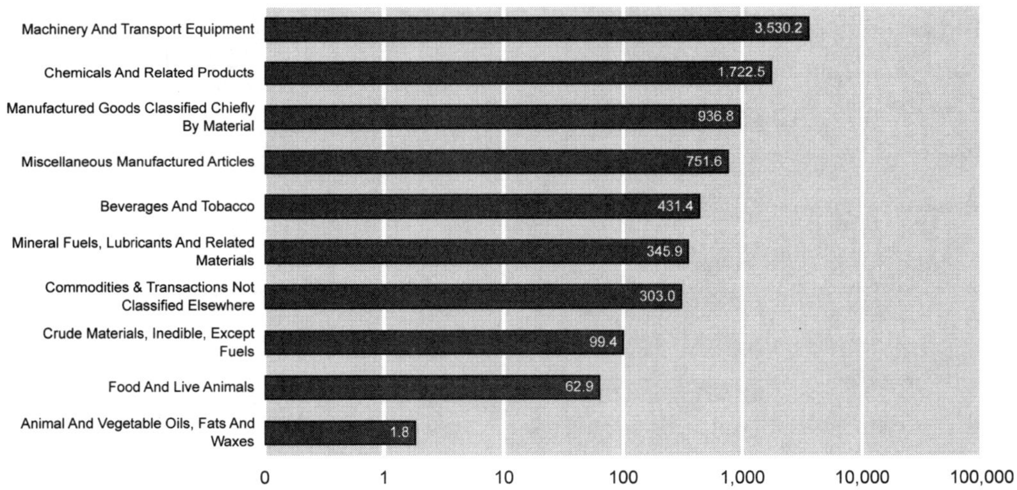

Source: Bureau of Economic Analysis, International Monetary Fund; Office of Trade and Industry Information

Switzerland & the United States
Investment and Trade Figures

Investment
The investment balance favors the U.S.— direct investment in Switzerland totaled $148.2 billion in 2009 versus $189.4 billion of Swiss investment in the U.S. Switzerland has one of the largest asset bases in the U.S. of any nation at nearly $1.7 trillion (mainly in services like insurance and financial services). The employment balance significantly favors the United States.

Switzerland - U.S. Global Linkages, 2008
($ billions)

	U.S. in Switzerland	Switzerland in U.S.
Foreign Direct Investment* (2009)	148.2	189.4
Total Assets of Affiliates	441.1	1,654.9
Foreign Affiliate Sales	275.3	212.5
Value Added of Affiliates	27.9	48.8
Affiliate Employees	81,500	394,400

*Based on a historic-cost basis, data for 2009; all data for majority-owned nonbank affiliates

Trade
Swiss exports to the U.S. totaled $17.4 billion in 2009, representing 10% of all Swiss exports, and 25% when taken as a share of exports to regions outside the EU. In the same year, Switzerland imported American goods worth nearly $9 billion, 5.8% of the global total, yet when imports from the EU were excluded, U.S. goods comprised 26.4% of Swiss imports.

Top Ten U.S. Imports from Switzerland, 2009 (in $ millions)

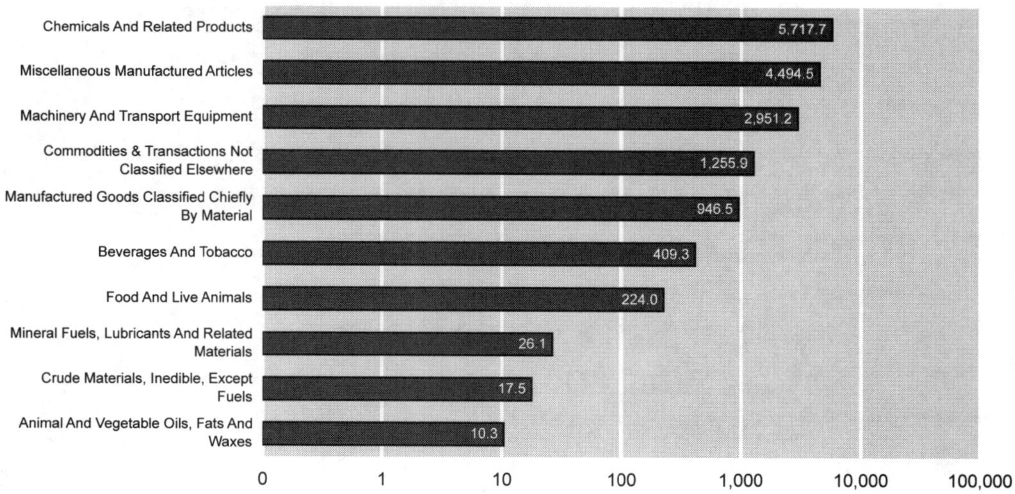

Source: Bureau of Economic Analysis, International Monetary Fund; Office of Trade and Industry Information

United Kingdom & the United States
Investment and Trade Figures

Investment

The U.S.-U.K. investment balance is fairly even, however the U.S. had a slightly larger presence in the U.K. in 2009. Sales of American and British affiliates totaled more than $1 trillion. U.S. affiliates employed more than 1 million workers in the U.K. while the U.K employed over 950,000 workers in the U.S.

United Kingdom - U.S. Global Linkages, 2008
($ billions)

	U.S. in United Kingdom	United Kingdom in U.S.
Foreign Direct Investment* (2009)	471.4	453.9
Total Assets of Affiliates	1,605.1	2,171.5
Foreign Affiliate Sales	622.4	543.8
Value Added of Affiliates	166.0	108.8
Affiliate Employees	1,174,200	957,400

*Based on a historic-cost basis, data for 2009; all data for majority-owned nonbank affiliates

Trade

Bilateral trade flows are strong between the United Kingdom and the United States. Exports to the U.S. totaled $51.9 billion in 2009, 14.7% of total exports from United Kingdom and 32.7% when intra-EU exports are excluded from the global sum. Top exports to the U.S. include chemical products and heavy machinery. The U.S. was similiarly a key supplier to the United Kingdom in 2009, with $46.9 billion in imports from the U.S accounting for 9.7% of imports from the world and 20.3% excluding intra-EU trade.

Top Ten U.S. Imports from United Kingdom, 2009 (in $ millions)

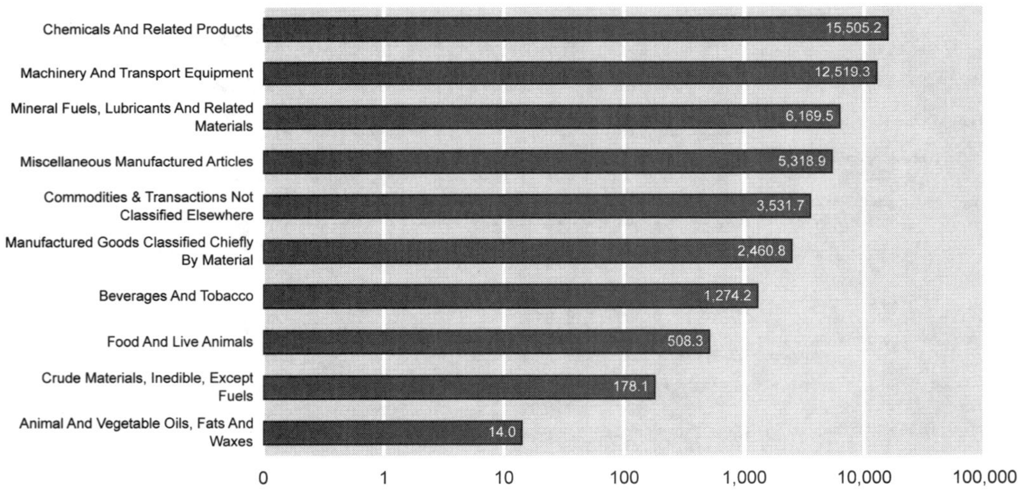

Source: Bureau of Economic Analysis, International Monetary Fund; Office of Trade and Industry Information

Notes on Terms, Data, and Sources

Employment, Investment, and Trade Linkages for the 50 U.S. States and Europe

Data for investment as well as investment related jobs are from the U.S. Commerce Department's Bureau of Economic Analysis. Investment data measure gross property, plant, and equipment of affiliates. Europe includes Belgium, France, Germany, Italy, Netherlands, Sweden, Switzerland, and the United Kingdom. Trade data are from the International Trade Administration's Office of Trade and Industry Information at the U.S. Commerce Department. Europe includes Albania, Andorra, Armenia, Austria, Azerbaijan, Belarus, Belgium, Bosnia-Herzegovina, Bulgaria, Croatia, Czech Republic, Cyprus, Denmark, Estonia, Faeroe Islands, Finland, France, Germany, Georgia, Gibraltar, Greece, Iceland, Ireland, Italy, Latvia, Liechtenstein, Lithuania, Luxembourg, Macedonia, Malta, Moldova, Monaco, Montenegro, Netherlands, Norway, Poland, Portugal, Romania, Russia, San Marino, Serbia, Slovakia, Slovenia, Spain, Svalbard, Sweden, Switzerland, Tajikistan, Turkey, Ukraine, United Kingdom, Vatican City. The top ten exports to Europe bar chart employs a logarithmic scale to facilitate cross state comparisons.

Investment and Trade for the EU 27, Norway and Switzerland and the U.S.

Investment data are from the Bureau of Economic Analysis. Trade data are from the IMF Trade Statistics. Data for the top ten U.S. imports bar charts are from the Office of Trade and Industry Information of the International Trade Administration. They employ logarithmic scales to facilitate cross-country comparisons.

Terms

Throughout this report, the term "EU" refers to all 27 member states of the European Union. The term EU15 refers to the older EU member states: the United Kingdom, Ireland, Belgium, Luxembourg, the Netherlands, Austria, Spain, Italy, Greece, France, Germany, Portugal, Sweden, Finland, and Denmark. The term EU12 refers to the newer EU member states: Estonia, Latvia, Lithuania, Poland, the Czech Republic, Slovakia, Hungary, Slovenia, Malta, Cyprus, Romania and Bulgaria.

In the report we refer to 12 world regions. China, Japan, Russia and India are countries that we consider "regions" unto their own. The other regions include the following countries:

Africa: Algeria, Angola, Benin, Botswana, Burkina Faso, Burundi, Cameroon, Cape Verde, Central African Republic, Chad, Comoros, Congo, Dem. Rep. of, Congo, Rep. of, Cote d'Ivoire, Djibouti, Equatorial Guinea, Eritrea, Ethiopia, Gabon, Gambia, Ghana, Guinea, Guinea-Bissau, Kenya, Lesotho, Liberia, Libya, Madagascar, Malawi, Mali, Mauritania, Mauritius, Mayotte, Morocco, Mozambique, Namibia, Niger, Nigeria, Reunion, Rwanda, Senegal, Seychelles, Sierra Leone, Somalia, South Africa, Sudan, Swaziland, Tanzania, Tunisia, Uganda, Zambia, Zimbabwe.

Caribbean: Anguilla, Antigua and Barbuda, Aruba, Bahamas, Barbados, Bermuda, British West Indies, Cayman Islands, Cuba, Dominica, Dominican Republic, French Guiana, Grenada, Guadeloupe, Haiti, Jamaica, Martinique, Montserrat, Netherlands Antilles, Puerto Rico, Sao Tome and Principe, St. Kitts and Nevis, St. Lucia, St. Pierre and Miquelon, St. Vincent and the Grenadines, Trinidad and Tobago, Turks and Caicos Islands, U.S. Virgin Islands.

Rising Asia: Afghanistan, Bangladesh, Bhutan, Brunei Darussalam, Cambodia, Hong Kong, Indonesia, Kazakhstan, Kyrgyzstan, Laos, Macao, Malaysia, Maldives, Mongolia, Myanmar, Nepal, North Korea, Pakistan, Palau, Philippines, Singapore, South Korea, Sri Lanka, Taiwan, Tajikistan, Thailand, Turkmenistan, Uzbekistan, Vietnam.

Latin America: Argentina, Belize, Bolivia, Brazil, Chile, Colombia, Costa Rica, Ecuador, El Salvador, Falkland Islands, Guatemala, Guyana, Honduras, Nicaragua, Panama, Paraguay, Peru, Suriname, Uruguay, Venezuela.

Middle East: Bahrain, Egypt, Iran, Iraq, Israel, Jordan, Kuwait, Lebanon, Oman, Palestinian Territories, Qatar, Saudi Arabia, Syria, United Arab Emirates, Yemen.

North America: Canada, Mexico, United States.

Oceania: American Samoa, Australia, Christmas Island, Cocos (Keeling) Islands, Cook Islands, East Timor, Fiji, French Polynesia, Guam, Kiribati, Marshall Islands, Micronesia, Nauru, New Caledonia, New Zealand, Niue, Norfolk Island, Papua New Guinea, Pitcairn, Samoa, Solomon Islands, Togo, Tokelau, Tonga, Tuvalu, United States Minor Outlying Islands, Vanuatu, Wallis and Futuna Islands.

Wider Europe: Albania, Andorra, Armenia, Azerbaijan, Belarus, Bosnia and Herzegovina, Croatia, Faroe Islands, Georgia, Gibraltar, Greenland, Guernsey, Iceland, Isle of Man, Jersey, Liechtenstein, Macedonia, Moldova, Monaco, Montenegro, Republic of, Norway, San Marino, Serbia, Switzerland, Turkey, Ukraine, Vatican.

About the Authors

Daniel S. Hamilton and **Joseph P. Quinlan** have authored and edited a series of award-winning books and articles on the modern transatlantic economy, including *The Transatlantic Economy* (annual editions, 2005-2011); *Germany and Globalization* (2009); *France and Globalization* (2008); *Globalization and Europe: Prospering in the New Whirled Order* (2008); *Sleeping Giant: Awakening the Transatlantic Services Economy* (2006); *Protecting Our Prosperity: Ensuring Both National Security and the Benefits of Foreign Investment in the United States* (2006); *Deep Integration: How Transatlantic Markets are Leading Globalization* (2005); and *Partners in Prosperity: The Changing Geography of the Transatlantic Economy* (2004). Together they were recipients of the 2007 Transatlantic Leadership Award by the European-American Business Council and the 2006 Transatlantic Business Award by the American Chamber of Commerce to the European Union.

Daniel S. Hamilton is the Austrian Marshall Plan Foundation Professor and Founding Director of the Center for Transatlantic Relations at the Paul H. Nitze School of Advanced International Studies, Johns Hopkins University. He also serves as Executive Director of the American Consortium on EU Studies (ACES), designated by the European Commission as the EU Center of Excellence Washington, DC. He has served as Deputy Assistant Secretary of State and Associate Director of the Secretary of State's Policy Planning Staff. Recent books include *Europe 2020: Competitive or Complacent?* (Washington, DC: Center for Transatlantic Relations, 2011); and *Shoulder to Shoulder: Forging a Strategic U.S.-EU Partnership* (Washington, DC: Center for Transatlantic Relations, 2010)

Joseph P. Quinlan is a Senior Fellow at the Center for Transatlantic Relations, with extensive experience in the U.S. corporate sector. He is a leading expert on the transatlantic economy and well-known global economist/strategist on Wall Street. He specializes in global capital flows, international trade and multinational strategies. He lectures at New York University, and his publications have appeared in such venues as *Foreign Affairs*, the *Financial Times* and the *Wall Street Journal*. His most recent book is *The Last Economic Superpower: The Retreat of Globalization, the End of American Dominance, and What We Can Do About It* (New York: McGraw Hill, 2010).